D0548135

Nutrition and the Elderly

242616

Nutrition and the Elderly

Policy Development, Program Planning, and Evaluation

TX
361
A3767
C. 2

Barbara Millen Posner
Boston University

Lexington Books
D.C. Heath and Company
Lexington, Massachusetts
Toronto

Library of Congress Cataloging in Publication Data

Posner, Barbara Millen.
    Nutrition and the elderly.

    Includes bibliographical references and index.
    1. Aged—Nutrition. 2. Nutrition policy—United States. 3. Food
relief—United States. I. Title.
[DNLM: 1. Nutrition—In old age. 2. Home care services—United States.
3. Financing, Government—United States.
WT30.3.P855n]
TX361.A3P67   362.6   77-17683
ISBN 0-669-02085-0

Copyright © 1979 by D.C. Heath and Company

All rights reserved. No part of this publication may be reproduced or
transmitted in any form or by any means, electronic or mechanical,
including photocopy, recording, or any information storage or retrieval
system, without permission in writing from the publisher.

Second printing, December 1980

Published simultaneously in Canada

Printed in the United States of America

International Standard Book Number: 0-669-02085-0

Library of Congress Catalog Card Number: 77-17683

22.95

To Marshall
My Husband and Most Steadfast,
Enthusiastic Adviser and Friend

Contents

Contents

List of Figures

List of Tables

Foreword

The Nutrition Program authorized by Title VII of the Older Americans Act of 1965, as amended (NPOA) was conceived in 1969, authorized in 1972, planned in detail over the ensuing year, first funded and implemented in 1973, and since then has expanded certain components of its legislative mandate in proportion to its increasing resources. Since 1973, much data has been generated quantifying dollar input and meal service output. With total resources of 0.5 billion dollars, NPOA now serves over 115 million meals annually. The mirage created by these huge numbers is dispelled, however, when meals served annually divided by registered participants reveals that NPOA provides, on the average, less than one meal per participant per week. In addition, further investigation reveals a lack of emphasis on health-related aspects of nutrition and on the delivery of primary health care among the aged cohorts who devour annually over half the nation's health resources while constituting less than 15 percent of the total population.

Reasons underlying the bias towards meals delivery at the near exclusion of health care needs are detailed in the Boston-based research described in this book. The results of this research parallel findings of the U.S. General Accounting Office. Therefore, Dr. Posner's quantification of Boston's experiences serve to highlight the need for comparable evaluation research in other locations. Until federal evaluation is reconceived and adequately funded, research at the community and state levels serves as the only mechanism for identifying and alleviating deficiencies responsible for NPOA's performance inadequacies.

Complying with the apparent mimicry by the Massachusetts Department of Elder Affairs' of the Federal Administration on Aging's approach to NPOA's evaluation, the Boston investigators relinquished the collection of objective data quantifying NPOA's impact on the health and nutritional status of NPOA participants. In spite of the unwelcome constraints on their research, the Boston investigator has collected, assembled, and analyzed an impressive quantity of information acquired from site, project, and state and federal records, from interviews with participants in three different project areas, and from observations made at the projects' sites. Dr. Posner's analyses provide abundant food for thought to all site, project, state, and federal personnel. Not only are deficiencies in ongoing procedures revealed, but quantitative changes in ongoing procedures are suggested.

Even more valuable are the conclusions based on data analyses that qualitative changes in NPOA procedures could result in far higher correlations of NPOA's legislatively mandated services with specific health, nutrition, income maintenance, education, counselling, and socialization needs of participants. By augmenting outreach, project management could locate elderly in greatest need not now participating in the program. Management could then supply escort and transportation (as indicated), bringing those persons in greatest need to project sites where they could take advantage of the full spectrum of NPOA services. Using triage and referral for already enrolled participants as well as new arrivals, project management could formally graduate those whose participation had led to greater self-sufficiency, those whose health-related and socioeconomic needs were least, and those whose participation rates were minimal. This process could segregate costly resources like meals, escort, transportation, and health care for those in greatest need. Nonetheless, under this procedure, NPOA's social and recreational activities would remain available as important contributions to the lives of all who desired them.

By assembling the data, the analyses, and the conclusions, Dr. Posner performs a service of pragmatic value, particularly useful for thoughtful managers of NPOA seeking information on how to increase the effectiveness and cost-effectiveness of their programs and projects. She provides a brief review of aging as a biologic process, of health factors modifying physiological aging, and of the impact of nutrition—the major environmental factor—on both aging and health. She emphasizes the need to view nutrition, health, and aging as an integrated triad, not as independent and unrelated entities. She develops within the constraints imposed on the Boston investigations a systems approach to analyzing and resolving major problems confronting NPOA.

The recommendations on which legislation authorizing NPOA was structured now approach their tenth anniversary. Dr. Posner's affirmation of their virtues, based on her interpretation of the Boston data, rekindles hope that this nation's greatest effort in providing publicly supported meal service delivery to adults will be reformed to focus on those in greatest need and to dedicate its great potential to improving the physical and emotional health of all older Americans. By setting an example, her report should encourage other state and community leaders to examine objectively their own NPOA programs and projects with the aim of extracting from relatively limited (in terms of total need) resources the maximum improvement in health and happiness of their present and future beneficiaries.

Before the 1981 White House Conference on Aging, such studies could provide a data base upon which to build recommendations for reform of Administration on Aging policies at the federal level, if by that time reformation has failed to result from congressional responses to presently available information such as that presented by Dr. Posner in this book.

Donald M. Watkin, M.D., M.P.H., F.A.C.P.

Preface

In 1973, the United States Congress appropriated nearly $100 million to establish the first nutrition intervention specifically for the nation's aged population, the Nutrition Program for Older Americans (NPOA), mandated by the 1972 Title VII amendment to the Older Americans Act of 1965. Funding for this program has nearly tripled since then, making Title VII the most significant program operated by the Administration on Aging (AoA), Department of Health, Education and Welfare. Expenditures for the nutrition program are expected to exceed $300 million by the end of 1978 and may reach $400 million by 1980. In addition, estimates of federal, state, and local investment indicate that at present, about $0.5 billion will be spent annually on the implementation of the NPOA.

The Title VII program has become one of the most visible domestic nutrition interventions. Its legislative mandate called for the development of a nationwide network of community-based meals programs located in congregate settings within easy access to the elderly. The result of this specific program implementation strategy has been the location of 9,732 meal sites in 1,047 Title VII nutrition project areas in all 50 states and 6 U.S. territories. To date, an estimated 2.9 million persons over the age of 60 have been served a congregate or home-delivered meal which has been designed to provide at least one-third of an older individual's daily recommended nutrient intake.[1]

As of the end of the first quarter fiscal year 1978, the AoA estimated that 22,024 persons were paid employees of the Title VII program and 127,200 persons were volunteering services. Some 66% of participants nationally were low-income and over one-fifth were minority elderly. Congregate meals, which constituted 83% of total meals served, were developed in a mix of Title VII sites, including senior centers (25% of total sites), religious facilities (25%), schools (5%), public housing (14%), restaurants (3%), and other locations such as community centers (28%).

Tremendous community support of the nutrition program has been cultivated and firmly rooted at the local level. Moreover, the successful development of the Title VII administrative infrastructure and rapid implementation of the meal delivery scheme has also provided the tangible evidence needed for political support of the nutrition program at the state and federal levels.

Despite its current visibility and popular support, however, the Title VII program has historically encountered obstacles which have adversely affected its implementation and effectiveness. Congressional vetoes prevented the initial appropriation of Title VII funds in 1972. Once funding became available for the subsequent year, it was politically imperative to accelerate the Title VII implementation process. It was necessary to generate, in the short run, tangible evidence of the feasibility of the Title VII congregate meal delivery mechanism. To facilitate this goal, full and open Title VII grant application processes at the state and local levels were curtailed. Efforts were focused on funding those programs which could become fully operational within a short start-up period. Emphasis was also placed on the development of the program's most readily quantifiable output—the congregate meal. Requirements to develop the program's supportive social service component were temporarily suspended to allow concentration on rapidly expanding the number of persons to whom meals were delivered.

The resultant rapid growth and development of the Title VII meal program was justified under politically motivated, short-term goals for program visibility and legitimacy. However, the price paid for this quick implementation and concentration on the congregate meal included lesser participation by the target group elderly, greater reliance on meal service vendors rather than project-operated kitchens for meal service delivery, and deviation from the long-term Title VII goals for health promotion among the aged through improved nutrition. Other researchers and policy analysts have recognized the political necessity, yet the detrimental effects of rapid implementation and focus on the program's congregate meal component.[2] They have noted that program policy was directed away from such critical program issues as needs for supportive services among the aged, quality of services provided, outreach and direction of Title VII services to target group aged, coordination of services with other community-based programs for the aged, and program monitoring and evaluation. These authors emphasized the need for a redirection of thinking relative to implementation of the NPOA. Some initial steps have been taken in this direction. Nonetheless, specific recommendations for future Title VII intervention design, stemming from objective evaluations of Title VII program's operating strategy and impact, are notably absent from the literature. This book attempts to fill a part of the void.

Within this context, the research explores the nature and scope of nutrition problems among the aged, the determinants of these problems, demographic trends which indicate the importance of seeking the earliest possible solution to these problems, and intervention design considerations for the Title VII program. To determine the nature and scope of nutrition problems among the aged, numerous national and local research studies among the aged were reviewed and summarized. Available research was also reviewed to identify demographic trends leading to the passage of Title VII and other legislation for programs for the aged, trends which will continue to impact on needs for social intervention programs. Government documents, congressional hearings, earlier research, discussions and interviews with many directly involved with the Title VII program provided the information needed to weave together the complex historical development of the Title VII program. To develop program design considerations, an in-depth objective evaluation of the Title VII program in the Boston area was completed in fiscal year 1976. Results of the Boston evaluation were compared with results of other Title VII research endeavors to identify consistent results and to summarize these for future programming. Finally, the results of the Boston research were shared with program practitioners to determine which design considerations would be most practical and feasible.

It was not within the scope of this research to evaluate the Title VII program relative to alternative program delivery strategies, for example, a food stamp program or commodity food distribution program. Rather, this research focused internally on the Title VII program in an attempt to quantify program outputs and impact to date; illuminate past policies which may have affected the degree of impact; and identify possible strategies for improved service delivery and goal attainment within the congregate, community-based service delivery mechanism. This intraprogram focus seemed justified in light of considerable political and financial commitment which has been made at the federal, state, and local levels to the current Title VII operating strategy.

This book can serve as a reference and planning tool for those involved in delivery of services to the aged, those studying nutrition intervention strategies, and those involved in the development and evaluation of program policies, particularly nutrition program policies.

Acknowledgments

There are many persons to whom I would like to express my sincere gratitude for their advice and guidance throughout this research. They include Dr. James Austin, Professor Jelia Witschi, and Dr. Robert Reed of the Harvard School of Public Health; Mr. Joe Carlin and Mr. George Malloy of the Region I Administration on Aging; Dr. Donald Watkin, former medical director of the National Program for Older Americans; Commissioner Maureen Schaffner of the Boston Area Agency on Aging and her diligent staff Ms. Ina Resnekoff, Ms. Aluma Motenko, and Ms. Linda Grant; as well as the local Title VII Nutrition program directors. Without these individuals and the perseverence of Miss Claire Wasserboehr who typed the manuscript, completion of the research would not have been possible.

Notes

1. National Academy of Sciences, Food and Nutrition Board: *Recommended Dietary Allowances*, 8th ed., Washington, D.C., 1974.

2. U.S. Senate Select Committee on Nutrition and Human Needs: "Nutrition and the Elderly," June 19, 1974; Watkin, D.M.: "The NPOA: A Successful Application of Current Knowledge in Nutrition and Gerontology," *World Rev. Nutr. Diet.* 26:26-40, 1977; and Lakoff, S.A.: "The Future of Social Intervention," in *Handbook of Aging and the Social Sciences*, chapter 25, eds. R.H. Binstock and E. Shanas, New York: Van Nostrand Reinhold Co., 1976.

1

The Problem Focus and Components of the Research

Factors Affecting the Nutritional Status of the Elderly

Preview of Malnutrition in the Aged

Malnutrition is one of the most pervasive and potentially debilitating problems of the aged in the United States. It may be present as biochemical or clinical deficiency with or without dietary involvement; it may arise from altered absorption, storage, or metabolism of nutrients secondary to acute or chronic disease, or result from chronic dietary excesses. Malnutrition has also been precipitated by various drugs and modes of disease therapy, and can be caused by physical, psychological, or socioeconomic barriers to optimal dietary intake.

Most nutritional problems among the aged are associated with chronic disease and disability because 85% of those 65 years of age and older in the United States have some form of chronic disease.[1] Half of these diseases, including coronary heart disease, hypertension, diabetes, arteriosclerosis, and obesity, are thought to be rooted in malnutrition.[2] Therefore many health problems of the aged which can have a secondary impact on nutritional status arise from chronic overnutrition. Nonetheless, nutritional deficiencies are also found to some extent since it is estimated that over half of the aged consume diets which contain less than recommended levels of nutrients.[3] Perhaps unique to those who are 60 or older, malnutrition is not confined to one economic, racial, or demographic stratum.[4]

Inadequate or excessive nutrition (food and nutrient intake) takes its toll on the aged by contributing to or exacerbating chronic and acute diseases, hastening the development of some of the degenerative diseases associated with aging, and promoting susceptibility to and delaying recovery from illness, thereby promoting dependency among the aged.

Beyond its physiological impact, food also has important psychological and social significance. Food can be a medium for socialization as well as a substitute for or enhancer of love.[5] Both what individuals consume and with whom they eat have great importance. Loss of appetite or lack of incentive to procure or prepare meals are often the symptoms of underlying loneliness, depression, social isolation, loss of self-esteem or dignity. Failure to understand both the physical and psychological dimensions of food will result in a failure to meet the nutritional needs of the aged.[6]

The design of effective interventions to mitigate the problems of malnutrition among the aged is a complex task that must draw upon expertise from many disciplines. To begin, it is helpful to identify the factors which may influence the nutritional status of elderly populations. Generally, these fall into three categories which are summarized in table 1-1, including the nature of the diet, the individual's characteristics (host factors); and the socioeconomic, physical, and social environment.

Diet and Standards of Dietary Adequacy

Focusing on diet, the nutrient composition of foods, the complementary or inhibitory effects of the nutrients they contain, and the manner in which foods are processed or prepared will interact and determine the exogenous supply of nutrients. A food usually contributes multiple nutrients to the diet, though it is frequently classified according to its contribution of a single nutrient. For example, red meats are rich sources of protein as well as fat (particularly saturated fat), potassium, phosphorus, iron, riboflavin, and niacin. Nutrients or other food components can interact and enhance or inhibit the absorption or utilization of other nutrients. For example, vitamin D and ascorbic acid aid calcium absorption, whereas large amounts of phosphate, phytate, or fat can inhibit calcium absorption. Extensive nutrient loss can occur during preparation and storage of food. Some nutrients can be destroyed by heat (vitamin A, thiamin, pantothenic acid, ascorbic acid), oxidation (vitamin A, ascorbic acid), prolonged cooking in water (thiamin, niacin), or exposure to sunlight (riboflavin, ascorbic acid).

Dietary adequacy is achieved when the exogenous supply of nutrients meets yet does not exceed an individual's metabolic requirements for nutrients. Standards of dietary adequacy for the healthy population have been prepared by the Food and Nutrition Board of the National Academy of Science and are presented in the report *Recommended Dietary Allowances* (RDA).[7] The standards for the population aged 51 and older and the adaptation of these standards for the Nutrition Program for Older Americans (NPOA) are summarized in tables 1-2 and 1-3.

It should be noted that these standards were designed to be adequate for nearly all healthy members of the U.S. population and they allow a margin of safety for individual variation in nutrient requirements. They were intended to act as goals for planning food supplies and evaluating the diet of groups of individuals. The RDA were never intended for use in evaluating individual dietary records, though they are frequently used for this purpose. In addition, the margins of safety added to the standards did not cover the modifications for requirements superimposed by disease.

There is currently little evidence to suggest that the process of aging itself has any impact on nutrient requirements, with perhaps the exception of reducing calorie needs. Nonetheless, the chronic and acute diseases, to which many aged succumb, may have profound impact on the individual's nutrient requirements. Therefore the RDA may have more limited use in evaluating the diets of the aged population. Certainly, the assessment of an aged individual's nutritional

Table 1-1
Diet, Host, and Environmental Factors That Influence Nutrition Status in the Elderly

Diet	Host	Environmental Factors
Level and adequacy of nutrient intake	Age	Socioeconomic
Protein, carbohydrate, fat	Sex	Inadequate income
Energy	Genetic makeup	Cultural food habits
Vitamins & minerals	Physical activity	Physical
Other dietary constituents	Exercise	Lack of preparation or storage facilities
Fiber	Loss of functional capacity	Distance to shopping
Phytate	Psychological and emotional stress	Social isolation
Water	Chronic conditions	Education
Food processing and preparation methods	*Circulatory:* Coronary heart disease, hypertension, cerebrovascular disease, diabetes	Media and quackery
	Digestive: Gallbladder disease, ulcer, abdominal hernia, enteritis & colitis, gastritis, constipation	Nutrition information
	Musculoskeletal: Paralysis, absence of extremities, arthritis & rheumatism, osteoporosis	Living situation
	Respiratory: Emphysema, bronchitis, asthma	
	Oral problems including dentition	
	Acute pathological states	
	Infection	
	Trauma	
	Neoplasia	
	Burns	
	Drugs and medication	
	Surgical intervention	
	Educational attainment	

Table 1–2
Recommended Dietary Allowances
(persons 51+ years)

	Male	Female
Calories (Kcal)	2,400.0	1,800.0
Protein (g)	56.0	46.0
Calcium (mg)	800.0	800.0
Iron (mg)	10.0	10.0
Vitamin A (IU)	5,000.0	4,000.0
Niacin (mg)	16.0	12.0
Thiamine (mg)	1.2	1.0
Riboflavin (mg)	1.5	1.1
Vitamin C (mg)	45.0	45.0
Vitamin D	–	–
Vitamin E (IU)	15.0	12.0
Folacin (μg)	400.0	400.0
Vitamin B_6 (mg)	2.0	2.0
Vitamin B_{12} (μg)	3.0	3.0
Phosphorus (mg)	800.0	800.0
Iodine (μg)	110.0	80.0
Magnesium (mg)	350.0	300.0
Zinc (mg)	15.0	15.0

Source: Reproduced from *Recommended Dietary Allowances*, 8th ed., 1974, with the permission of the National Academy of Sciences, Washington, D.C.

status will require records of nutrient intake as well as clinical and biochemical evaluations.

Host Factors

Nutrient requirements vary greatly across individuals and even for an individual at different times. Requirements may vary with a long list of factors, including age, sex, makeup, body size, physical activity and condition, level of stress, and environmental conditions. With the exception of environment, these characteristics are often termed host factors.

The effect of age appears to be a reduction in calorie needs which parallels the decline in metabolically active, lean body mass. The requirements for many nutrients are less for aged women than men because of the former's smaller body size or lesser proportion of metabolically active tissue. Genetics can predetermine susceptibility or resistance to disease. The major effect of physical activity or loss of functional capacity will be on altering calorie needs, though prolonged bed rest can affect metabolism and nutrient requirements. Psychological and emotional stress may impose problems related to reduce appetite or loss of motivation to eat.

Table 1–3
Dietary Regulations, Title VII Older American's Act[a]
Nutrition Programs for the Elderly

	1/3 RDA (1974)[b] (51+ years)
Calories (Kcal)	800.0
Protein (gm)	19.0
Vitamin A (IU)	1,667.0
Vitamin C (mg)	15.0
Niacin (mg)	5.0
Riboflavin (mg)	0.6
Thiamine (mg)	0.4
Calcium (mg)	267.0
Iron (mg)	3.3
Vitamin E (IU)	5.0
Folacin (μg)	0.1
Vitamin B_6	0.7
Vitamin B_{12}	1.0
Phosphorus (mg)	267.0
Iodine (μg)	37.0
Magnesium (mg)	117.0
Zinc (mg)	5.0

Source: Reproduced from *Recommended Dietary Allowances*, 8th ed., 1974, with the permission of the National Academy of Sciences, Washington, D.C.

[a]Legislation requires that meals served furnish one-third of the recommended dietary allowances for the age group. The 1974 allowances are the current suggestions for the nutritional basis of daily meals.

[b]Highest figure: male or female.

Chronic and acute diseases have a wide range of negative effects on the nutritional status of the aged. They can be generally categorized into those which affect digestion, absorption, and utilization of nutrients (selected chronic circulatory or musculoskeletal problems, pancreatic or hepatic insufficiency, intestinal or bacterial growth, structural gastric or bowel alterations), those which interfere with nutrient intake (e.g., oral problems including poor dentition), and those which increase the excretion of specific nutrients (diabetes, osteoporosis, infection, neoplasia, burns, trauma, prolonged bed rest). Surgical intervention may require preoperative and postoperative nutritional therapy. Dumping syndrome, metabolic bone disease associated with vitamin D deficiency and decreased absorption of calcium, and iron, folate, or vitamin B_{12} deficiency-induced anemias can follow gastric resection. Altered functional capacity of the small intestine with age or postsurgically may produce decreased absorption of thiamine, vitamins B_{12} and A, carotene, and folic acid and dietary fat. Negative nitrogen balance generally accompanies trauma.

Drugs often have a favorable effect on nutritional status by limiting the disease process, enhancing appetite, and correcting underlying metabolic defects.

On the other hand there are many examples of adverse drug/diet interrelationships. For example, folate deficiency can be produced in some persons using anticonvulsants. Antibiotic therapy has been found to produce vitamin deficiency by its action on bacterial microflora in the intestine. Chronic use or abuse of medications can produce gastrointestinal abnormalities which affect nutritional status. Prolonged use of laxatives can result in altered absorption of fat-soluble vitamins, diarrhea, weight loss, and fatigue.

Educational attainment may indirectly affect nutritional status to the extent that it influences an individual's knowledge of appropriate food preparation or consumption, dietary management, and susceptibility to media messages and quackery. Finally, psychological or emotional trauma may impose problems by reducing appetite or incentive to prepare or consume meals.

Environmental Factors

In addition to the influence of host and diet factors, several environmental factors are known to affect the nutritional status of the elderly. The primary influence of socioeconomic factors (income, cultural food patterns) and physical barriers to adequate nutrition (lack of preparation facilities, distance to shopping) will be on the nature and composition of the diet. Social isolation may influence an individual's appetite or desire to prepare food, while available educational information may influence the selection of food and preparation of nutrient needs.

The living situation, particularly living alone or in isolated rural or urban settings (about one-third of the 6.1 million elderly persons who live alone are thought to be socially isolated), may result in financial or psychological barriers to adequate nutrition.

Relative Importance of Factors

The extent to which dietary, host, and environmental factors influence the nutritional status of the aged is only partially understood. Some of the major studies of dietary intake among the aged are discussed in chapter 2, whereas the impact of disease on requirements for specific nutrients is elaborated in chapter 4.

Considering all the factors known to influence the nutritional status of the elderly, perhaps none are more important than the acute and chronic diseases and the financial burdens imposed by limited income. A firm estimate cannot be made of the absolute number of elderly persons with nutritional problems secondary to these factors. However, disease and inadequate income are perhaps the two most prevalent problems facing the elderly in the United States today.

Because of their close association with nutritional status and dietary intake, the dimensions of these problems are discussed.

Prevalence of Chronic and Acute Conditions

Chronic Conditions

The prevalence of chronic diseases in the elderly and the total population is summarized in table 1–4. In those 65 and older, chronic diseases are consistently more prevalent, such as circulatory conditions, including heart disease, hypertension, and cerebrovascular disease (stroke) which affect over 9.3 million; followed by musculoskeletal conditions, including arthritis which affects over 8 million. It also appears that about one-fifth of the aged (over 6 million) have serum cholesterol levels above 260 milligrams per 100 milliliters,[8] a level which markedly increases their risk of a heart attack[9] and therefore deserves attention.[10] About two in every five persons aged 65 and older (over 12 million) are obese (over 20% ideal body weight),[11] a state which elevates their risk of and exacerbates many chronic conditions, including coronary heart disease, hypertension, and diabetes. In addition, about 30% of those 65 and older (over 9 million) are thought to have osteoporosis, a disease characterized by bone loss, alterations in calcium metabolism, and susceptibility to bone fracture.[12]

The presence of chronic conditions apparently varies with an individual's sex, income, race, and level of educational attainment. For example, the prevalence of all heart conditions and hypertensive disease are inversely related to income and education of the family head.[13] The rate of hypertension in females is nearly twice that in males, while the rate of hypertension in whites is less than twice that in other races.[14] The rate of coronary heart disease is similar across income and educational strata, more prevalent in elderly males than females, and more prevalent among whites than other races. Women over the age of 65 have about four times the rate of osteoporosis as males. Respiratory conditions were more frequent in males and those with low incomes. All chronic digestive conditions (included in this discussion) were more prevalent in elderly females than males 65 and older and generally more frequent among those with low incomes.

Limitations in Functional Capacity

Limitations in functional capacity associated with chronic disease by age, living situation, income, and race are summarized in table 1–5. Overall, 43.2% of persons 65 and older (over 18 million) have some limitation in functional capacity

Table 1–4

Prevalence of Selected Chronic Conditions in Total U.S. Population and Persons 65 Years and Older

Chronic Conditions	Persons Aged 65+ (condition in thousands)	Persons Aged 65+ (no./1000)	Total Population
Circulatory			
Heart conditions[a]	3,959	198.7	50.4
Hypertensive disorders[b]	3,972	199.4	60.1
Coronary heart disease	1,674	84.0	16.2
Cerebrovascular disease	960	48.2	7.5
Arteriosclerosis	512	25.7	3.4
Musculoskeletal			
Arthritis	7,095	380.3	92.9
Paralysis, partial or complete	446	23.1	6.9
Rheumatism	432	23.2	6.1
Diseases of the bone	181	9.7	4.5
Respiratory			
Chronic bronchitis	782	41.2	32.7
Emphysema	602	31.7	6.6
Digestive			
Constipation	1,775	96.3	23.8
Abdominal cavity hernia	1,084	58.8	16.3
Upper gastrointestinal disorder	695	37.7	13.1
Enteritis & colitis	627	34.0	9.3
Gallbladder condition	605	32.8	10.3
Duodenal & stomach ulcer	535	29.0	17.2
Gastritis & duodenitis	442	24.0	8.6

Source: DHEW, PHS, HRA, NCHS: "Prevalence of Chronic Circulatory Conditions, U.S., 1972" (vital and health statistics series 10-94); "Prevalence of Chronic Skin and Musculo-skeletal Conditions, U.S., 1969" (series 10-92); "Prevalence of Chronic Respiratory Conditions, U.S., 1970" (series 10-84); "Prevalence of Selected Chronic Digestive Conditions, U.S., July–December, 1968" (series 10-83).

[a]Includes: heart conditions, acute and chronic rheumatic fever, hypertensive heart disease, other specific heart disease, unspecified disorders of heart rhythm, and heart trouble not otherwise specified.

[b]Hypertensive disease, not elsewhere classified.

due to chronic disease compared with 12.7% of persons of all ages. While 5.3% are not limited in their capacity to perform major activities (ability to work or keep house), about one-fifth of the aged (21.6%) are limited in major activities and 16.3% are unable to carry out major activities.[15] Functional capacity is also related to living situation, income, and race. The aged who live with nonrelatives or have incomes below poverty and nonwhites are more apt to have major limitations in functional capacity.

Table 1-5
Percent Distribution of Persons by Activity Limitation Status Because of Chronic Conditions: According to Age and Characteristic, United States, 1972

Age	No. of Persons (000)	No Activity Limitation	Limitation Not Major Activity [a]	Limitation in Major Activity	Unable to Carry Out Major Activity
			(% distribution)		
All persons, all ages	204,148	87.3	3.1	6.6	3.0
All persons, 65+	19,924	56.8	5.3	21.6	16.3
Persons 65+					
Living alone	5,612	58.3	7.3	24.5	9.9
Living with nonrelative	425	49.9	0.0	22.8	23.3
Income under $3,000	6,144	48.0	6.3	27.2	18.5
Nonwhite	1,749	48.2	4.7	23.2	24.0

Source: DHEW, PHS, HRA, NCHS: "Limitation in Activity and Mobility due to Chronic Conditions, U.S., 1972" (data from national health survey, series 10-96, 1974.)
[a]Major activity refers to ability to work, keep house, or engage in preschool or school activities.

Acute Conditions

In addition to chronic conditions, acute conditions (infections and parasitic diseases, respiratory infections, digestive disorders, injuries) take their toll on the elderly population. Their major impact on the health and nutritional status of the aged relates to their ability to limit functional capacity, confine the elderly to bed, and alter digestion, absorption, utilization, metabolism, and requirement for nutrients. The age-specific incidence of acute conditions across all age strata in the United States is lowest in persons 65 and older, 91.3 per 100 persons per year compared with 346.9 among those under 6 years of age.[16] On the other hand, the duration of disability associated with acute conditions is greatest in the elderly. Persons over 65 experience 13.3 days of activity loss per acute condition, including 5.8 days spent in bed as compared with 3.1 days of restricted activity including 1.3 days in bed among those under 6 years of age.[17] Therefore, while the rate of acute conditions is low in the aged, the effect of the conditions is more debilitating than in earlier years.

Poverty and Income Status of the Aged

Poverty appears to be the most important environmental determinant of inadequate nutrition among the elderly. It is associated with chronic disease, but its impact on nutritional status is indirect. Poverty alone cannot precipitate a nutritional deficiency. Poverty affects the availability of an adequate diet and may also reduce the availability of health care needed to diagnose, treat, and manage the chronic and acute diseases linked to nutritional status.

Poverty statistics for the population aged 65 and older by sex, race, and living situation are summarized in table 1-6.[18] Fifteen percent of those over 65 or 3.3 million had incomes below the Bureau of Census Poverty Index in 1975 ($2,572 for one person living alone or with nonrelatives, $3,232 for two persons, head of household). Of these, 2.6 million (79%) were white, the majority of whom (66%) were living alone or with nonrelatives. In addition, 20% of the impoverished elderly (652,000) were blacks, over half of whom were living alone or with nonrelatives, and 4% (137,000) were Spanish-speaking, of whom about two-fifths were living alone or with nonrelatives. The median income of families with heads over age 65 was less than three-fifths (59%) the median income for all American families in 1975 ($8,054 versus $13,719, respectively).

The proportion of elderly families with female heads that fell below the poverty level (26.4%) was almost three times the poverty rate in families with male heads (9.8%). Examination of the interracial and sex differences indicates that the poverty rate among elderly households with female heads is consistently higher than those with male heads. The poverty rate among black elderly families with female heads of households is over twice that of white families with

Table 1-6
Persons 65 Years and Older with Incomes below Poverty Level and Rate of Poverty, Elderly Family Status, Race, Household Head, and Ethnic Origin, 1975

	In Families		Living Alone or with Nonrelatives	
	No. of Persons below Poverty (000)	Poverty Rate (%)	No. of Persons below Poverty (000)	Poverty Rate (%)
Total				
All races	3,317	15.3	2,215	31.0
White	2,634	13.4	1,736	28.0
Black	652	36.3	366	61.1
Spanish	137	32.7	56	52.5
Heads of Household				
Male				
All races	1,411	9.8	410	27.7
White	1,106	8.4	299	23.8
Black	292	27.6	103	93.0
Heads of Household				
Female				
All races	1,905	26.4	1,716	31.9
White	1,527	23.7	1,437	27.1
Black	260	48.7	263	65.7

Source: Bureau of Census, *Money Incomes and Poverty Status of Families and Persons in the United States*, 1975 and 1975 revisions; September 1976.

female heads. The poverty rate for black households with male heads is slightly greater than that in white families with female heads (27.6% versus 23.7%, respectively) yet three times the poverty rate in white families with male heads (8.4%). Poverty was most prevalent among elderly black females who were living alone or with nonrelatives (65.7%). In fact, poverty among male and female elderly of both sexes who were living alone or with nonrelatives in 1975 was consistently higher than in families.

The absolute number of elderly living in families with white or black female heads that fell below the poverty line (1.9 million) was greater than the number of elderly below poverty living in families with male heads (1.4 million). In addition, there were 410,000 elderly males who were living alone or with non-relatives and fell below the poverty line in 1975, some 75% of whom were white and about 25% were black. There were 1.7 million elderly females living alone or with nonrelatives who were below the poverty level in 1975; the majority of these (1.4 million) were white, while 263,000 were black.

Quantifying Dimensions of Inadequate Nutrition

The nutritional status of the elderly individual and the quantitative impact of diet, host, and environmental factors are at best inadequately understood. Young[19] and Watkin[20] stressed the difficulties inherent in determining the scope of nutritional problems among the aged, the intricacies of studying the requirements for nutrients as age progresses, and our inadequate understanding of nutrient requirements among the aging. It can be argued convincingly that insufficient evidence exists upon which to determine quantitative dimensions of nutritional problems among the aged and to rank determinants of the problems by their relative importance. Nonetheless, if one accepts the premises that current methods of assessing dietary intake and biochemical status are sufficiently valid for making population estimates, and nutritional deficiency develops along the patterns of inadequate nutrient intake → biochemical lesion → clinical deficiency,[21] the available scientific literature can be reviewed to draw preliminary estimates of the risk of nutritional deficiency among the aged. Consistent with this approach is the statement of the National Academy of Science, Food and Nutrition Board,[22] "the farther habitual intake falls below the RDA standard for a particular nutrient and the longer the low intake continues, the greater the risk of deficiency." Furthermore, if the correlates of nutritional risk can be identified, the prevalence of factors increasing the risk of nutritional deficiencies can be quantified. The following chapter reviews the literature on the nutritional status of the aged and the nature and scope of their nutritional problems.

Notes

1. Watkin, D.M.: "Biochemical Impact of Nutrition on the Aging Process," in *Nutrition, Longevity, and Aging*, eds. M. Rockstein and M. Sussman, New York: Academic Press, 1976.

2. "Toward a National Policy on Aging," Proceedings of the 1971 White House Conference on Aging, vol. 2, 1971.

3. DHEW: First Health and Nutrition Examination Survey, United States, 1971-1972, "Dietary Intake and Biochemical Findings," pub. no. (HRA) 74-1219-1, National Center for Health Statistics, January 1974; Ten-State Survey, "Highlights," *Nutrition Today*, July/August 1972; and USDA, Agricultural Research Service: "Dietary Levels of Households in the United States, 1965," report no. 18, 1966.

4. DHEW: "Dietary Intake and Biochemical Findings"; Ten-State Survey; USDA: "Dietary Levels of Households"; Davidson, C.S., et al.: "The Nutrition of a Group of Apparently Healthy Aging Persons," *Am. J. Clin. Nutr.* 10:181-99, 1962; Dibble, M.V., et al.: "Evaluation of the Nutrition Status of Elderly Subjects, with a Comparison between Fall and Spring," *J. Am. Ger. Soc.* 11, 15: 1031-61, 1967; Fry, P.C., et al.: "Nutrient Intakes of Healthy Older Women," *J.A.D.A.* 42:218-22, 1963; Guthrie, H.A., et al.: "Nutritional Practices of Elderly Citizens in Rural Pennsylvania," *The Gerontologist* (Winter 1972): 330-35; LeBovit, C.: "The Food of Older Persons Living at Home," *J.A.D.A.* 46:285-89, 1965; Lyons, S., and Trulson, M.F.: "Food Practices of Older People Living at Home," *J. Ger.* 11:66-72, 1956; McGandy, R.B., et al.: "Nutrient Intakes and Energy Expenditures in Men of Different Ages," *J. Ger.* 21:581-87, 1966; Steinkamp, R.C., et al.: "Resurvey of an Aging Population: Fourteen-Year Followup," *J.A.D.A.* 46:103-10, 1965; Watkin, D.M.: "Aging, Nutrition and the Continuum of Health Care," *Ann. N.Y. Acad. Sci.* 300:290-97, 1977; and Young, C.M., et al.: "Food Usage and Food Habits of Older Workers," *Arch. Ind. Hyg. Occ. Med.* 100:501-11, 1954.

5. Weinberg, J.: "Psychologic Indications of the Nutritional Needs of the Elderly," *J.A.D.A.* 60:293-96, 1972.

6. Ibid.

7. National Academy of Sciences, Food and Nutrition Board: *Recommended Dietary Allowances*, 8th ed., Washington, D.C., 1974.

8. DHEW: "A Comparison of Levels of Serum Cholesterol of Adults 18-74 Years of Age in the United States 1960-62 and 1974-74," advance data no. 5, Feb. 22, 1977.

9. Kannel, W.B., et al.: "Serum Cholesterol Lipoproteins and the Risk of Coronary Heart Disease," The Framingham Study, *Ann. Int. Med.* 641:888-99, 1964.

10. There appears to be no general agreement about the applicability of cholesterol data among the aged. The Framingham data indicated that in men 30 to 49 years of age, the risk of heart attack was five times greater in those with serum cholesterol levels above 260 mg/100 ml than for those with cholesterol levels below 220 mg/100 ml. Concern for high cholesterol levels and dietary cholesterol and saturated fat modification to reduce serum cholesterol levels, at least in those under 80 years, seems prudent.

11. Master, A.M., et al.: "Analyses of Weight and Height of Apparently Healthy Populations, Ages 65 to 94 Years," *Proc. Soc. Exper. Biol. Med.* 102: 367-70, 1959.

12. Lutwak, L.: "Continuing Need for Dietary Calcium throughout Life," *Gerontology* 29:171-78, 1974.

13. DHEW: "Prevalence of Chronic Circulatory Conditions, U.S. 1972," National Health Survey, series 10, no. 94, PHS, September 1974.

14. Ibid.

15. DHEW: "Limitations in Activity due to Chronic Conditions, U.S., 1974," National Health Survey, series 10, no. 111, PHS, June 1977.

16. DHEW: "Acute Conditions: Incidence and Associated Disability, U.S. July 1974–June 1975," National Health Survey, series 10, no. 114, PHS, February 1977.

17. Ibid.

18. U.S. Department of Commerce, Bureau of the Census, "Money Incomes and Poverty States of Families and Persons in the United States: 1975 and 1974 Revisions," series P-60, no. 103, September 1976.

19. Young, V.R.: "Protein Metabolism and Needs in Elderly People," in *Nutrition, Longevity and Aging*, M. Rockstein and M.L. Sussman, New York: Academic Press, 1976.

20. Watkin: "Biochemical Impact of Nutrition," in *Nutrition, Longevity, and Aging,* M. Rockstein and M.L. Sussman, New York: Academic Press, 1976.

21. Hegsted, D.M.: "Dietary Survey Methodologies," *J.A.D.A.* 60:13, 1975.

22. National Academy of Sciences, Food and Nutrition Board: *Recommended Dietary Allowances.*

Nutrition Status of the Elderly

National Nutrition Literature

Three major sources of national data concerning the nutritional status and dietary intake of the aged have been published, including the First Health and Nutrition Examination Survey,[1] the Ten-State Survey,[2] and the 1965 USDA Household Food Consumption Survey.[3] These studies and those derived from local selected samples of elderly individuals are summarized in table 2-1.

The criteria for evaluating dietary adequacy are summarized with the conclusions. In most cases, the standards used were the RDA that were available at the time of the study. The HANES survey, however, had its own set of standards which are also summarized in table 2-2, along with other standards of dietary adequacy. Because of the varying criteria of dietary adequacy and differing techniques used to determine dietary intake and nutritional status, it is difficult to compare data from the various studies.

In the 1971 HANES survey, dietary and biochemical data were collected from a national probability sample of persons 1 to 74 years of age. The observations indicated that half (56.2%) or about 18 million persons 60 years of age and older were consuming diets inadequate in one or more nutrients. The most frequent deficits were dietary iron, vitamin A, ascorbic acid, and calcium. Low hemoglobin and hematocrit levels, suggestive of iron-deficiency anemia, were found among aged black persons in the following proportions: in 27.6% and 35.2% respectively. In addition, 7% and 15.4% of aged white individuals had low hemoglobins and hematocrits, respectively. Clinical signs of nutritional deficiency were uncommon, but obesity was prevalent, particularly among elderly black females and white males.

The Ten-State Survey[4] involved populations with the lowest quartiles of income at the time of the 1960 census from five relatively high-income and five relatively low-income states (Washington, California, Texas, Louisiana, South Carolina, Kentucky, West Virginia, Michigan, Massachusetts, New York). Nutritional deficits of dietary origin were prevalent among those aged 60 and older and included iron in both sexes; vitamin A in Spanish-American men and women; riboflavin in black and Spanish-Americans of both sexes; and ascorbic acid in males of all racial origins. Anthropometric measurements were similar to HANES data indicating the common occurrence of obesity in black as well as white women. Biochemical data corroborated with dietary findings relative to poor iron status of the aged.

Table 2-1
Summary of Nutrition Status in Noninstitutionalized Elderly

Author	Year	Location of Study	Study Population	Methods	Conclusions
U.S. Department of Agriculture	1955	National		24-hr recall	Older persons have poorer diets in all nutrients compared to younger households.
U.S. Department of Agriculture	1965	National	14,519 individuals 1,643 elderly	24-hr recall	Mean intake was adequate; diets of older males were low in ascorbic acid, vitamin A, thiamin, riboflavin, & calcium; women, 65–74, had diets low in calcium, thiamin, & riboflavin; smaller & low-income households had poorest diets.
Ten-state nutrition survey	1972	Ten states	24,000 families	Physical exams, anthropometry, x-ray, hemo-globin %, HCT subgroup, dietary analysis	Biochemistries showed undernutrition in elderly was not restricted to low-income strata or ethnic minorities; iron and ascorbic acid were in deficit.
HANES	1971–1972	National	10,127 individuals 1,938 elderly	24-hr recall, hemoglobin %, hematocrit, serum albumin	In elderly blacks, 36% had intake below 1,000 calories and were low in iron; overall, 12% under 25 g protein daily, 41% under 450 mg calcium, 38% under 30 mg ascorbic acid, & 56% under 3,000 IU vitamin A.
Jordan, Kepes, Hayes, Hammond	1954	Westchester County, N.Y.	100 elderly living alone	Diet history	Proportion of diets low in citrus fruits, 40%; milk, 43%; vegetables, 59%; protein, 34%.
Lyons & Trulson	1956	Boston	100 low to moderate income elderly	Diet history, illness/social history	Proportion below 2/3 RDA: males: calories, 39%; calcium, 23%; iron, 13%; thiamin, 32%; riboflavin, 23%; niacin, 10%; females: calories, 14%; calcium, 23%; iron, 33%; thiamin, 17%; riboflavin, 16%; ascorbic acid, 20%.
Davidson, Livermore, Anderson, Kaufman	1962	Boston	104 middle-upper-income elderly	7-day recall & record	Proportion below RDA: B_2, 37%; niacin 57%; calcium 30%; iron 40%; vitamins A 7%; B_1 21%; C 16%.

Authors	Year	Location	Sample	Methods	Findings
Fry, Fox, Linkswiler	1963	Lincoln, Nebr.	32 women, 65–80, living alone	Weighed intake; 7-day recall	Mean intake met RDA; high individual variation; proportion of diets low in individual nutrients: iron, 12%; calcium, 16%; vitamin A, 29%.
LeBovit	1965	Rochester, N.Y.	283 low-income households	7-day record	25% below RDA for one or more of 7 nutrients, 30% without food supplies to meet RDA for calcium and vitamin C.
Steinkamp, Cohen, Walsh	1965	San Mateo, Calif.	54 men, 58 women 50+	1-day food record	25% males, 50% females below RDA for calcium; 25% of sample low in vitamin A and ascorbic acid.
Dibble, Brin, Peel, Thiele, Chen, McMullen	1967	Syracuse, N.Y.	214 elderly 50+	Food intake; blood: vitamin A, ascorbic acid, transketolase; urine: thiamin, riboflavin	Deficient to low serum ascorbic acid levels in 7%; under 5% deficient for vitamin A or carotene; transketolase activity normal; thiamin and riboflavin in urine suboptimal in 41% and 17% of cases.
Brin, Dibble, Peel, McMullen, Bourguin, Chen	1965	Onondaga, N.Y.	254 institutionalized and noninstitutionalized elderly	Blood: HCT, ascorbic acid, vitamin A; urine: thiamin	18% low HCT, 22% low serum ascorbic acid levels, 4% low vitamin A, 6% low thiamin; institutionalized more often low nutrient status.
McGandy, Barrows, Spanias, Meredith, Stone, Norris	1966	Baltimore	252 professionals	7-day record anthropometry; BMR	Mean intake met RDA for all nutrients; decline in iron, thiamin, riboflavin, & niacin intake with advancing age accounted for by reduced intake with falling BMR and activity levels.
Young, Streib, Greer	1954	Ithaca, N.Y.	640 elderly	24-hr recall, 1-day food record	10% men & 7% women had adequate diets; foods & nutrients in short supply: milk, protein, ascorbic acid, & vitamin A; intake more adequate as educational level increased.
Guthrie, Black, Madden	1972	Rural Pennsylvania	109 elderly	24-hr recall	Low income particularly at risk of deficit; proportion of low-income diets below 2/3 RDA: calories 55%, protein 42%, calcium 70%, thiamin 51%, riboflavin 57%, ascorbic acid 51%.
Kohrs	1976	Jefferson City, Mo.	547 elderly, Title VII program participants & nonparticipants	24-hr recall, diet history, selected biochemistries	Infrequent Title VII participants and program nonparticipants more likely at risk of vitamin A and ascorbic acid deficiency; participants consume more calories, protein, calcium; sex, occupation, educational levels related to diet in some groups of elderly.

The 1965 U.S. Department of Agriculture, Household Food Consumption Survey[5] provides the base for comparing the dietary intake of various age and socioeconomic strata in the country. The survey demonstrates decreased mean nutrient intake with advancing age in males and females. Though mean intake of all age groups appeared adequate when compared with the recommended dietary allowances,[6] mean intake data failed to disclose the variability in nutrient consumption and the proportion of the population consuming one or more nutrients below recommended levels. Diets of older males were most frequently inadequate in ascorbic acid, vitamin A, riboflavin, and calcium, whereas diets of elderly women were most frequently low in calcium, thiamin, and riboflavin. A significant association was also found between inadequate nutrient intake and low income.

It should be noted that the implications of many biochemical findings and the etiology of both clinical and biochemical abnormalities are not completely understood;[7] however, the available national data on clinical/biochemical status and dietary intake emphasize the high relative risk of malnutrition among the aged.

Problem Scope

The national dietary intake surveys indicate that the 32 million persons currently over age 60 constitute a population very vulnerable to nutrient deficiencies. The aged are clearly the segment of the population most prone to acute and chronic diseases and associated decreased functional capacity and number disproportionately among those who are poor, poorly educated, uninformed about good dietary practices, and socially isolated.

It seems appropriate to conclude that no less than 3 million elderly Americans (one-tenth of the population aged 60+) and as many as 18 million (56.2%) may be consuming diets that are below standard. This would suggest that a large number of the aged consume diets that are incapable of providing the level of nutrients needed for the maintenance of adequate nutritional status, physical health, and well-being; inappropriate for therapeutic regimens for managing acute and chronic diseases; and that may predispose them to or exacerbate many chronic diseases. It also seems clear that two major factors—disease and poverty—weigh most heavily on the maintenance of adequate nutritional status among the aged.

The remaining relevant literature includes studies that were done with local nonrandom samples of aging individuals. These studies cannot assist in quantifying the scope of nutritional problems nationally, but shed light on the factors predisposing to inadequate nutrition.

Local Nutrition Studies

Lyons and Trulson[8] studied a random probability sample of 100 persons, 65 and older, in a low-income to moderate-income area in Boston and documented dietary deficits of males and females. Highly variable dietary intake was found: one-quarter of the sample consumed less than the daily recommended allowance of one or more nutrients. Calories, iron, riboflavin, and ascorbic acid were the most frequently found nutrients in deficit in the diets of elderly women. The diets of elderly males were often low in calcium, thiamin, riboflavin, and calories. Similarly, Jordan et al.[9] compared dietary histories from 100 elderly living alone in Westchester County, New York, with the Jolliffe check list for a satisfactory diet[10] and found 40% of the diets inadequate in citrus fruit, 43% low in milk or cheese, 59% low in vitamin-A-rich vegetables, and 43% low in protein. Food habits leading to comparatively poor dietary intake were associated with poor health, social isolation, and economic constraints. LeBovit[11] examined the intake of 283 predominantly low-income households and found the diets poorest in those with older persons, lowest incomes, and where persons were living alone, particularly males. Lack of interest in eating and poor appetite were serious problems in this sample. Diets of a quarter of the households were below two-thirds of the recommended dietary allowances (RDA) for one or more nutrients. Ascorbic acid and calcium were in shortest supply.

Davidson et al.[12] studied 104 middle-income and upper-income volunteers in the Age Center of New England (Boston), aged 51 to 97. Dietary information was collected by seven-day recall and a one-week record of food intake. Information from the two weeks was summarized and compared with the RDA. Additional information about eating habits, interest in food fads, availability of foods, and significant changes in consumption over time was collected. The authors concluded that most of the elderly shopped for food and ate meals alone; food habits did change with advancing age because of high food costs, inaccessible food shopping centers, and loss of desire to prepare meals. Those living alone, retired, and with lower incomes had less variety of food in their diets as well as comparatively less vitamin A, ascorbic acid, iron, and calcium intake than other elderly. The authors also concluded that the most socially isolated were in greatest need of nutrition intervention because of dietary intake which placed them at greatest risk of nutrient deficit. In the Boston study, the socially isolated persons were most often female, very old, and above ideal body weight.

Fry and coworkers[13] used weighed intakes and seven-day records to determine the intake of 32 women, aged 65–80, living in Nebraska. Significant variation in intake existed for all nutrients. Mean intake met the RDA for all nutrients, while calcium and iron fell below recommended levels in the diets of many individuals.

Table 2-2
Daily Dietary Intake Standards for the Aged

	1964 RDA[a] (55-75)[f]		1968 RDA[a] (55-75)[f]		1974[b] RDA[a] (51+)[f]		FAO/WHO[c] (60+)[f]		HANES Survey[d] (60+)[f]		1980 RDA (51+)[f]	
	Male	Female	Male	Female	Male	Female	Male	Female	Male	Female	Male	Female
Calories (Kcal)	2,200.0	1,600.0	2,400.0	1,600.0	2,400.0	1,800.0	2,380.0	1,680.0	34/kg	24/kg	2,400.0	1,800.0
Protein (g)	70.0	58.0	65.0	55.0	56.0	46.0	70.0	58.0	1/kg	1/kg	56.0	44.0
Calcium (g)	800.0	800.0	800.0	800.0	800.0	800.0	400.0	400.0	400.0	400.0	800.0	800.0
Iron (mg)	10.0	10.0	10.0	10.0	10.0	10.0	10.0	10.0	10.0	10.0	10.0	10.0
Vitamin A (IU)	5,000.0	5,000.0	5,000.	5,000.0	5,000.0	5,000.0	3,500.0	3,500.0	3,500.0	3,500.0	1,000.0[e]	800.0[e]
Niacin (mg)	15.0	13.0	14.0	13.0	16.0	12.0	16.0	11.0	(information not available)		16.0	13.0
Thiamin (mg)	0.9	0.8	1.3	1.0	1.2	1.0	.95	.67	"		1.2	1.0
Riboflavin (mg)	1.3	1.2	1.7	1.5	1.5	1.1	1.30	.90	"		1.4	1.2
Vitamin C (mg)	70.0	70.0	60.0	55.0	45.0	45.0	30.00	30.00	60.0	60.0	60.0	60.0

Source: Adapted from P. O'Hanlon and M.B. Kohrs, "Dietary Standards of Older Americans," *Am. J. Clin Nutr.* 31:1257-69, 1978.

[a]RDA = *Recommended Dietary Allowances*, published by the National Academy of Science, National Research Council, in 1964 (6th ed.) 1968 (7th ed.), and 1974 (8th ed.).

[b]Basis for Ten-State Study (1968-70): 70 kg male; 58 kg female.

[c]FAO = Food and Agricultural Organization, World Health Organization. Guidelines used for the Ten-State Nutrition Survey (1970).

[d]HANES = First Health and Nutrition Examination Survey (1971-72).

[e]Micrograms of retinal equivalents.

[f]Age

A 14-year longitudinal study of 273 persons in San Mateo, California, was conducted by Steinkamp et al.[14] Data from 114 individuals who had completed three previous dietary histories were analyzed. Individual intake showed no significant trend over time. There was a general trend toward lower consumption in persons over 75 years, while the proportion of calories from protein, carbohydrate, and fat remained constant in all diets. A quarter of males' and one-half of females' diets were below two-thirds the RDA for calcium; one-quarter of participants' diets were low in vitamin A and ascorbic acid.

Seasonal variation in dietary intake was studied by Dibble and others.[15] The nutritional status of 214 elderly volunteers was evaluated using dietary and biochemical information, supplemented with socioeconomic statistics. Significantly more women were found to have poor iron status, defined by ICNND hematocrit standards.[16] Those in the deficient category all had diets below two-thirds the RDA for iron. Dietary iron, thiamin, and riboflavin were suboptimal in 43%, 41%, and 17% of the diets of the total sample, respectively. Significant fall to spring variation in intake was not found. The authors concluded that 10% of the elderly population had suboptimal status for three out of five nutrients.

McGandy[17] evaluated seven-day records, anthropometric data, basal metabolic rates, and activity patterns of 252 professional volunteers, aged 20 to 99 in Baltimore. He found no significant differences in nutrient intake between age groups. The progressive decline in iron, thiamin, riboflavin, and niacin intake was accounted for by age-incremental declines in calorie intake which followed falling basal metabolic rate and energy expenditure. It was emphasized that the individuals studied were of high socioeconomic status. This fact may have eradicated any difficulty in procuring food.

Young et al.[18] in Ithaca, New York, utilized 24-hour recall to evaluate the dietary practices of 1,640 industrial employees, aged 64. The intakes were compared for different educational levels and income strata. In only 10% of males and 7% of females did diets meet standards of adequacy. The foods or nutrients most often in deficit were milk (35–39%), protein (40–51%), and ascorbic acid (30–40%). Over 40% of the males and 30% of the females had diets without protective food rich in vitamin C (ascorbic acid). Two-thirds of the older workers had no rich dietary source of vitamin A or carotene. Educational level seemed positively correlated with dietary intake, whereas a significant association between dietary intake and income was not seen.

Brin et al.[19] analyzed urine and blood samples and concluded that most volunteers in a group of 234 elderly in Onondaga, New York, were fairly well nourished. However, 18% had low hematocrit levels, 8% deficient ascorbic acid levels, and 6% deficient thiamin. The institutionalized elderly seemed more at risk of being in the low to deficient categories for all nutrients.

Guthrie and coworkers[20] examined the 24-hour diet recall of 109 elderly individuals from low-income and higher-income households. Those with low incomes had diets poorer in iron, protein, and riboflavin than individuals with incomes above poverty. Both groups had less adequate diets than low-income families of all ages. Guthrie and coworkers concluded that both age and income adversely affect dietary adequacy and suggested that the elderly poor are more vulnerable nutritionally than either the elderly or the poor of all ages.

Whereas there is only one study of the dietary intake and nutritional status of elderly participants and nonparticipants of the Title VII National Nutrition Program for Older Americans, others with more limited scope have been done.[21] (The national Title VII evaluation will hopefully add data in this area, but it is not expected until 1980.) Using the ten-state biochemical guidelines of nutritional risk and the RDA to assess dietary adequacy, Kohrs[22] studied 547 elderly from one of three groups: program participants who ate Title VII congregate meal the day of food record completion; program participants who had not eaten Title VII congregate meal on days of food record completion; and elderly Title VII program nonparticipants.

Program participants appeared to consume more calories, protein, and calcium than nonparticipants. Education, sex, and occupation were related to dietary intake in nonparticipants and participants not eating at the program site on the day of the food record. Males consumed significantly more calories, protein, iron, thiamin, and niacin than females. Education had a significant positive relationship to intake of protein, thiamin, and niacin, and was inversely related to saturated fat intake in nonparticipants and participants who did not attend on the day of food record. Unskilled laborers were likely to consume more protein, calcium, and thiamin among nonparticipants and likely to consume less calories, thiamin, niacin, and saturated fats among participants. Among those who came to the program on the day of food record, socioeconomic characteristics did not correlate with nutrient intake.

Persons who attended the program less than twice a week and nonparticipants were more apt to be biochemically at risk of inadequate vitamin A and ascorbic acid status. Iron status among females who came more than twice a week was poorer than nonparticipants' or those who attended the program less frequently. Prevalence of iron deficiency was 0.8% and 1.2% among all females and males, respectively. Less than 1% of the elderly studied were protein or riboflavin deficient.

The local nutrition studies further support the national data which indicate the scope of nutritional problems among the aged. Together they emphasize the complexity of determinants of nutritional problems and suggest that the following factors interact to affect the dietary intake and nutritional status of the aged: poor health, social isolation, economic constraints, motivation to eat and appetite, functional capacity, process of aging, and educational attainment.

Future Research Needs

In addition to assisting in the determination of the scope and nature of the nutritional problems of the aged, the available nutrition literature emphasized the needs for research in the following areas: quantification of nutrient require-ments of healthy elderly individuals as well as those with diseases; development of valid and reliable methods of assessing the health and nutritional status as well as dietary adequacy among aging populations; and detailed assessment of physio-logical, dietary, and environmental determinants of the nutritional status and nutrient intake of the aged.

Future research endeavors may provide the framework for monitoring the health status of the elderly population. They will assist in defining appropriate standards of dietary adequacy for the healthy aged population as well as those with chronic diseases. Research will assist in quantifying the impact of disease on the absorption, metabolism, and requirements for nutrients among the aged. Such research will also guide practitioners in their treatment of diseases and will provide the basis for recommendations concerning optimal diet at all ages.

Until this research is accomplished, practitioners must rely on the available data to make decisions concerning the management of nutritional problems among the aged. Though the data are sparse, there is no question that the aged are more at risk of nutritional problems relative to other age groups in the country. They therefore deserve priority consideration when domestic nutrition interventions are designed.

Design of Nutrition Interventions

To design effective nutrition interventions, it is necessary to search beyond the data on the nature and scope of nutritional problems among the aged and ex-amine in detail two additional characteristics of the elderly population, that is, its changing demographic composition and the requirements for nutrients among the aged.

The demographic characteristics of the elderly population have important implications for addressing the issue of urgency of needs among the aged. Chap-ter 3 discusses the aging of the population in the United States, emphasizing the critical need to act soon in developing intervention plans concerning the aged.

An understanding of the nutrient requirements of the elderly is important in setting guidelines for nutrition interventions as well as establishing criteria for evaluating the delivery of food and nutrients to them. Nutrient requirements of the aged and factors which impact on requirements, including specific chronic diseases, are discussed in chapter 4.

Notes

1. DHEW: First Health and Nutrition Examination Survey, United States, 1971-1972, "Dietary Intake and Biochemical Findings," pub. no. (HRA) 74-1219-1, National Center for Health Statistics, January 1974.

2. Ten-State Survey, "Highlights," *Nutrition Today*, July/August 1972.

3. USDA, Agricultural Research Service: "Dietary Levels of Households in the United States, 1965," report no. 18, 1966.

4. Ten-State Survey.

5. USDA: "Dietary Levels of Households."

6. National Academy of Sciences, Food and Nutrition Board: *Recommended Dietary Allowances*, 8th ed., Washington, D.C., 1974.

7. Gershoff, S.N., et al.: "Studies of the Elderly in Boston. I: The Effects of Iron Fortification on Moderately Anemic People," *Am. J. Clin. Nutr.* 30: 226-34, 1977.

8. Lyons, J.S., and Trulson, M.F.: "Food Practices of Older People Living at Home," *J. Ger.* 11:66-72, 1956.

9. Jordan, M., et al.: "Dietary Habits of Persons Living Alone," *Geriatrics* 9:230-32, 1954.

10. Jolliffe, N.: "The Preventive and Therapeutic Use of Vitamins," *J.A.M.A.* 129:613-17, 1945.

11. LeBovit, C.: "The Food of Older Persons Living at Home," *J.A.D.A.* 46:285-89, 1965.

12. Davidson, C.S., et al.: "The Nutrition of a Group of Apparently Healthy Aging Persons," *Am. J. Clin. Nutr.* 10:181-89, 1962.

13. Fry, P.C., et al.: "Nutrient Intakes of Healthy Older Women," *J.A.D.A.* 42:218-22, 1963.

14. Steinkamp, R.C., et al.: "Resurvey of an Aging Population: Fourteen-Year Followup." *J.A.D.A.* 46:103-10, 1965.

15. Dibble, M.V., et al.: "Evaluation of the Nutrition Status of Elderly Subjects, with a Comparison between Fall and Spring," *J. Am. Ger. Soc.* 15: 1031-61, 1967.

16. Interdepartmental Committee on Nutrition for National Defense: *Manual for Nutrition Surveys,* Bethesda, Md.: National Institutes of Health, 1963.

17. McGandy, R.B., et al.: "Nutrient Intakes and Energy Expenditures in Men of Different Ages," *J. Ger.* 21:581-87, 1966.

18. Young, C.M., et al.: "Food Usage and Food Habits of Older Workers," *Arch. Ind. Hyg. Occ. Med.* 100:501-11, 1954.

19. Brin, M., et al.: "Some Preliminary Findings on the Nutrition Status of the Aged in Onondaga, New York," *Am. J. Clin. Nutr.* 17:240-58, 1965.

20. Guthrie, H.A., et al.: "Nutritional Practices of Elderly Citizens in Rural Pennsylvania," *Gerontologist* (Winter 1972):330-35.

21. Hosokawa, M.C., et al.: "Central Missouri Nutrition Assessment Project," 1975; idem: "Nutrition Project Assessment," Central Missouri AAA, 1976; Hardman, A.P., and Bringwatt, R.J.: "Program Integration: An Approach Using Titles III and VII of the Older Americans Act and Title XX of the Social Security Act," paper presented at the Gerontological Society 30th Annual Scientific Meeting, Nov. 18-22, 1977; Martin, J.D., and Folkemer, D.: "Nutrition and

Social Experience: A Descriptive Evaluation of Title VII Lunch Programs in Maryland," paper presented at the American Gerontological Society Annual Convention, New York City, October 1976; and Postma, J.S.: "The Characteristics and Needs of the Eugene-Springfield Elderly Nutrition Congregate Meals Program Participants and Their Perceptions of the Program's Effects and Operation," doctoral dissertation, University of Oregon, 1974.

22. Kohrs, M.B.: "Influences of the Congregate Meal Program in Central Missouri on Dietary Practices and Nutritional Status of Participants," Jefferson City, Mo.: Lincoln University, Department of Agriculture and Natural Resources, Human Nutrition Research Program, August 1976a; Kohrs, M.B., et al.: "Contribution of the Nutrition Program for Older Americans to Nutritional Status," paper delivered at American Gerontological Society Meetings, New York City, 1976b; Kohrs, M.B.: "Nutrition Data from an 'Aging Program': Implications for Planning," paper presented at the Society for Nutrition Education Annual Meeting, Kansas City, Mo., 1976c; and Hosokawa et al.: "Central Missouri Nutrition Assessment."

The Aging of the U.S. Population

3

Definition of Aging

Aging refers to the irreversible biological changes that occur progressively within individuals over their life span.[1] Though the process of aging begins at conception, the term aging generally refers to changes that occur later in life, following the reproductive period.

Aging has been defined in terms of physical functional capacity and chronological age. Physically and functionally, it is clear that aging occurs at markedly different rates across individuals, though the physical signs of deterioration eventually occur in all persons. This makes the description of normal aging difficult, if not impossible.

When using chronological age as the criteria of aging, adjustments are not made for these varying rates of physiological change. Therefore chronological age may yield less than satisfactory results when used to differentiate individuals. In demography, chronological age is generally used to describe the aging of populations. It is assumed that for large populations, the aging process follows a pattern and functional and physiological age follows chronological age closely.

With these assumptions in mind, the aging of the U.S. population is examined. To begin with, the age strata 65 years and older is generally used to refer to the elderly or aged individuals. For our purpose, however, statistics for the population 60 and older are used to the extent they are available since this age group and their spouses, regardless of age, are eligible for participation in the Title VII Nutrition Program for Older Americans.

Size of the Aged Population

Trends in growth of the population aged 65 and older are in figure 3-1. The age distribution and percent increase in persons 55 and older from 1900 to 2040 are in table 3-1. The population 60 and older in the United States numbered 4.9 million in 1900 and had risen to 31.6 million in 1975.[2] Not only has the number of elderly individuals increased, but the American population itself has aged. The proportion of persons 60 years of age and older increased from 6.4 to 14.8% of the population during the same time period. Each year from 300,000 to 400,000 persons reached age 60. This trend has increased and it is now estimated that over 450,000 persons reach age 60 each year.[3]

27

Table 3-1
Total Population in the Older Ages and Decennial Increases: 1900 to 2040

(Numbers in thousands. Estimates and projections as of July 1. Total resident population of the 48 States and District of Columbia (excluding Alaska and Hawaii) for 1900 to 1930. Estimates for 1940 and later years refer to the total population of the 50 States and District of Columbia and include Armed Forces overseas. A minus sign (−) denotes a decrease.)

Year	55 Years and Over		60 Years and Over		65 Years and Over		75 Years and Over		85 Years and Over	
	Number	% Increase in Preceding Decade	Number	% Increase in Preceding Decade	Number	% Increase in Preceding Decade	Number	% Increase in Preceding Decade	Number	% Increase in Preceding Decade
Estimates										
1900	7,125	(X)	4,901	(X)	3,099	(X)	899	(X)	[1]122	(X)
1910	9,087	27.5	6,274	28.0	3,986	28.6	1,170	30.1	[1]167	36.9
1920	11,548	27.1	7,952	26.7	4,929	23.7	1,449	23.8	[1]210	25.7
1930	15,182	31.5	10,484	31.8	6,705	36.0	1,945	34.2	[1]272	29.5
1940	19,725	29.9	13,822	31.8	9,031	34.7	2,664	37.0	370	[2]36.0
1950	25,793	30.8	18,500	33.8	12,397	37.3	3,904	46.5	590	59.5
1960	32,299	25.2	23,828	28.8	16,675	34.5	5,621	44.0	940	59.3
1970	38,749	20.0	28,751	20.7	20,085	20.4	7,598	35.2	1,432	52.3
1975	42,180	(X)	31,643	(X)	22,400	(X)	8,527	(X)	1,877	(X)
Projections[3]										
1980	45,570	17.6	34,267	19.2	24,523	22.1	9,112	19.9	2,071	44.6
1990	49,412	8.4	39,127	14.2	28,933	18.0	11,402	25.1	2,487	20.1
2000	53,537	8.3	40,589	3.7	30,600	5.8	13,521	18.6	3,217	29.4
2010	65,733	22.8	48,012	18.3	33,239	8.6	13,893	2.7	3,841	19.4
2020	79,481	20.9	60,664	26.4	42,791	28.7	15,381	10.7	3,826	−0.4

2030	(II)	82,546	3.9	67,037	10.5	51,590	20.6	20,716	34.7	4,409	15.2
	(III)	82,418	3.7								
Range {	(I)	82,730	4.1								
2040	(II)	84,783	2.7	65,854	-1.8	50,266	-2.6	24,218	16.9	5,993	35.9
	(III)	79,809	-3.2	63,822	-4.8	50,149	-2.8				
Range {	(I)	91,053	10.1	68,318	1.9	50,431	-2.2				

Source: *Census of Population, 1930*, Population Vol. II, *General Report*; and *Current Population Reports*, Series P-25, Nos. 311, 519, 614, and 601. In Bureau of Census Series P-23, No. 59, May 1976.

X Not applicable.

[1] Estimates for 1900-30 as of April 1.

[2] Pertains to 10 1/4 year period.

[3] Base date of projections is July 1, 1974.

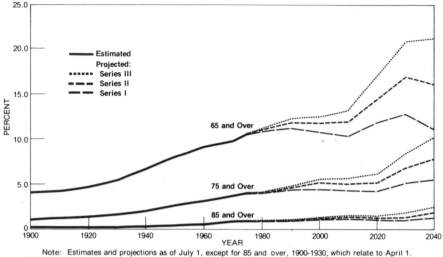

Note: Estimates and projections as of July 1, except for 85 and over, 1900-1930, which relate to April 1. Points are plotted for years ending in zero except for 1975.

Source: U.S. Bureau of Census, series P-23, no. 59, May 1976.

Figure 3-1. Percent of Total Population in Older Ages: 1900 to 2040

By the year 2000, population projections suggest that the number of persons over 60 will increase to 42 million or 30% greater than at present. About 20% of the population will be 60 years of age or older and eligible for Title VII services as currently defined.[4]

In addition to trends in the population as a whole, the population 65 years and older has also been aging. The proportion of the population that is 65-69 is growing smaller relative to those 75 and older.[5] In 1900, the 65-69 category was 42.3% of those 65 years and older, whereas the 75 and older was 29%. In 1975, the 65-69 group was 35% of the population 65 years and older, whereas the 75 and older group had risen to 38.1%[6]

Determinants of Population Aging

Three primary forces lie behind the growth in size and proportion of the elderly population: rise in fertility rates, that is, post-World Wars I and II; declining age-specific death rates; and influx of immigrants, particularly up to World War I.[7]

Fertility Rates

A general rise in the birthrate in the nineteenth century and during the first part
of the twentieth century has accounted for the growth of the elderly population
and will continue to account for its growth until about 1990.[8] The declining
fertility of the 1960s will have the additional effect of increasing the number of
persons 60 years of age and older relative to the younger population. After
1990, the rate of growth in the elderly population will decline somewhat until
the first two decades of the next century, when the effects of the post-World
War II baby boom are felt. During this time, the population aged 60 and older
will surge forward again. After the year 2020, growth rate projections suggest a
marked decline in the rate of growth of the aged population. The fertility rates
and the resultant increase in birth cohorts have had the single largest impact on
the size and proportion of the elderly population relative to the other age strata.
The effects of declining death rates and increased life expectancy have had a
much lesser effect.

Life Expectancy

Trends in Life Expectancy: During the first half of this century, the average life
expectancy at birth increased 20 years. Since then, trends in life expectancy
have plateaued and in some cases declined. Since 1950, the average life expectancy has increased only one year for men and three years for women.[9]

Marked improvements in life expectancy were realized early in this century
because of improved sanitation, reduced infant mortality, and major break-
throughs in prevention and management of infectious diseases and malnutrition.
Progress in prevention and treatment of chronic diseases has not kept pace.
Therefore chronic diseases and their associated disabilities continue to decrease
life expectancy and the overall quality of life, and prevent the existence of
disease-free living. In the future, chronic diseases will continue to take their toll
unless major improvements in their management and prevention are discovered.
Therefore the effect of fertility on the size of the aged population will continue
to dominate.

Leading Causes of Death: The leading causes of death for those 65 years of age
and older in 1975 were heart diseases, cancer, and cerebrovascular diseases
(mainly stroke). Death rates from these and other leading causes are in table 3-2.
Heart disease, cancer, and stroke accounted for 75% of the 6,000 deaths per
100,000 persons 65+ in 1973. These were followed by deaths due to influenza

Table 3–2
Death Rates for the Ten Leading Causes of Death, for Ages 65 and Over,
by Age: 1973

Rank	Cause of Death	65 Years and Over	65 to 74 Years	75 to 84 Years	85 Years and Over
	All causes	5,874.4	3,440.0	7,932.1	17,429.4
1	Diseases of heart	2,643.2	1,461.6	3,609.2	8,382.1
2	Malignant neoplasms	946.7	768.1	1,187.9	1,435.3
3	Cerebrovascular diseases	839.3	355.1	1,233.5	3,197.9
4	Influenza and pneumonia	210.3	82.1	295.6	910.4
5	Arteriosclerosis	146.0	32.4	190.6	890.2
6	Accidents	127.7	77.5	160.6	404.2
	Motor vehicle	33.2	29.4	40.7	34.7
	All other	94.5	48.1	119.8	369.5
7	Diabetes mellitus	126.3	85.4	179.7	245.9
8	Bronchitis, emphysema, and asthma	97.7	79.4	126.2	133.2
9	Cirrhosis of liver	37.9	44.6	28.8	19.9
10	Infections of kidney	22.9	11.1	32.2	81.6
	All other causes	676.4	442.7	887.8	1,728.7

Source: Prepared on basis of data from U.S. Public Health Service, National Center for Health
Statistics, *Vital Statistics of the United States, Mortality, Part A, 1973* (forthcoming). (See
table 5–8.) In Bureau of Census Series P-23, No. 59, May 1976.

and pneumonia, arteriosclerosis, accidents, diabetes, bronchitis, emphysema and
asthma, cirrhosis of the liver, and kidney infections.

An Ounce of Prevention: It has been estimated that "if the major cardiovascu-
lar-renal diseases (principally diseases of the heart, cerebrovascular diseases,
arteriosclerosis, hypertension, nephritis and nephrosis) were eliminated, there
would be an 11.8 year gain in life expectancy at birth and even an 11.4 year gain
in life expectancy at age 65."[10] It has also been estimated that if heart disease
itself were eliminated (holding all other death rates constant), the gain in life
expectancy would be 5.9 years and 5.1 years, respectively. (Age-specific death
rates from other causes in the elderly cohorts may increase; however, these
projections can be viewed in light of their ability to identify major causes of
reduced life expectancy.) The gains would be particularly prevalent for women.

Sex and Racial Differences in Life Expectancy: Women tend to live longer than
men; life expectancy at birth in 1974 was 75.9 years for females and 68.2 years
for males. Expectation of remaining years of life at age 65 was 17.5 years for
females and 13.4 years for males.[11] Looking at death rates among males relative
to females 65 and older, for only arteriosclerosis and diabetes do death rates in
elderly females exceed those of males.

An interesting hypothesis for the differences between males and females in life expectancy is that "women have superior vitality, and, with elimination of infections and parasitic illnesses and maternal mortality and the consequent emergence of the chronic degenerative diseases, such as disease of the heart, cardiovascular disease and malignant neoplasms as the leading causes, this vital superiority has been increasingly evidenced."[12] Interesting as this hypothesis may be, however, it is still without definitive quantitative documentation and will have to await future scientific testing.

Life expectancy also varies with race. In the U.S. white population, the average life expectancy of 72.7 years in 1974 was well above that for other races (67 years).[13] Much of the difference in life expectancy, however, occurs among those under 65, and by age 75 the expected number of remaining years is approximately the same across all races.

Death rates among blacks and other races when compared with whites 65 years and older are greater for cancer, cerebrovascular diseases, motor vehicle accidents, diabetes, and kidney infections. Heart disease, the number one killer, is more prevalent among whites.

Summary

The aging of the U.S. population presents a variety of problems which deserve priority attention. Problems related to health, economics, and nutrition rank high on the list of things which jeopardize the quality of life among the aged. The segment of the population aged 60 and older is rapidly expanding and will continue to grow until the turn of the twentieth century. As their population increases, the severity of their problems will become more apparent and demand attention of policymakers. Furthermore, since persons 65 years and older comprise 10% of the population and an even greater share of the public polity— 15% of the voting population—their concerns are certain to reach and impress the legislators.

Having discussed some of the prevalent problems among the U.S. elderly population and the urgency demographic trends place on early solutions to these problems, the focus now shifts to an examination of standards for adequate nutrition among the aged and factors which affect nutrient requirements. These standards have important implications for the development of nutrition interventions among the aging.

Notes

1. Shock, N.W.: *Trends in Gerontology*, 2d ed., Stanford University Press, Palo Alto, 1977.

    2. U.S. Department of Commerce, Bureau of the Census: "Demographic Aspects of Aging and the Older Population in the United States," series P-23, no. 59, May 1976; and Brotman, H.B.: "Life Expectancy: Comparison of National Levels in 1900 and 1974 and Variation in State Levels, 1969–1971," *Gerontologist* pp. 1, 12–22, 1977.

    3. Department of Commerce: "Demographic Aspects of Aging."

    4. Ibid.

    5. Ibid.

    6. Ibid.

    7. Ibid.

    8. Ibid.

    9. Ibid.

    10. Ibid.

    11. Ibid.

    12. Ibid.

    13. DHEW: "Differential in Health Characteristics by Color, U.S., July 1965–June 1967," PHS, Health Services and Marital Health Administration, October 1969, Vital and Health Statistics from National Health Survey.

Nutrient Requirements and Dietary Guidelines for the Aged Population

Introduction

The essential role of certain food for human survival has been understood for centuries. It was not until the development of the science of nutrition in the twentieth century, however, that the vital role of specific nutrients for growth, health, and vigor was elucidated.[1] More recently, the social and psychological aspects of food, particularly relative to the aged, have been emphasized.[2] Much less well understood are the effects that the process of aging has on nutrient requirements. Part of the problem arises in attempting to define normal aging.[3]

Many physiological functions remain relatively constant as age increases, including the maintenance of fasting blood sugar levels, circulating thyroid hormone, plasma volume, and osmotic pressure in the resting state. Following stress, however, the speed of recovery to resting values may be slower in the aged.[4] Many other physiological functions decrease with advancing age, including cardiac performance, renal and pulmonary function, muscle strength, and nerve conduction velocity.[5] Superimposed on these changes are additional factors which may have adverse impact on adaptation to physiological or psychological changes. These factors include chronic and acute diseases, dietary imbalance, economic deprivation, and social isolation.[6]

The physiological process of aging varies across individuals. For this reason, chronological age, which is used to discuss demographic changes in the population, may not adequately reflect differences in functional age. Krehl[7] emphasized that the concept of individuality is particularly relevant to the aged. It may not be appropriate to group people indiscriminately into a group of so-called aged. In some older persons, an active, independent, disease-free existence may be a reality. In others, the long list of complaints may include chronic or acute illness, alcohol addiction, loss of dentition, social isolation, and poverty. All these problems can have impact on nutritional status and nutrient requirements of the aged. (See chapter 1 for a discussion of factors affecting nutrient requirements.)

The purpose of this chapter is to explore the nutrient requirements of the aged and the impact major physical and psychological problems may have on requirements for selected nutrients.

At the present time the recommended dietary allowances[8] are the best guidelines for planning diets and assessing the adequacy of the nutrient intake of the healthy aged population (table 1-2). These guidelines are integrated into the following discussion. They are supplemented with data that pinpoint where these recommendations may require modifications when evaluating the diets of elderly individuals, particularly those with chronic diseases.

Adequate Nutrition

Adequate nutrition plays an essential role in animals and humans of all ages. It is necessary for the support of baseline metabolic requirements, optimal physical performance, and increased needs that may arise from physical, biological, or emotional stress or trauma. Furthermore, adequate nutrition is needed for normal tissue and bone growth and development prenatally and perinatally as well as during childhood and adolescence. Adequate nutrition, however, plays its most significant role during youth and middle age, at which time it assists in the prevention of chronic diseases that become serious disabilities among the aged.[9] Among the healthy aged as well as those who succumb to disease and disability, diet plays an important role in the nourishment of older persons but also factors prominently into many aspects of everyday living. Perhaps no component of living, other than diet, is so intermixed with life's events. Food is used for reward, punishment, nourishment, celebrating, and so forth. The social aspects of meals consumed with others, particularly relative to the aged, have been aptly summarized by Sherwood,[10] "the congregate meal can be used to advantage as a medium of social interaction through which knowledge, attitudes, and values are communicated and inculcated and desired changes are successfully realized." She continued that "consideration should also be given (1) to the use of mealtime as a recreational activity in progress for the aged; and (2) use of food and drink as sources of mutual gratification and feelings of personal identity."

The nutrients, their major function, and factors influencing changes with aging are detailed below.

Calories and Obesity

Basal metabolic rate, lean body mass (metabolically active tissue), and physical activity all decline with advancing years. These represent a general slowing down of physical processes. Correspondingly, it has been recommended that calorie intake decline 10-20% from that consumed in the second decade of life. Mann[11] and Mayer[12] have aptly noted that while calorie needs decrease with age, micronutrient requirements remain constant. Therefore the quality of the diet, that is, density of micronutrients in food relative to total food intake, must be increased. This poses unique demands on the aged individual whose income may be limited. Often too as Todhunter[13] points out, decreased calorie intake does not follow declining needs with the net result expressed as varying degrees of overweight or obesity.

Weg's[14] comments regarding calorie needs of the aged should not go unmentioned. She reviewed the data on declining work efficiency with age and speculated that older persons may require more calories to perform the same amount of work. In light of reduced physical exertion with age, this finding may have little practical relevance. Furthermore, the prevalence of obesity in the aged population suggests a need to be concerned about excessive calorie intake. Perhaps the more pertinent comment would be made by stressing the increased calorie needs imposed by unique situations, including surgical stress, injuries, infections, and burns among the aged.

Lean body mass declines progressively throughout life and is accompanied by loss of height and diminishing bone mass. Concomitantly, body fat increases. Loss of lean body mass has implications for nutrition (e.g., decreased calorie needs) and pharmacology (drug dosage adjustment).[15] Obesity or excessive weight, on the other hand, is associated with increased risk of surgical morbidity and mortality, cardiovascular diseases (atherosclerosis and hypertension), renal and gallbladder diseases, and carbohydrate intolerance and diabetes. Obesity is also an aggravating factor in arthritis.[16] Obesity affects up to two-fifths of the aged; its development appears to be sex-related and its prevalence age-related.

Master et al.[17] found that among men 65 years of age and older the proportion of moderate to severe overweight decreased from about 30% at age 65 to about 10% at ages 90-94. Similarly, in women the proportion who were obese decreased from 40% at age 65 to 10% in the 90-94 years.

In a study of 605 married couples (husbands 60-64 years old) in Providence, Rhode Island, Burnight and Marden[18] found that 33% of males and 32.8% of females were overweight by some 16 to 25 pounds over the desirable weight. (Desirable body weight was defined in terms of Metropolitan Life Insurance Tables for persons 20-24 years of age.) In addition, some 18.7% and 35.8% of males and females, respectively, were obese (35 pounds or more in excess of desirable body weight). These studies concur with the findings of national studies indicating the high prevalence of obesity in older Americans.

The best measures of obesity are the body mass index (wt/ht^2; weight over height squared) and skinfold thickness. Recently, the potential value of ultrasound techniques in determining the degree of adiposity has been noted.[19] Hypertrophy, or increase in fat cell size, is found in all types of obesity. Hyperplasia, increase in fat cell number, is seen in children and adults who were obese by age one, an apparently critical period in the induction of adipose cellularity due to overeating.

Obesity among the aged has critical impact on the health of individuals. Master and Lasser[20] found a clear association between moderate overweight and relatively high mortality with the aged. They concluded that only a 10% variation in weight above or below mean weight for age and sex could be considered healthy, while weights varying 20% or more from mean weights for age and sex should be considered unhealthy. The 10% and 20% limits for standard weight for males and females 65 years of age and older are in table 4-1. These can be used as the basis for assessing the need for therapeutic weight (gain or loss) intervention among the aged.

Weight control has long been recognized as an important component of preventive medicine.[21] Life expectancy can be prolonged by adequate (but not excessive) nutrition and physical activity.[22] While the benefits of weight loss are well known, the poor response of some individuals to weight-loss regimens is equally apparent. Long-term maintenance when achieved, rarely exceeds 30% of individuals regardless of the mode of intervention. Obesity intervention at an early age seems important, though concern at all ages is justified.

Protein

Food protein provides the amino acids needed for the synthesis and maintenance of hard and soft tissues (muscle, bones, teeth) as well as for synthesis of hormones, nonessential amino acids, proteins, hemoglobin, and other nitrogen-containing substances.[23] Since some of the amino acids, the so-called essential amino acids (proline, valine, methionine, arginine, tyrosine, isoleucine, leucine, lysine) cannot be synthesized by adults, they must be supplied by diet and are perhaps the most critical from a nutritional point of view. After the requirement for these amino acids has been fulfilled, the body needs for additional nitrogen can be provided in a variety of forms.[24]

Young[25] found that total protein synthesis and breakdown expressed per unit body weight declined as age increased, paralleling the decline in metabolically active tissue. Protein metabolism per unit body weight in the elderly was 63% that of young adults but similar in both groups when expressed in relation to energy metabolism and higher when expressed per unit of creatinine.[26] The latter findings suggested an increase in the contribution to total body protein metabolism of the synthesis and breakdown of visceral organs (intestine and liver) relative to skeletal muscle.[27] Overall these findings indicate a decrease in protein synthesis and a reduction in the level and intensity of muscle protein metabolism with age. Young has speculated that this may "lower the body's capacity for metabolic adaptation to environmental changes, and thus, its ability to overcome unfavorable situations."[28] He also noted that utilization of high-quality protein may be reduced in the aged. In any case, reversing earlier conclusions[29] that the FAO/WHO safe practical allowances of protein (0.52 gram per kilogram of body weight per day) were adequate, Young recently concluded they were no longer considered adequate for aged persons.[30]

Table 4-1
±10 and ±20% Limits for Standard Weight per Inch of Height

Height, Inc.	65-69 ±10%	65-69 ±20%	70-74 ±10%	70-74 ±20%	75-79 ±10%	75-79 ±20%	80-84 ±10%	80-84 ±20%	85-89 ±10%	85-89 ±20%	90-94 ±10%	90-94 ±20%
Men												
61	156-128	170-114	153-125	167-111	151-123	164-110						
62	158-130	173-115	155-127	169-113	153-125	167-111						
63	161-131	175-117	157-129	172-114	155-127	169-113	148-122	162-108	146-120	160-106		
64	164-134	179-119	161-131	175-117	157-129	172-114	150-122	163-109	148-122	162-108		
65	166-136	181-121	164-134	179-119	160-130	174-116	152-124	166-110	153-125	167-111	143-117	156-104
66	169-139	184-123	167-137	182-122	163-133	178-118	155-127	169-113	156-128	170-114	146-120	160-106
67	172-140	187-125	170-140	186-124	166-136	181-120	158-130	173-115	160-130	174-116	150-122	163-100
68	175-143	191-127	174-142	190-126	169-139	184-123	162-132	176-118	163-133	178-118	154-126	168-112
69	179-147	196-130	178-146	194-130	174-142	190-126	165-135	180-120	167-137	182-122	158-130	173-115
70	184-150	200-134	182-148	198-132	178-146	194-130	169-139	185-123	172-140	187-125	164-131	179-119
71	189-155	206-138	186-152	203-135	183-149	199-133	175-143	191-127	176-144	192-128	169-139	185-123
72	195-159	212-142	190-156	208-138	188-154	205-137	180-148	197-131	182-148	198-132		
73	200-164	218-146	196-160	214-142	192-158	210-140	187-153	204-136				
Women												
58	146-120	160-106	138-112	150-100	135-111	148- 98	122-100	133- 89	121- 99	132- 88		
59	147-121	161-107	140-114	152-102	136-112	149- 99	130-106	142- 94	124-102	136- 90		
60	148-122	162-108	142-116	155-103	139-113	151-101	133-109	145- 97	128-104	139- 93		
61	151-123	164-110	144-118	157-105	141-115	154-102	136-112	149- 99	132-108	144- 96		
62	153-125	167-111	147-121	161-107	144-118	157-105	141-115	154-102	136-112	149- 99	131-107	143- 95
63	155-127	169-113	151-123	164-110	147-121	161-107	145-119	158-106	141-115	154-102	131-107	143- 95
64	158-130	173-115	154-126	168-112	151-123	164-110	150-122	163-100	146-120	160-106	132-108	144- 96
65	162-132	176-118	158-130	173-115	154-126	168-112	154-126	168-112	152-124	166-110	136-112	149- 99
66	166-136	181-121	162-132	176-118	157-128	172-114	158-130	173-115	156-128	170-114	142-116	155-103
67	170-140	186-124	166-136	181-121	161-131	175-117						
68	175-143	191-127	170-140	186-124								
69	180-148	197-131	176-144	192-128								

Source: A.M. Master, R.P. Lasser, and G. Beckman, "Tables of Average Weight and Height of Americans Aged 65 to 94 Years," *J.A.M.A.* 172(7): 114-18, 1960. Copyright 1960, American Medical Association.

Irwin and Hegsted,[31] as well as Miller and Stare,[32] concluded that experimental data on protein requirements in the aged were equivocal and evidence for changing requirements with age inconclusive. Currently the recommended dietary allowances of protein for young adults and the aged are the same (0.8 g/kg body weight/day). When calorie intake is adequate, it is thought that protein intake can be met by a combination of animal protein (meat, fish, poultry, milk, eggs, cheese) as well as vegetable or animal protein (cereal products, legumes, vegetables). The vegetable proteins are deficient in one or more essential amino acids, but by careful mixture of foods containing complementary essential amino acids, amino acid deficiency can be avoided. Young has gone one step further by considering all factors that could influence requirements for amino acid and protein and has suggested[33] an intake of 1 gram of protein per kilogram of body weight per day for the elderly.

Inadequate protein (protein deficiency) could result in hunger edema, pellagra, nutritional liver disease, and nutritional anemia.[34] Edema results from low plasma protein concentrations, particularly plasma albumin. Pellagra becomes evident when the amino acid tryptophan is absent or low, thereby inhibiting its conversion to niacin; or when dietary niacin intake is inadequate. Liver disease is seen clinically in chronic alcoholics whose intake of calories and protein is low as well as in those with impaired protein metabolism. Protein deficiency with superimposed vitamin deficiencies (folic acid, vitamin B_{12}) can result in macrocytic anemia, whereas alone, it can result in microcytic anemia (with adequate iron stores).

Stress—particularly anxiety, infections, physical injury, burns, and metabolic decrease—can increase nitrogen excretion, impose unique nitrogen demands for recovery, and thereby increase requirements for protein.[35] Surgery can also increase protein catabolism and impose increased protein needs for tissue replacement and wound healing.[36] Reduced appetite can run concurrent with stress and surgery, making attention to protein and other nutrient needs an acute concern among the aged. In light of these details and until more data become available, it would appear sensible to adhere to the suggestion of 1 gram of protein per kilogram of body weight per day when planning diets for the aged. Among the aged with physical or emotional stress, dietary intake will require individual adjustment.

Fat

Risk Factors in Heart Disease

There is a worldwide body of epidemiological evidence in support of the positive correlation between rising intake of total dietary fat and increasing mortality from heart disease, rates of coronary heart disease, and myocardial infarctions (heart attacks).[37] The strength of these associations is statistically convincing. Additional support of the association is provided by studies of segments of populations migrating from one habitat to another.[38] It has also been confirmed that modification of dietary cholesterol content,[39] substitution of polyunsaturated fat for saturated fat,[40] and modifications of dietary fat and cholesterol[41] can all reduce serum cholesterol levels, a principal risk factor in coronary heart disease.

While diet is but one of the risk factors in heart disease, it appears to interact with other risk factors (cigarette smoking, hypertension, inactivity, obesity, family history) to increase the relative risk of heart disease among individuals. Diet, nonetheless, appears to have an independent adverse effect on risk of heart disease.

Therefore current therapeutic intervention among persons with abnormal serum lipid levels or concomitant weight problems involve dietary modifications. Furthermore, dietary fat intervention is viewed as a primary method of reducing the adverse effects of and, importantly, in preventing several chronic diseases, including heart disease, diabetes, osteoporosis, obesity, and cancer. It has been estimated[42] that up to 25% of deaths from heart and vascular disease, 50% of the cases of diabetes and carbohydrate disorders, 75% of the cases of osteoporosis, 80% of the obesity cases, and 20% of deaths from cancer could be prevented with improved nutrition in this country, including modification of dietary fat and cholesterol.

Though no conclusive statements can be made as to the definitive quantitative impact of dietary modification on the outcome of coronary heart disease or other chronic diseases, both domestic and international expert committees have found the implicating evidence conclusive enough to incorporate recommendations for the modification of dietary cholesterol, total fat, and saturated and polyunsaturated fats in their recommendations for heart disease prevention in the general population.[43] Evidence indicates that similar modifications would be prudent in the aged. Woodlow[44] studied 195 randomly selected elderly residents in the Philadelphia Geriatric Center and found that average serum cholesterol and triglyceride levels rose 5 to 10% with each decade in life until age 70, plateaued and declined after age 80. Elevated serum lipids at all ages, even during the eightieth and ninetieth decades, appeared to be a significant risk factor in death and myocardial infarction (heart attack).

About one-fifth of the population aged 65 and older have cholesterol levels of 260 milligrams per 100 milliliters, a level which in younger persons is known to increase the risk of heart attack five times over persons with serum cholesterol levels of 200 mg/100 ml.[45] While higher levels of serum cholesterol might be acceptable in the aged, others have argued that even a cholesterol level of 200 mg/100 ml may prove to be abnormal.[46]

Dietary Considerations

Fat provides a concentrated source of calories as well as the satiety value of a diet. It also carries the fat-soluble vitamins (A, D, E, K) and is the source of the essential fatty acid, arachidic acid, or its precursor, linoleic acid. Dietary fat actually includes three major types of fatty acids: saturated, polyunsaturated, and monosaturated. Each has important effects on serum cholesterol levels and is therefore an important constituent of dietary guidelines for the aged. Perhaps the most recent comprehensive discussion of dietary guidelines for the population has been presented in a report[47] of the former U.S. Senate Select Committee on Nutrition and Human Needs. The report was the end result of numerous hearings concerning nutrition and disease. It proposed a number of dietary recommendations which seem suitable for both the young adult and the aged population. Their guidelines focus on fat and other major dietary components:

1. Avoid overweight, consume only as much energy (calories) as expended; if overweight, decrease energy intake and increase energy expenditure
2. Increase consumption of complex carbohydrates and "naturally occurring" sugars from (their current) 28% of energy intake to about 48% of energy intake
3. Reduce consumption of refined and processed sugars by about 45% to account for about 10% of total energy intake
4. Reduce overall fat consumption from approximately 40 to 30% of energy intake
5. Reduce saturated fat consumption to account for about 10% of total energy intake; and balance that with polyunsaturated and monosaturated fats, which should account for about 10% of energy intake each
6. Reduce cholesterol consumption to about 300 mg a day
7. Limit the intake of sodium by reducing the intake of salt to about 5 grams a day

While these recommendations have been controversial[48] and are subject to change as new scientific evidence becomes available, it is reasonable to conclude that they can be followed by the aged without hazardous effects. Certainly, potential positive impact on health and disease is possible if dietary modifications are kept within the limits specified in the report.

The most significant impact of the dietary goals will be realized if instituted at an early age. Nonetheless, it seems suitable to utilize these guidelines in combination with therapeutic dietary interventions among the aged in an attempt to prevent the occurrence, extension, or complication of chronic and acute diseases.

Carbohydrates

Diabetes

Carbohydrate intolerance and diabetes seem in the aged to be secondary to decreased peripheral tissue sensitivity to insulin, reduced numbers of insulin receptor sites in target tissues (adipose tissue or muscle), obesity (chemical diabetes), and pancreatic insufficiency.

Older diabetics are unique in that they manifest metabolic problems, that at least in maturity-onset diabetes, may be a cause or consequence of the aging process.[49] Depending on the clinical presentation of the disease and need for medications (insulin or hypoglycemics), therapy will vary somewhat. The older asymptomatic clinical diabetic (with an abnormal glucose tolerance but normal fasting and postprandial blood sugar) should be advised to lose weight or maintain ideal body weight, engage in light regular exercise, and reduce the sources of refined sugar in the diet while maintaining adequate intake of protein, vitamins, and minerals. The goals and dietary recommendations for those receiving insulin or drugs can be summarized as follows: maintenance of ideal body weight, and acceptable levels of blood sugar and serum lipids; avoidance of hypoglycemia; avoidance of glycosuria; and performance of light exercise.

The diabetic diet, even for those using insulin, has been liberalized in recent years. Trends have been toward more flexible intake of carbohydrates, though refined sugars or concentrated sweets should be avoided. Up to 55% of calories can be provided by carbohydrates, preferably complex carbohydrates (starches), though simple sugars from fruits are also advisable. A minimum of 150-200 grams of carbohydrate per day can be well tolerated. Protein intake has been discussed in the section on protein and in conjunction with recommendations for fat in the previous section should focus on protein from lean red meats, fish, poultry, and legumes or vegetables. There is no need for vitamin or mineral supplementation unless persistent polyuria (frequent urination) is an accompanying feature of the disease. Under these circumstances, treatment should focus on decreasing polyuria (this generally occurs when the diabetic therapy is instituted) and supplementation with potassium, and possibly the B vitamins. In all diabetics, regular meal spacing is advisable, particularly for those receiving insulin and oral hypoglycemics.[50]

General Carbohydrate Considerations

Carbohydrates are a major source of calories in the diet today, accounting for about 45% of total calorie intake. No recommended intake of carbohydrate has been made by the National Research Council, though the Senate Select Committee has encouraged substitution of fat calories with carbohydrate calories, particularly complex carbohydrates. As mentioned when the goals were detailed in the previous section, it appears that they are suitable for the young adult as well as the aged population.

Calcium and Vitamin D

Absorption and Metabolism

Calcium is a major essential mineral found primarily in the skeleton (99% of the total body calcium is in the skeleton) where it serves two major functions: a support function as a component of bone hydroxyapatite, and a reserve for the remaining 1% of body calcium that is found in extracellular fluid and cell membrane.[51] Calcium in the membrane serves as a chemical regulator and supports the transport of nutrients and energy into the cell. Calcium in the extracellular fluid is important in the conduction of nerve impulse and muscle contraction and also participates in blood clotting.

Calcium homeostasis, involving control of calcium ions in the extracellular fluid and maintenance of bone integrity, is under the regulation of parathyroid hormone (PTH), vitamin D, or its active form 1,25-dihydroxy-vitamin D_3, the serum level of inorganic phosphate (PO_4), and the renal tubular absorption of both calcium and PO_4. Maintenance of calcium levels in the serum prevents an untoward effect of hypocalcemia, including tetany, seizures, muscular irritability, hypotension, and even cardiac failure.

Parathyroid hormone acts on bone and kidney to produce the net effect of increasing the level of calcium and decreasing PO_4 in the plasma. This is accomplished by increasing bone (phosphorus plus calcium) resorption and decreasing renal tubular resorption of PO_4, increasing renal tubular resorption of calcium, and adding the conversion of inactive vitamin D to its active metabolite in the kidney, whereby intestinal absorption of calcium increases.

Vitamin D stimulates calcium and phosphate absorption in the intestine and may augment bone resorption to maintain serum levels of both calcium and phosphorus. Vitamin D may also stimulate the synthesis of calcium-binding protein which increases calcium entry into cells. Despite its action on bone resorption, vitamin D can stimulate bone mineralization in rickets and is thought to affect osteoporosis favorably (a major problem of the aged) by ensuring that the fluid bathing the bones has favorable levels of calcium and phosphorus as well as promoting collagen maturation, which is conducive to crystal deposition in the bone (in the case of rickets).

Calcitonin inhibits bone resorption, though renal tubular and fecal calcium and phosphate excretion continue. Phosphate can inhibit the absorption of calcium in the intestine if consumed in large amounts.

Throughout the day, after a meal calcium absorption occurs aided by vitamin D and calcium enters the extracellular fluid, raising its concentration. Calcitonin is secreted, inhibiting bone resorption. Postabsorptively, calcitonin secretion drops and PTH secretion increases. PTH stimulates bone resorption and other processes to maintain serum calcium levels.

The body's requirements for calcium and phosphorus intake among the aged is 800 mg per day[52] and can be supplied by milk and dairy foods, eggs, deep-green leafy vegetables, and dry fruit. Absorption of calcium may vary from 10 to 50% and can be inhibited by excessive protein intake, magnesium, phosphate, and high fat intake (150-200 grams).

Vitamin D is necessary for calcium homeostasis; however, there is no adult recommended dietary allowance. This is because the vitamin D provitamin (7-dehydrocholecalciferol) is found in the skin and converted to active vitamin D upon exposure to sunlight. Unless exposure to sunlight is restricted, vitamin D intake is probably not necessary among the healthy aged, thought intakes of 400 IU (international units) per day are not associated with any adverse effects. Excessive doses of vitamin D can be toxic.

Osteoporosis

Osteoporosis is a metabolic bone disease frequently seen in the aged, particularly aged women, which appears to be closely related to calcium intake, vitamin D, and a variety of other factors possibly including fluoride. Osteoporosis is characterized by a reduction in total bone mass. Clinically, symptoms include severe backache, pain, progressive loss of height, and susceptibility to fracture, particularly vertebral fracture. Osteoporosis may affect as many as 30% of men over 60 and women over 55 years and is four times more prevalent in females (postmenopausal osteoporosis) than males (senile osteoporosis). About 12 million elderly women suffer with this disease.[53]

The exact cause of osteoporosis is not known; it is thought to involve a genetic component that cannot be manipulated as well as dietary and hormonal components which may be amenable to intervention. Chronic suboptimal calcium intake may promote the development of osteoporosis in the aged. The disease also seems to be more prevalent in areas where fluoride intake is low. The sex-related incidence of the disease suggests a hormonal involvement. However, estrogen therapy in elderly females with osteoporosis has not proven as successful as researchers thought it might be, which suggests that chronic suboptimal calcium intake and resultant bone resorption may be more important.

The therapy for osteoporosis is controversial and has involved estrogen therapy (believed to retard but not reverse osteoporosis), calcium (2-3 grams per day), vitamin D (50-10,000 IU per week), and possibly fluoride (25 mg per day). The long-term goal in preventing osteoporosis is to prevent bone resorption by supplying adequate dietary intake in the absence of calcium inhibitors (phytates, fat, etc.). Moderate exercise may also have a beneficial effect on bone calcium retention, whereas bed rest and stress may have a negative impact.

Anemia in the Aged

Iron

The human body contains about 3.5 grams of iron, 70% of which is functional; it is in the hemoglobin of the red blood cells, in the myoglobin of muscles, and in a number of enzymes. The rest is stored in the liver, spleen, and bone marrow.[54]

The recommended dietary allowance of iron for elderly males and post-menopausal women is 10 mg per day.[55] This amount is needed to cover the 1 mg per day iron requirement due to the loss of iron-containing cells, assuming that about 10% of dietary iron is absorbed in the intestine. To the extent that it is not economically feasible for some aged to obtain this level of intake from iron-rich foods (heme iron from animal meats), dietary supplement with iron preparations may be needed. Ascorbic acid will increase its absorption while phosphates and oxalates will decrease its absorption.

Folacin

Folacin is the term for the vitamin folic acid and other compounds which exhibit biologic activity of folic acid (monopteroylglutamic acid). The adult requirement is 400 μg (micrograms) per day. A normal jejunum is required to split complex forms of folic acid in food prior to its absorption. Foods such as bananas, lima beans, liver, and Brewer's yeast contain folic acid that is readily available. Other foods such as orange juice, romain lettuce, egg yolk, cabbage, defatted soy bean, and wheat germ contain lower amounts of folic acid with lower availability. Folic acid deficiency is seen in patients with tropical sprue, alcoholism, and gastrectomy (jejunum).

Vitamin B_{12}

Vitamin B_{12} is essential for the functioning of all cells, but especially those of the bone marrow, the nervous system, and the gastrointestinal tract.[56] It is also concerned with the metabolism of the major nutrients protein and carbohydrate, and vitamin folacin.[57] The vitamin is unique in that its absorption requires the presence of an intrinsic factor, a protein found in the gastric juice of the gastrointestinal tract. Absorption takes place in the ileum. Persons with surgical gastric resection in which the ileum has been removed require B_{12} therapy due to the resultant loss of production capabilities of the intrinsic factor. The RDA for B_{12} is 3 micrograms. The best sources of vitamin B_{12} are meat, fish, and liver; it is not found in vegetable foods and this fact leads to the higher incidence of B_{12} deficiency (megaloblastic anemia) in strict vegetarians.

Forms of Anemia

Some 20% of the predominantly low-income aged studied in the Ten-State Nutrition Survey[58] were found to have deficient hemoglobin levels, a general indication of anemia. Examination of the relatively low serum iron and transferrin saturation levels among the aged, particularly in light of high serum folate levels, suggested that iron deficiency was the cause of the anemia. However, the HANES survey[59] and a recent study among the elderly in Boston[60] involving in both cases elderly with low to moderate incomes failed to confirm the previous conclusions of prevalent iron deficiency among the aged. While low to moderately low hemoglobin levels were found among the elderly, serum iron and transferrin saturation levels were not concomitantly low. These facts led Gershoff et al.[61] to conclude that low hemoglobin levels were not the result of iron deficiency, folate deficiency, or occult bleeding.

Despite these controversial findings, anemia, particularly iron-deficiency anemia, is thought to occur regularly among the aged, though a combination of anemias may exist. Pernicious anemia (B_{12} deficiency) occurs almost exclusively in the aged. Folic acid deficiency is common and may be associated with ascorbic acid deficiency.[62]

Anemia is best defined as a reduced oxygen-carrying capacity of the blood induced by a reduced hemoglobin concentration. Symptoms of anemia—e.g., shortness of breath, fatigue, decreased exercise tolerance—rarely occurs before hemoglobin levels fall below 10 mg/100 ml. It is important to evaluate the cause of anemia since iron, vitamin B_{12}, folacin, or other factors (blood loss, impaired red cell production) may all be determinants and can be treated.

The most common type of anemia is microcytic, hypochronic anemia (iron-deficiency anemia). The cause in adults is generally chronic blood loss, though in rare cases defective iron absorption may be the determinant. With chronic bleeding, iron stores are exhausted leading to the iron-deficient state and anemia. Iron-deficiency anemia can be treated with iron supplement (300 mg ferrous sulfate per day) but, most importantly, causes of chronic blood loss should be diagnosed and treated if possible.

Megaloblastic anemia can occur from vitamin B_{12} or folate deficiency. As previously mentioned, B_{12} deficiency is generally caused by the lack of intrinsic factor or ileal resection, though gastrointestinal disorder may precipitate the deficiency (e.g., achlorhydria). In contrast, folate deficiency is more often associated with chronic alcoholism, severely restricted diets, pregnancy, or certain types of drug therapy (dilantin, triamterene, trimethoprim, primidone, barbiturates). Drugs may inhibit conversion of food folates to absorbable forms, or may inhibit conversion of folacin to its active form.

Treatment of the various anemias will of course vary with etiology and may involve dietary supplements. The extent to which iron, vitamin B_{12}, or folic acid supplement is needed among the elderly is not known. A recent study of the unsuccessful use of iron-fortified foods with the aged,[63] however, indicates that widespread iron fortification to prevent iron-deficiency anemia is not warranted.

Water-soluble Vitamins

Deficiencies of the water-soluble vitamins are rarely seen among the aged, though it is not uncommon to find that dietary intake of water-soluble vitamins, particularly ascorbic acid, is below recommended levels. The dietary findings are usually not linked to any clinical manifestations of disease or malfunction. For this reason, it is difficult to determine the true importance of the dietary findings. Nonetheless, even the early nutrition literature attributed water-soluble vitamin supplement to improved health among the aged. For example, vitamin B-complex (thiamin, riboflavin, niacin) and ascorbic acid supplements were attributed to general vitality and vigor among the aged, as well as improvement in symptoms associated with nonspecific senility and atherosclerosis.[64] More recently, vitamin C has been promoted as a means of preventing the common cold. Scientific evidence, however, does not suggest that water-soluble-vitamin deficiencies contribute to any of these disorders, nor does it support any proposed large-scale water-soluble-vitamin supplementation efforts.

Those who advocate large doses of the water-soluble vitamins do so on the basis of incomplete data and speculation. The potentially detrimental effects of excessive doses have been ignored. Excessive intakes of some water-soluble vitamins, including ascorbic acid and niacin, have been associated with the precipitation or aggravation of clinical disorders, including gastrointestinal irritation and possible liver damage (niacin), development of specific types of urinary tract stones (ascorbic acid), and interference in anticoagulant therapy (ascorbic acid).

The recommended dietary allowances for the water-soluble vitamins are in table 1-2. It should be kept in mind that these standards are appropriate for healthy populations. Metabolism can be significantly altered during acute and chronic diseases and with some disease therapies such that dietary supplement may be required. The decision to supplement, however, will require individual evaluations of nutritional status and physician prescription. In cases where diets provide adequate nutrient intake, supplementation with multivitamin or single vitamin preparations can be expensive and of no real benefit.

Fat-soluble Vitamins

Fat-soluble-vitamin deficiencies have been found, though very rarely, among adults in the United States. These deficiencies resulted from inadequate intake of specific vitamins or consumption of substances, such as mineral oil, which interfere with absorption of fat-soluble vitamins.[65] Deficiencies have also been found in association with malabsorption syndromes such as steatorrhea.[66] Healthy individuals rarely exhibit deficiencies of these vitamins. (The role of vitamin D in osteoporosis has been discussed.) In spite of these facts, many fat-soluble vitamins, most notably vitamin E, have been popularized erroneously as a means of preventing the process of aging. The aging process is progressive and relentless. It is apparent that dietary modifications and life-style changes, particularly early in life, may prove to increase the average age at death and delay the development of some chronic diseases and their associated disabilities, such as heart disease. Nonetheless, aging is a biologic process that continues relentlessly until death.

Some food faddists highly skilled in the art of communication but lacking any scientific training have made claims in which they state megavitamin therapy will prevent aging. These self-proclaimed nutritionists prey on the illness and disability of the aged and the desire of all persons to live a disease-free existence. There is no scientific evidence to support intake of vitamins among healthy persons in excess of the levels in table 1-2. In fact, excessive intake of some fat-soluble vitamins, such as vitamins A and D, may be harmful. Symptoms associated with fat-soluble-vitamin toxicity include vomiting and transient hydrocephalus (vitamin A), hypercalcemia and irreversible renal damage (vitamin D), abdominal discomfort, bone or joint pain (vitamin A), and scaly rough skin, peripheral edema, and mouth fissures (vitamin A).

Summary of Dietary Guidelines

The nutrition-related problems of the aged in the United States are pervasive and need attention. Unfortunately, the available literature is not yet sufficient to quantify the scope of the nutritional problems systematically. Guidelines have been prepared by the Food and Nutrition Board of the National Academy of Sciences to assist planning the diets of the aged population.[67] However, these guidelines were designed for the healthy population and therefore some of the major nutrition-related health problems were discussed. Care must be taken when evaluating the diet of individuals since many factors to which the aged are susceptible, including chronic and acute diseases, are known to affect nutrient requirements.

Nutrient needs of elderly persons will have to be determined in light of the unique health, economic, social, and environmental factors which may affect the availability, intake, and utilization of nutrients (see chapter 1 for a discussion of the determinants of nutritional status among the aged and table 8-1 for guidelines in assessing target group elderly for nutrition interventions.[68]

The remainder of the book focuses on the development and implementation of the federal Title VII Nutrition Program for Older Americans (NPOA).

Notes

1. Todhunter, E.A.: "Nutrition," background paper for the 1971 White House Conference on Aging, 1971.

2. Weinberg, J.: "Psychologic Implications of the Nutritional Needs of the Elderly," *J.A.D.A.* 60:293-96, 1972; and Sherwood, S.: "Sociology of Food and Eating: Implications for Action for the Elderly," *Am. J. Clin. Nutr.* 28:1108-10, 1973.

3. Todhunter, "Nutrition."

4. Shock, N.W.: *Trends in Gerontology*, 2d ed., Stanford University Press, Palo Alto, 1977.

5. Ibid.

6. Mann, G.V.: "Relationship of Age to Nutrient Requirements," *Am. J. Clin. Nutr.* 26:1096-97, 1973.

7. Krehl, W.A.: "The Influence of Nutritional Environment on Aging," *Gerontology* 29:65-85, 1974.

8. National Academy of Sciences, Food and Nutrition Board: *Recommended Dietary Allowances*, 8th ed., Washington, D.C., 1974.

9. Watkin, D.M.: "Mutual Relationships among Aging," *Nutr. Health,* 1978, in: *Nutrition: A Comprehensive Treatise*, ed. by Plenum Press, New York, 1979.

10. Sherwood: "Sociology of Food and Eating."

11. Mann: "Relationship of Age to Nutrient Requirements."

12. Mayer, J.: "Aging and Nutrition," *Gerontology* 29:57-59, 1974.

13. Todhunter: "Nutrition."

14. Weg, R.B.: *Nutrition and the Later Years*, University of Southern California Press, 1978.

15. Forbes, G.B., and Reina, J.C.: "Adult Lean Body Mass Declines with Age: Some Longitudinal Observations," *Metabolism* 19:653-63, 1970.

16. Hollifield, G., and Parson, W.: "Overweight in the Aged," *Am. J. Clin. Nutr.* 7:127-31, 1959.

17. Master, A.M., et al.: "Tables of Average Weight and Height of Americans 65 to 94 Years," *J.A.M.A.* 172:114-18, 1960.

18. Burnight, R.G., and Marden, P.G.: "Social Correlates of Weight in the Aging Population," *The Milbank Mem. Fund Quart.* 45(2), part 1, 1967.

19. Sanchez, C.L., and Jacobson, H.N.: "Anthropometry Measurements: A New Type," *Am. J. Clin. Nutr.* 31:1116-17, 1978.

20. Master, A.M., et al.: "Analyses of Weight and Height of Apparently Healthy Populations, Ages 65 to 94 Years," *Proc. Soc. Exper. Biol. Med.* 102: 367-70, 1959.

21. U.S. Senate Select Committee on Nutrition and Human Needs: "Dietary Goals for the United States," 1977; Keys, A.: "Official Collective Recommendations on Diet in the Scandinavian Countries," *Nutr. Rev.* 26:259, 1968; *Primary Prevention of the Atherosclerotic Diseases*, report of the Inter-Society Commission for Heart Disease Resources, *Circulation* 42:A-55, 1970; McIndoe, J.: "Coronary Heart Disease," report to the National Heart Foundation of New Zealand, Dunedin, 1971; Committee on Food and Nutrition, American Health Foundation: "Position Paper on Diet and Coronary Heart Disease," *Prev. Med.* 1:255, 1972; Council on Food and Nutrition of the American Medical Association and the Food and Nutrition Board of the National Academy of Sciences, National Research Council: "Diet and Coronary Heart Disease," *J.A.M.A.* 22: 6047-48, 1972; American Heart Association: *Diet and Coronary Heart Disease*, Committee on Nutrition of the Central Committee for Medical and Community Programs of the American Heart Association, document #EM379PE, 1973; and Keys, A., et al.: "Lessons from Serum Cholesterol Studies in Japan, Hawaii, and Los Angeles," *Ann. Int. Med.* 48:83, 1958.

22. Watkin, D.M.: Nutrition for the Aging and the Aged, chapter 25, in *Modern Nutrition in Health and Disease*, sixth ed., eds. R.S. Goodhart and M.E. Shils, Philadelphia: Lea and Febiger, 1979.

23. Todhunter: "Nutrition"; and National Academy of Science, Food and Nutrition Board, *Recommended Dietary Allowances.*

24. Swenseid, M.E., et al.: "The Effect of Sources of Non-essential Amino Acids of Nitrogen Balance in Young Adults," *J. Nutr.* 71:105-08, 1960; and Nutrition Foundation: "Evidence of Liver Damage in Subjects Fed Amino Acid Diets Lacking Arginine and Histidine," *Nutr. Rev.* 28:229-32, 1970.

25. Young, V.R.: "Protein Metabolism and Needs in Elderly People," in *Nutrition, Longevity, and Aging*, eds. M. Rockstein and M.L. Sussman, Academic Press, New York, 1976.

26. Ibid.

27. Ibid.

28. Ibid.

29. Ibid.

30. Ibid.

31. Irwin, M.I., and Hegsted, D.M.: "A Conspectus of Research on Protein Requirements of a Man," *J. Nutr.* 101:385-429, 1971.

32. Miller, J.M., and Stare, F.J.: "Nutritional Problems and Dietary Requirements," in *Surgery of the Aged and Debilitated Patients*, ed. T.H. Powers, Philadelphia: Saunders, 1968.

33. Young, "Protein Metabolism."

34. Dreizen, S.: "Clinical Manifestations of Malnutrition," *Gerontology*, 29:97-103, 1974.

35. Young: "Protein Metabolism"; Beisel, W.R., and Rappaport, M.I.: "Interrelations between Adrenocortical Functions and Infectious Illness," *New Eng. J. Med.* 280:541, 596, 1969; and Balsey, M., et al.: "Nutrition in Disease and Stress," *Geriatrics* 26:87-93, 1971.

36. Ibid.; and Randall, H.T.: "Diet and Nutrition in the Care of the Surgical Patient," in *Modern Nutrition in Health and Disease*, 5th ed., eds. R.S. Goodhart and M.E. Shils, Lea and Ferbiger, Philadelphia, 1975.

37. Keys et al.: "Serum Cholesterol Studies"; Connor, W.E.: "Dietary Cholesterol and the Pathogenesis of Atherosclerosis," *Geriatrics* 16:407, 1971; Paul, O., et al.: "A Longitudinal Study of Coronary Heart Disease," *Circulation* 28:20, 1963; and Kannel, W.B., et al.: "Serum Cholesterol Lipoproteins and the Risk of Coronary Heart Disease," The Framingham Study, *Ann. Int. Med.* 74: 1-12, 1971.

38. Keys et al.: "Serum Cholesterol Studies"; and Scrimshaw, N.A., and Guzman, A.: "Diet and Atherosclerosis," *Lab. Invest.* 18:623-28, 1968.

39. Hegsted, D.M., et al.: "Quantitative Effects of Dietary Fat on Serum Cholesterol," *Am. J. Clin. Nutr.* 17:281-95, 1965; and Connor, W.E., et al.: "The Effects of Dietary Carbohydrate on the Serum Lipids in Human Subjects," *Circulation* 40(4), suppl. 3:61, 1969.

40. Keys et al.: "Serum Cholesterol Studies"; Groen, J., et al.: "The Influences of Nutrition, Individuality and Some Other Factors, Including Various Forms of Stress, on Serum Cholesterol: An Experiment of Nine Months' Duration in 60 Normal Human Volunteers," *Voedig* 13:556-86, 1952; Kinsell, L.W., et al.: "Dietary Modification on Serum Cholesterol and Phospholipid Levels," *J. Clin. Endocrin. Metab.* 12:909-13, 1952; Ahrens, E.H., Jr., et al.: "Effect on Human Serum Lipids of Substituting Plant for Animal Fat in the Diet," *Proc. Soc. Exper. Biol. Med.* 86:872-78, 1954; and Keys, A., et al.: "Serum Cholesterol Response to Changes in the Diet. II: Effect of Cholesterol in the Diet," *Metabolism* 14:759-65, 1965.

41. National Diet/Heart Study Research Group: "The National Diet Heart Study," final report, *Circulation* (suppl.) 37:1-419, 1968; Shorey, R.L., et al.: "Alteration of Serum Lipids in a Group of Free-Living Adult Males," *Am. J. Clin. Nutr.* 27:268, 1974; Tabaqchali, S., et al.: "Experience with a Simplified Scheme of Treatment of Hyperlipidaemia," *Brit. J. Med.* 3:337, 1974; Miettinen, O., et al.: "Effect of Cholesterol Lowering on Mortality from Coronary Heart Disease and Other Causes," *Lancet* ii:836, 1972; and Geill, T., et al.: "Dietary Fats and Thrombosis," *Nature* 185:330, 1960.

42. Weir, C.E.: Benefits of Human Nutrition Research, in "Dietary Goals for the United States," Senate Select Committee on Nutrition and Human Needs, 1977.

43. Senate Committee: "Dietary Goals"; Keys: "Recommendations on Diet"; Commission for Heart Disease: *Atherosclerotic Diseases*; McIndoe: "Coronary Heart Disease"; Committee on Food: "Coronary Heart Disease"; Council on Food: "Coronary Heart Disease"; and American Heart Association: *Coronary Heart Disease.*

44. Woodlow, A.: "Hyperlipidemia and Its Significance in the Aged Population," *J. Am. Ger. Soc.* 23:407–10, 1975.

45. Kannel et al.: "Serum Cholesterol Lipoproteins."

46. Levy, R.I. (moderator): "Diet and Drug Treatment of Primary Hyperlipidemia," *Ann. Int. Med.* 77:264, 1972.

47. Committee on Nutrition: "Dietary Goals."

48. Senate Select Committee on Nutrition and Human Needs: "Dietary Goals for the United States—Supplemental Views," 1977; Senate Select Committee on Nutrition and Human Needs: "Diet Related to Killer Diseases, II: part 1, Cardiovascular Disease," 1977; Senate Select Committee on Nutrition and Human Needs: "Diet Related to Killer Diseases, part 2, Obesity," 1977; Senate Select Committee on Nutrition and Human Needs: "Diet Related to Killer Diseases, III: Response to Dietary Goals of the United States: RE Meat," 1977; Senate Select Committee on Nutrition and Human Needs, "Diet Related to Killer Diseases, IV: Dietary Fiber and Health," 1977; Senate Select Committee on Nutrition and Human Needs: "Diet Related to Killer Diseases, VI: Response to Dietary Goals of the United States: RE Eggs," 1977; and Senate Select Committee on Nutrition and Human Needs: "Diet Related to Killer Diseases, VII: Nutrition: Aging and the Elderly," 1977.

49. Hillman, R.W.: "Sensible Eating for Older Diabetics," *Geriatrics* 29:123–32, 1974.

50. Ibid.

51. Lutwak, L.: "Symposium on Osteoporosis—Nutritional Aspects of Osteoporosis," *J. Am. Ger. Soc.* 17:115–19, 1969.

52. NAS: *Recommended Dietary Allowances.*

53. Lutwak: "Symposium on Osteoporosis."

54. Todhunter: "Nutrition."

55. NAS: *Recommended Dietary Allowances.*

56. Todhunter: "Nutrition."

57. Ibid.

58. Ten-State Survey, "Highlights," *Nutrition Today*, July/August, 1972.

59. DHEW: First Health and Nutrition Examination Survey, United States, 1971–1972, "Dietary Intake and Biochemical Findings," pub. no. (HRA) 74-1219-1, National Center for Health Statistics, January 1974.

60. Gershoff, S.N., et al.: "Studies of the Elderly in Boston," *Am. J. Clin. Nutr.* 30:226–34, 1977.

61. Ibid.

62. Krehl: "Influence of Nutritional Environment."

63. Gershoff et al.: "Studies of Elderly."

64. Stephenson, W., et al.: "Some Effects of Vitamins B and C on Senile Patients," *Brit. J. Med.* 2:839–44, 1941; Wexberg, E.: "Neurometabolic Deficiencies in Old Age," *Am. J. Psychiat.* 97:1406, 1941; and Jolliffe, N.: "Treatment of Neuropsychiatric Disorders with Vitamins," *J.A.M.A.* 117:1496–1500, 1941.

65. Watkin: Nutrition for the Aging.

66. Ibid.

67. NAS: *Recommended Dietary Allowances.*

68. Dietary goals which have been prepared by the Senate Select Committee on Nutrition and Human Needs seem suitable for adaptation to general diet planning for the aged.

69. Watkin, D.M.: "Aging, Nutrition and the Continuum of Health Care," *Ann. N.Y. Acad. Sci.* 300:290–97, 1977.

70. Watkin, D.M.: "A Year of Developments in Nutrition and Aging," *Med. Clin. North Am.* 54:1589–97, 1970.

71. Watkin, D.M.: "Biochemical Impact of Nutrition on the Aging Process," in *Nutritional and Aging Longevity*, eds. M. Rockstein and M.L. Sussman, Academic Press, New York, 1976.

72. Watkin, D.M.: "The NPOA: A Successful Application of Current Knowledge in Nutrition and Gerontology," *World Rev. Nutr. Diet.* 26:26–40, 1977.

73. Food and Agricultural Organization/World Health Organization: "Energy and Protein Requirements," WHO report series no. 522, Geneva, 1973.

Nutrition Program
for Older Americans

Historical Development

Title VII Nutrition Program for the Aged (NPOA) was launched in response to the growing awareness of and concern for the nutritional needs of the aged[1] and to the specific recommendations of the White House Conference on Food, Nutrition, and Health,[2] the Administration on Aging,[3] the White House Conference on Aging,[4] and the President's Task Force on Aging.[5] These recommendations called for the development of congregate and home-delivered food systems whereby nutritious meals could be distributed to the aged, and supportive social and health services could be provided to older Americans. They also urged the development of technical and financial-aid programs to assist local groups and community agencies in providing services to the elderly. The Title VII program was not the first attempt to intervene in the nutritional and health status of the elderly, though it was the first to identify the aged as a single target population.

The food distribution and food stamp programs which had been instituted during the 1960s and operated by the U.S. Department of Agriculture had become available to the aged. It was recognized, however, that these programs, while serving some aged, were inadequate in meeting the unique needs of specific groups of elderly, including the socially isolated, the chronically disabled, and the very poor.[6] As a result, in 1968 Congress authorized $2 million annually for a three-year nutrition research and demonstration project under Title IV of the Older Americans Act of 1965. The purpose of these programs was to study alternative approaches to meal delivery in congregate settings. Also included in the legislative mandate were provisions for the delivery of health services, leisure time activities, consumer and nutrition education, outreach, escort, and transportation services, as well as program evaluation.[7] The R&D programs were carried out in 32 settings through 1971 under the sponsorship of the Administration on Aging. While a comprehensive quantitative evaluation of the programs was never accomplished, it was concluded that congregate meals were both feasible and well-received community-based mechanisms for delivering food to the aged.[8] Limited data on the characteristics of congregate meal program participants suggest that Title IV programs attracted elderly persons with potential nutritional problems, particularly those with low incomes and minority individuals. In addition, it was evident that nutrition and related problems, including inadequate diet, lack of nutritional knowledge, poor health, social isolation, limited access to transportation, social and rehabilitative services, and leisure activities existed among those served. The severity of these problems seemed to be reduced by participation in the congregate meal programs.[9]

Despite no quantitative evaluation of the Title IV programs, their popularity among program participants and in the public at large was so overwhelming that efforts to discontinue them in 1971 were futile.[10] They were continued with emergency funds appropriated by Congress in 1971 and 1972. The Title IV experience succeeded in providing momentum behind the passage of legislation to expand the congregate nutrition program nationwide.

In 1971 the Title VII amendment[11] was attached to the Older Americans Act of 1965 to establish the Nutrition Program for Older Americans (NPOA). The statute was signed into law on March 22, 1972.

Unfortunately, the 1972 actions of the 92d Congress resulted in a stalemate since appropriations of Title VII funds were vetoed in April 1972 along with the entire fiscal year 1973 Labor-DHEW Appropriation Bill. The 93d Congress passed an appropriation bill in 1973 which was again threatened by veto, this time, because riders were attached to the appropriation bill requiring a halt to the bombing of Cambodia. In mid-June a compromise was reached to end the bombing on August 15, 1973. Therefore at the very end of fiscal year 1973, the president signed a bill providing a $100 million Title VII appropriation, precisely at the termination of the year for which it had been originally intended. Simultaneously, Congress passed and the president signed a continuing resolution for extension of the 1973 fiscal year funding levels to fiscal year 1974. The Department of Health, Education and Welfare with $200 million adopted a "forward funding" scheme under which only $100 million of the potential $200 million could be used in FY 1974 to implement the Title VII program in all 56 U.S. jurisdictions.

Thus, the Title VII program was born in 1973. Then the complex task began of implementing the Nutrition Program for Older Americans in line with the rules and regulations that had been published in 1972.[12]

While the spirit and intent of the Title VII legislation were evident in the regulations, minor changes had occurred during their drafting which had major influences on the focus and implementation strategy of Title VII nationally. All references to professional medical, health, and nutrition personnel were removed from drafts of the regulations. This left the task of determining the qualification requirements of Title VII staff, advisory personnel, and project advisory councils to the State Agencies on Aging. Though quite subtle, these changes, in concert with subsequent controversial decisions, diverted program philosophy and activities away from the Title VII health goals stated in the original legislative mandate.

Subsequent to the 1973 appropriation of the Title VII implementation funding, two decisions helped to further shift the program's focus away from its health and supportive service components toward an almost singular concentration on the Title VII meals delivery component. In July 1973 all Title VII programs were required to become operational on the first day of their budget year and fully operational to the level approved in their grant application within 90 days. This decision was modified in September 1973 by a moratorium on the implementation of the Title VII supportive services for 90 and up to 180 days with the consent of the Commissioner on Aging if justified by the state. These moves were deliberately made to speed implementation of the readily quantifiable program output, that is, the number of meals served daily; provide local, state, and national program visibility; and assure utilization of appropriated Title VII funds.[13]

The price paid for rapid implementation of the Title VII program, however, was lesser participation by target group beneficiaries—the disabled, isolated, those with transportation problems, the poorest of the poor, very old, and minorities; greater reliance on meal service vendors; and lesser reliance on Title VII project-operated kitchens for the delivery of Title VII home-delivered and congregate meals.[14] Lakoff concluded[15] that these decisions led to a deviation from the long-term Title VII program goals related to health and nutrition to satisfy short-term political motives for program visibility.

Recognizing the need for a redirection of Title VII policy, the Senate Select Committee on Nutrition and Human Needs reviewed the Title VII program and recommended[16] that "the time has come to broaden the reach and responsiveness of the Title VII program . . . to act on recommendations that have been ignored." The Committee proposed the following activities which could lead to greater program goal realization: program evaluation, development of Title VII supportive service components, allocation of administrative monies to cover expenses, assurance of elderly individuals' rights, outreach to low-income and minority elderly, and more direct interaction between program staff and elderly participants.

Since the last quarter of 1975 onward, additional emphasis has been placed on improvement of staffing Title VII supportive services so all Title VII sites can have the required personnel. Meal service capacity has been increased to assist particularly those sites which had been rationing meals. The nutrient standard method of menu planning and monitoring[17] was implemented to attempt to reduce the number of meals served by commercial caterers and to increase the number of project-operated meal service facilities. Furthermore, a national longitudinal evaluation of the Title VII program was begun. Many of the Senate Select Committee recommendations relative to the Title VII program were considered and attempts were made to incorporate them into program operating policy. Nonetheless, Watkin, former medical director of NPOA, concluded[18] that the opportunity to develop the Title VII program's position as the vanguard of national health efforts relative to the aging has not been accomplished, is only now at hand, and must be consolidated.

Efforts in this direction must be implemented with interrelationships between aging, nutrition, and the continuum of health care firmly in mind[19] and knowledge of the Title VII program's impact to date and possible future directions for program planning well in hand.

Data relative to Title VII impact and future planning directives can be provided by program evaluation research. Unfortunately, the literature in this area is sparse. Conclusive results of the national Title VII program evaluation will not be available until 1980.[20] Therefore program planning knowledge, which is essential for the ongoing development and revision of Title VII operating policy, will have to be generated from local program evaluations. To the extent that the knowledge they produce can be generalized, information relevant to the Title VII program planning nationally will be available.

Basic research will be needed to examine both the interrelationships between aging, health, and environmental factors such as nutrition as well as the application of this knowledge to the extension and improvement of a quality for all persons in the future.

Program Goals

National Goals

It was the spirit and intent of Title VII legislation to serve the elderly who, because of "physiological, psychological, social, and economic changes that occur with aging" adopt a pattern of living "which causes malnutrition."[21] The following federal goals for the Nutrition Program for the Elderly were stated:

1. To provide persons aged 60 years and older and their spouses regardless of age, particularly those with low income and minority individuals, with low-cost, nutritionally sound meals in strategically located centers ... where they can obtain other social and rehabilitative services
2. To promote better health among the older segment of the population through improved nutrition
3. To reduce the social isolation of old age
4. To offer older Americans an opportunity to live out their remaining years in dignity

It was additionally stated that no person meeting the age specifications could be denied services for any reason.

A conceptual framework for the nutrition program is in figure 5-1. The congregate meal is the central program focus. These programs draw elderly individuals together in settings conducive to the delivery of a wide range of federally mandated supportive services, including nutrition education, shopping assistance, transportation and escort services, information referral, outreach, and recreational services. (These services are defined in the appendix.) These nutri-

---

Community Sources of Information & Bases of Referral into Title VII Program

Title VII outreach[a]   Community agencies and programs
Media   Family
Word of mouth   Hospital and health centers
                                       Walk-in

Title VII Elderly Nutrition Program

Congregate Meals

Outreach[a]   *Education & Counseling*
Information & referral[a]   Nutrition[a]
Home-delivered meals[a]   Health and welfare[a]
Transportation[a]   Crime prevention
Recreation[a]   Housing
                                       Legal
                                       Health Services
                                       Screening
                                       Prevention
                                       Treatment
                                       Rehabilitation

Area of Potential Program Impact

Health	*Nutrition*	*Economic*	*Social*	*Psychological*
Information	Nutrient intake	Income supple-	Reduce isola-	Improve life
Accessibility	Nutritional	mentation	tion	satisfaction
of health	status		Peer group	Improve morale
care	Food prepara-		interaction	Improve self-
Referral	tion		Recreation	esteem
Prevention of	Knowledge		Interaction with	Dignity
unnecessary	Food purchasing		professional	
hospitaliza-			Title VII	
tion and insti-			staff	
tutionalization				
Early discharge				

[a]Legislatively mandated Title VII supportive services

Figure 5-1. Conceptualization of Title VII Elderly Nutrition Program

tion programs are considered as one step toward assuring the adequacy of the diets consumed by older persons in the United States and as a means of providing a variety of community-based services to reduce the debilitating consequences of chronic disease.

The success or failure of the Title VII program in meeting the health and nutritional needs of the elderly rests on its ability to attract and serve the target beneficiaries. The viability of the program will depend on the ability of program practitioners to achieve program goals and to compete effectively with other programs for funding.

State Goals

States and territories that desire Title VII funds must submit plans to the Administration on Aging. Title VII requires that each state fulfill the following administrative objectives before receipt of funds:

1. Establish or designate a single state agency for administration, coordination, and implementation of the programs (State Agency on Aging)
2. Set forth the policies and procedures to assure (a) that Title VII funds are expended as grants in cash or in kind to public and community agencies or political subdivisions of the state for implementation of the Title; and (b) proper and efficient administration of state Title VII programs, which include:
   a. Completion of reports to the Administration on Aging
   b. Assurance of fiscal control
   c. Establishment and maintenance of personnel standards
   d. Preference given to projects serving low-income individuals and in addition to the extent feasible projects serving minority elderly in proportion to their number in a given state
   e. Incorporation of nutrition services into coordinated services program for the elderly established under Title VII of the Older Americans Act

Local Goals

State Title VII funds are disbursed by the State Agency on Aging to grant recipients or contractors who fulfill legislatively mandated objectives. The goals established at the federal level for those local community agencies, public or nonprofit institutions or agencies, organizations or political state subdivisions who receive Title VII funds include the following:

1. To establish nutrition projects which serve at least one hot meal a day in congregate settings or where necessary and feasible via a home-delivered meal system.
2. To assume the provision of a nutritious meal that includes a minimum of one-third the recommended dietary allowances.
3. To serve individuals 60 years of age or older who may not eat adequate meals because they cannot afford to do so, they lack the skills to select and prepare nourishing and well-balanced meals, they have limited mobility which may impair their capacity to shop or cook for themselves, and they have feelings of rejection and loneliness which obliterate the incentive necessary to prepare and eat a meal alone. (Persons with these characteristics are referred to as "target" individuals; in addition, minority individuals have

been added to target eligible definitions and are to be served to the extent possible in proportion to their concentration in the state or territory.)

4. To set nutrition project sites in close proximity to eligible individuals as feasible and to, where appropriate, furnish transportation to and from meal sites.
5. To utilize methods of administration, including outreach, to assure maximum participation by eligible individuals.
6. To provide special menus where feasible and appropriate to meet the special dietary needs arising from health requirements or religious or ethnic backgrounds.
7. To provide information and referral, health and welfare counseling, shopping assistance, nutrition education, and recreational services not otherwise available.
8. To include the training required to enable personnel to carry out the provisions of Title VII.
9. To seek the advice of experts in the field of aging services delivery as well as the elderly themselves, to establish and administer the program.
10. To provide an opportunity to evaluate the effectiveness, feasibility, and cost of each particular type of project.
11. To give staffing preference to persons 60 years of age or older.
12. To comply with standards of future regulations.[22]

Discussion of Goals

Obvious differences exist in the focus of the goals that have been defined at the federal, state, and local levels of Title VII operation. The federal focus is primarily on the outcome or potential benefits of the program. Federal goals define four major areas in which the program is designed to have impact: health, nutrition, social isolation, and dignity of older persons. These goals also identify the characteristics of eligible and target group elderly as well as the primary mode of program delivery, that is, the congregate meal system. State goals are more administratively oriented than federal goals. State goals focus on development of the statewide infrastructure, implementation and management of statewide Title VII operation, and communication with the federal agency. Local goals can best be thought of as program operating goals containing specific program inputs needed to make Title VII operational. They are void of any reference to program effects or benefits but tend to provide greater specificity to some of the national goals, including specification of the nutritional quality of the meals and an elaboration of the characteristics of program target beneficiaries.

The differences among Title VII goals at the various levels of program operation raise problems for evaluation research. The primary objective of an evaluation is to measure the degree to which program goals are met. In the

Title VII program, multiple and distinct goals exist at the federal, state, and local levels. The problem is which goals to use as the evaluation reference. Title VII federal goals lack precision, time, dimensions, statements of priorities, and measurability, thus hampering evaluation research. Fortunately, all the goals as stated at the administrative (state) and operating (local) goals do not conflict with federal goals. However, there is no assurance that attainment of local or state goals will result in federal goal achievement. Therefore evaluation research that measures only the degree to which state or local goals are met will not necessarily document program outcomes or effects. By the same token, measurement of the degree to which federal goals are met does not necessarily identify the determinants of the program impact at the administrative and operating level such that data relative to future program planning can be generated. For these reasons evaluation research can be most useful when it utilizes goals at the different levels, that is, those that relate to program effects (federal) as well as those that relate to program inputs or design factors that affect program performance.

Title VII Program Administrative Structure

Federal and Regional Title VII Administration

To effectively carry out Title VII legislation, the law mandates that the Commissioner on Aging, Director of the Administration on Aging (AoA) within the Department of Health, Education and Welfare (DHEW) administer the Title VII program through AoA in consultation with other departments of the federal government. AoA is divided into 10 regional offices nationwide, each containing three to eight states. The regional offices review and approve the annual operating plans of states in their regions and provide technical assistance to these State Offices on Aging in developing their Title VII plans. The relationship between the Administration on Aging, the regional offices, State Agencies on Aging, and local Title VII programs is in figure 5-2.

State Administration

Unlike Title IV programs, which because of their experimental nature required that they be responsible to and monitored solely by the federal government, Title VII programs include state government structures in their implementation strategy. From the total annual appropriations for Title VII each of the 50 states and, in addition, the District of Columbia, Guam, American Samoa, the Virgin Islands, and the Trust Territories of the Pacific Islands receive an allotment "which bears the same ratio to such sum as the population aged 60 and over in

Agencies	*Functions*
Department of Health, Education and and Welfare Office of Human Development Service Administration on Aging	Responsible for developing a national plan for implementation of the Older Americans Act, including establishing federal regulations, guidelines, and procedures; allots appropriated funds to states.
Regional Office of Human Development Service	Reviews and approves state operating plans; provides technical assistance to develop state plans.
State Agency on Aging	Responsible for developing state operating plans for carrying out the Older Americans Act in keeping with state and federal goals and guidelines; awards funds to local projects.
State Planning and Service Areas Area Agency on Aging	Develops, plans, and establishes comprehensive and cooridnated systems of delivering services to the elderly in the planning and service areas; provides technical assistance to local programs; responsible for evaluation of services in planning and service areas; limited capacity in direct service delivery.
Local Nutrition Project (Title VII Grantee) Nutrition Project Sites	Directly responsible to the state agency or Area Agency on Aging for all activities throughout the project area, including delivery of services mandated by the Older Americans Act to those the act intends to serve in accordance with state and federal guidelines.

Source: Adapted from U.S. Department of Health, Education and Welfare, Administration on Aging: "Guide to Effective Program Operations." April, 1973.

Figure 5-2. Title VII Agency Relationship and Functions

such States bears to the population aged 60 years or over in all states."[23] Appropriations to a given state can be no less than half of one percent of the total federal appropriation and therefore the four territories, no less than one-quarter of one percent. These funds are made available for grants that support up to 90% of the cost of development and implementing the Title VII program.

Roles and responsibilities of the state agencies include:

1. Identification of eligible target group elderly in the state and approval of projects serving these individuals
2. Establishing minimum project size for effective program implementation
3. Approval of local project plans and awarding of Title VII grants
4. Monitoring and evaluation
5. Project menu review

6. Establishment of state sanitation and safety rules
7. Development of program accounting procedures in line with AoA guides
8. Volume purchasing if requested by local projects
9. Assuring maximum use of USDA food assistance programs
10. Developing guidelines for bonding project employees who handle money

For state implementation of Title VII, each State Agency on Aging, in accordance with Title III of the Older Americans Act, divides the state into planning and service areas (PSA) after review of pertinent data on the size and needs of the elderly in the geographic areas, resources available for serving the elderly, and the location of local governing bodies within the state. Within each PSA, the state agency designates an Area Agency on Aging (AAA). An advisory council composed of target group elderly and the general public is appointed by each AAA. In addition, with the advice of the advisory council they develop the plan for delivery of comprehensive services to the elderly in the PSA and submit this to the state agency.

The activities of the AAA also include determination of needs for services among the elderly in their geographic area, provision of information about available services to the elderly, implementation of periodic evaluation of services included in the area plan, and provision of technical assistance to service providers in the PSA, that is, the local Title VII nutrition projects. The Title VII mandate stipulates that the AAA cannot directly provide services to the elderly, with the exception of information and referral and, where feasible, legal services. The AAA's primary functions are planning, coordination, evaluation, and provision of technical assistance to local community service programs. They have no direct administrative authority over Title VII programs except in cases where AAAs have been made directly responsible for the disbursement of Title VII funds in the PSA. The AAA can, however, influence the allocation of Title VII funds from the State Office on Aging by making the results of their periodic evaluations known to the state.

General Administrative Structure Locally

Title VII nutrition projects at the local community level constitute the direct service component of the Title VII Elderly Nutrition program. Within a given PSA there is generally more than one autonomous nutrition project servicing specific local neighborhoods and communities. The projects for the most part have some professional administrative staff. Some of the direct providers of service associated with the Title VII program are also professionals by training, that is, dietitians, nurses, and social workers. In many cases, however, the paid staff and volunteers who actually oversee the delivery of congregate and home-delivered meals and the provision of other services at local meal sites in the nutrition project areas are nonprofessionals with some experience in operating community programs.

The activities of the local projects include planning, development, implementation, and management of all Title VII activities. Local project activities are overseen by advisory councils made up of target group elderly and the general public which are established by the local project.

The nutrition projects are directly accountable to the State Office on Aging for all Title VII activities. Nutrition project plans are submitted annually to the state office for their approval. These plans are expected to reflect the needs of the local elderly and the spirit of the Title VII legislation.

In 1976 Title VII regulations stipulated the baseline operating characteristics of an Elderly Nutrition program and limited activities of programs in selected service areas. Since then, some of these ceilings have been lowered. For example, experience indicated that the costs of capital assets rarely exceeded 3% and the ceiling was dropped. The generally accepted limit on home-delivered meals has become 15%. Some of the quantitative limits included (1) an average of 100 meals per day in a given project area unless the program is located in a rural area; (2) a ceiling on costs of capital assets including land, building, and equipment up to 10% of the cost of the project for the budget year; (3) limit of 5% on repairs, improvements, and renovations; and (4) limit on home-delivered meals to account for up to 20% of the total meals provided. The local projects are also mandated to collect certain information.

1. Range of supportive services offered
2. Cost of congregate and home-delivered meals and supportive services, program administration, salaries, and equipment
3. Source of income (federal, matching funds, project income, and in-kind contributions)
4. Number and characteristics of staff
5. Estimate of persons with incomes below poverty served
6. Number of minority, isolated, and other eligibles served
7. Number and frequency of congregate meals
8. Number of supportive services delivered
9. Frequency of participation by individual

Some of these report mandates have been dropped, including number of isolated aged served, frequency of participation, and number of supportive services delivered. In addition to the collection of this information, the local nutrition project was advised to interview project participants within two weeks after their becoming active members in the project to obtain certain information for project files, including address, phone, age, sex, religion, marital status, emergency information, planned degree of attendance, special health or dietary needs, transportation and other social service needs, activities and interests, and reasons for request of social services.[24]

Data are theoretically compiled on a daily basis and submitted in a summarized form on a quarterly basis to the State Office on Aging. The state office in turn summarizes the data for all programs and submits these to the Administration on Aging for monitoring purposes. The state agency also uses the information for its own monitoring purposes. The intended value of the data is to provide estimates of the growth in number of meals and services provided as well as the number and characteristics of the elderly served. Comparisons can theoretically be made between projects to determine the relative growth, efficiency of service delivery, and adherence to program operating guidelines.

The reports submitted to the state and federal offices are not meant to be the sole source of program assessment. Annual audits and periodic on-site evaluations generally add to the available data on program operation.

Title VII Program Growth

Funding became available for Title VII services late in 1973. Comprehensive national data for the period from 1973 to June 1974 are not available. Since July 1974 over $620 million has been expended on the delivery of Title VII services. Between fiscal year 1975 (7/1/74-6/30/75) and fiscal year 1976 (7/1/75-6/30/76) annual program costs rose from $96 million to $248 million. In the first quarter of fiscal year 1978 (ending 10/31/77), program costs $81.9 million) already exceeded the total operating costs for fiscal year 1975 (table 5-1). The Administration on Aging has reported a growth in number of nutrition projects by 65% from fiscal year 1975 to the first quarter of fiscal year 1978. During this same period, the number of meal sites has more than doubled nationally and the average daily number of meals served has increased 2.6 times. In fiscal year 1977, 2.9 million elderly persons were served an average of 382,919 meals per day (table 5-2). Then figures show that seven meals are delivered every ten weeks to participants.

The Title VII program is the major U.S. nutrition intervention for the aged. Since its implementation in 1973, Title VII has become the major operating program within the Administration on Aging (AoA). It has been funded at 5 to 10 times the level of most other AoA programs and accounts for half of the AoA's total expenditures. In 1978 the federal Title VII allocation is expected to reach $300 million, though when resources available from all sources (USDA, community resources, other federal monies) are considered, the total Title VII operating budget is $500 million.

The rapid growth of Title VII programs to a national program currently operating in 9,732 sites across the United States and in six U.S. territories has made the program politically visible. The community development which has

Table 5-1
Title VII Program Costs and Its Elements Nationally

Period	(1) = Total Program Costs	(a) + Total Meal Costs	(b) + Capital Costs	(c) + Social Service Costs	(d) Administrative Costs
FY[a] 1975 7/1/74–6/30/75	96,184,381	69,584,867 (72%)	1,654,501 (2%)	12,845,020 (13%)	12,099,993 (13%)
FY 1976 7/1/75–6/30/76	144,695,216	104,695,097 (72%)	2,484,410 (2%)	16,353,583 (11%)	21,162,126 (15%)
Cumulative 7/1/74–6/30/76	240,879,597	174,279,964 (72%)	4,138,911 (2%)	29,197,603 (12%)	33,262,119 (14%)
Transition quarter 1976 7/1/76–9/30/76	47,673,067	33,439,497	1,314,608	6,236,334	6,682,628
Cumulative 7/1/74–9/30/76	288,552,664	207,719,461 (72%)	5,453,519 (2%)	35,434,937 (12%)	39,944,747 (14%)
FY 1977 10/1/76–9/30/77	248,934,145	175,106,361 (70%)	7,701,150 (3%)	34,084,322 (14%)	32,042,312 (13%)
First quarter 1978 10/1/77–12/31/77	81,931,705	58,673,609 (72%)	1,814,349 (2%)	11,058,177 (13%)	10,385,570 (13%)

Source: Administration on Aging, regional office, Boston, Massachusetts, AoA IM-77-74, August 1978.
[a]FY = fiscal year.

Table 5-2
Title VII Nutrition Program for the Elderly[a]

Period	No. of Projects	No. of Sites	Total Persons Actually Served	Total No. of Meals Served	Average Daily Meals
FY[b] 1975					
7/1/74-6/30/75	652	4,710	1,276,922	48,539,400	183,861
FY 1976					
7/1/75-6/30/76	845	6,672	1,722,992	64,273,028	243,458
Transition quarter 1976					
7/1/76-9/30/76	880	6,944	677,427	21,315,845	327,513
FY 1977					
10/1/76-9/30/77	1,047	9,166	2,854,755	101,090,720	382,919
First quarter 1978					
1/1/77-3/31/77	1,074	9,732	1,534,534	31,490,779	477,133

Source: Administration on Aging, regional office, Boston, Massachusetts, AoA IM-77-74, August 1978.
[a]Performance to date.
[b]FY = fiscal year.

taken place around Title VII program implementation has generated tremendous federal, state, and local support.

The growth in the number of meal sites and aged served has provided the short-run evidence of the logistical feasibility of the national congregate meal delivery system for the aged. What has failed to develop during this same period is a monitoring and evaluation scheme which can assess on an ongoing basis the extent to which program goals were being achieved across Title VII programs and the relative merits of alternative program delivery schemes.

The evaluation research study presented in subsequent chapters attempts to provide input into the Title VII planning process by providing data on the current implementation status and impact of the program in the Boston area and by proposing alternative intervention design features.

Notes

1. Segal, J.: "Food for the Hungry: The Reluctant Society," Baltimore: Johns Hopkins Press, 1970; and Mayer, J., ed.: *U.S. Nutrition Policies of the Seventies*, San Francisco: W.H. Freeman & Co., 1973.

2. *White House Conference on Food, Nutrition, and Health*, Government Printing Office, 1969.

3. Watkin, D.M.: "A Year of Developments in Nutrition and Aging," *Med. Clin. Am.* 54:1589-97, 1970.

4. "Toward a National Policy on Aging," Proceedings of the 1971 White House Conference on Aging, vol. 2, 1971.

5. U.S. Senate Committee on Labor and Public Welfare: "Research in Aging and Nutrition Programs for the Elderly," 92d Congress, 1st sess., June 1971.

6. "National Policy on Aging."

7. PL 92258, 92d Congress, S 1163, Mar. 22, 1972.

8. Bechill, W.D.: "The Program Highlights of the Research and Development of Nutrition Programs Funded under Title IV of the Older Americans Act of 1965," University of Maryland School of Social Work and Community Planning, 1971.

9. Ibid.

10. Watkin, D.M.: "The NPOA: A Successful Application of Current Knowledge in Nutrition and Gerontology," *World Rev. Nutr. Diet.* 26:26–40, 1977.

11. Ibid.

12. PL 92258, 92d Congress.

13. Lakoff, S.A.: "The Future of Social Intervention," in *Handbook of Aging and the Social Sciences*, chapter 25, eds. R.H. Binstock and E. Shanas, New York: Van Nostrand Reinhold Co., 1976.

14. Watkin, D.M.: "The NPOA."

15. Lakoff, S.A.: "The Future of Social Intervention."

16. U.S. Senate Select Committee on Nutrition and Human Needs: "Nutrition and the Elderly," 1974.

17. Harper, J.M., and Jansen, G.R.: "Nutrient Standard Menus," *Food Technol.* 27:48–52, 1973; Jansen, G.R., and Harper, J.M.: "Nutritional Aspects of Nutrient Standard Menus," *Food Technol.* 28:62–67, 1974; and Frey, A.L., et al.: "Comparison of Type A and Nutrient Standard Menus for School Lunch. I: Development of the Nutrient Standard Method (NSM)," *J.A.D.A.* 66:242–48, 1975.

18. Watkin: "The NPOA."

19. Watkin, D.M.: "Biochemical Impact of Nutrition on the Aging Process," in *Nutritional and Aging Longevity*, eds. M. Rockstein and M. Sussman, Academic Press, New York, 1976.

20. Howard, L.: "The National Title VII Evaluation Study," paper presented at the Annual American Dietetic Association Meetings, October 1977.

21. PL 92258, 92d Congress.

22. Ibid.

23. Ibid.

24. DHEW Administration on Aging: "Guide to Effective Program Operations, NPOA," April 1973.

6

Title VII Nutrition Program Evaluation Research

Introduction

This chapter discusses the nutrition program planning process and the role evaluation plays in program planning. The rationale, objectives, and methods employed in this research are examined briefly.

The Planning Process

In general terms the nutrition program planning process consists of three major steps: problem diagnosis, intervention prescription, and evaluation. Each step contains key decision-making considerations. As the knowledge base grows in the area of nutrition programming, specific guidelines can be established to steer the formulaters through the planning stages. The intended outcome is the prescription and the implementation of policy through action plans. In slightly more detailed form, the steps in the process are:

PROBLEM DIAGNOSIS
↓
ANALYSIS OF ALTERNATIVES
↓
DETERMINATION AND SELECTION
↓
IMPLEMENTATION
↓
EVALUATION
↓
TERMINATION

Diagnosis refers to gathering, processing, and disseminating information about the nature and scope of a nutritional problem. The data generated through basic and applied research can serve as the basis of program decision making. Analysis of alternatives refers to the review of the pros and cons of potential program forms. The relative merits and defects of programs are weighed against alternative methods of solving the nutritional problem. In the dissemination and selection phase program goals and policies are identified. Specific intervention

71

components are also prescribed at this step in the planning process. During program implementation, the program design becomes operational. Evaluation refers to analyses of the costs and intended or unintended program effects, with the specification of the program determinants of the realized effects and benefits. The role of this phase is to provide information relevant to each planning stage. In so doing, program evaluation can initiate new or revised program definitions, policies, intervention designs, or operating procedures. Termination refers to the dissolution of a specific prescription or action plan. This step is essential prior to the adoption and implementation of a new program policy so conflicting activities do not coexist within program activities.

Good planning is generally necessary, though not always a sufficient condition for effective program performance. All too often, the planning process falters for one or more of the following reasons:

1. Incomplete collection of information related to the pertinent problem area
2. Inaccurate assessment of the nature, scope, or cause of the problem
3. Incomplete definition of problem-related areas amenable to change
4. Lack of clear, concise, and measurable long-term and short-term implementation goals and objectives
5. Faulty assessment of the political-logistic feasibility and constraints of policy application
6. Absence of program evaluation

The absence of program evaluation is a critical element and is frequently missing in social service intervention schemes, including nutrition programs. Evaluation research is one method of examining goal attainment and is essential for sound nutrition program planning.

Evaluation research attempts to bring systematic, logical, objective, and analytic procedures to the area of social programming. As Weiss[1] points out, evaluation research establishes clear and specific criteria of program success; collects evidence systematically from a representative sample of units of concern; usually translates the evidence into quantitative terms; compares it with criteria of success; and draws conclusions about the effectiveness, merit, and success of the phenomenon under study.

Title VII Evaluation Research

Since implementation of the Title VII program, the results of only one relatively comprehensive local program evaluation have been reported. Preliminary results of two evaluation contracts for a national evaluation of the Title VII program have begun to appear, but conclusive results may not be available until 1980.[2] Kohrs[3] conducted a cross-sectional study of Title VII participants and nonparticipants in Lincoln County, Missouri. Researchers completed medical histories, clinical examinations, and dietary evaluations on a sample of 547 persons. Nutritional status, dietary intake, and health appeared to be better among participants than nonparticipants and the researchers concluded that improvements seemed to increase with increasing levels of program participation. In addition, it was concluded that nutritional deficiencies which exist among the aged because of dietary inadequacies could be eliminated or improved by participation in the program. Theoretical estimates suggested that if 50% of the recommended dietary allowances (RDA) for a nutrient was provided by the Title VII program, up to one-third the weekly allowance could be provided if five-day participation was achieved by an elderly individual. If 80% of the RDA was provided in each meal (as was the case for some of the menus analyzed in the Missouri evaluation), eating Title VII meals three days a week could provide one-third the weekly recommended nutrient allowance.

The Missouri data suggest two very important concepts concerning the elderly nutrition program: that the Title VII program may have significant positive impact on the health and nutritional status of participants and that program impact is linked to the quality of meals provided and rate of program participation, with impact rising as program participation rises. It would seem worthwhile, however, to examine closely the research methodology that was employed to determine whether or not these conclusions are valid.

The design of the Missouri evaluation was preexperimental, that is, one which Campbell and Stanley[4] describe as the "static-group" comparison. In this type of research design, a group which has experienced an intervention (Title VII participants) are compared to groups which have not experienced the intervention (nonparticipants). Measurements are made after the intervention only. Since no measurements are taken prior to the intervention, no formal means exist for documenting whether or not the two groups were comparable before the intervention or whether or not the two groups would have been comparable had it not been for the intervention. Therefore the differences between the groups at the time the measurements were taken may have existed without the exposure of one group to the intervention. In addition, even if the characteristics of the two groups had been identical at one time, they may differ after the intervention because of selective dropout from either group. This factor may be of critical importance in evaluating Title VII programs since it has been estimated that Title VII dropout rates may be as high as 50% of participants per year.[5]

Therefore a number of confounding factors exist which may limit the conclusions that can be drawn from the static-group comparison used in the Missouri research. Nonetheless, the data are valuable because they clearly provide baseline biochemical data on the nutritional status of participants and nonparticipants. They also evaluate the Title VII meal relative to its contribution to an elderly individual's daily nutrient intake, and project the nutrient quality of menus provided at the program. Concern, however, does arise when attempts are made to draw conclusions about the direct effects of Title VII participation on nutritional status and improved nutrient intake among the aged.

Kohrs' study does make it clear that the Title VII meal has the potential of making significant contributions to the weekly nutrient intake of elderly participants. From 30 to 80% of the daily RDA for selected nutrients were found in a sample of 25 Title VII menus. Frequent program participation increased the likelihood of a positive program impact on nutrient intake. It is not clear, however, whether or not the nutrient intake and nutritional status of program participants improved over time or whether the Title VII meal substituted for meals otherwise consumed at home or in restaurants.

Impact of the program on the nutritional status and dietary intake of elderly participants will depend upon the prior nutritional status of the individual participant, consumption of the Title VII meal, the manner in which nutrients are utilized, health status of the individual, and the extent to which the total dietary intake and diet-related behavior of the individual is affected by participation.

Therefore, while the Missouri evaluation points the reader in a number of interesting directions, it does not conclusively document the quantitative impact of the Title VII program on elderly individuals, though its results have been used for this purpose.[6] Definitive estimates of the nature and dimensions of Title VII impact will hopefully be provided by the national Title VII evaluations which are being conducted under the Administration on Aging by Kirschner Associates and Opinion Research Corporation. This study utilizes criteria which increase the likelihood of providing the conclusive evidence of program impact that is sought by policymakers and program practitioners alike, including the following:

1. Longitudinal study design; the Title VII evaluation may proceed for up to five years to provide quantitative estimates of changes over time (results are expected in 1980).
2. Study sample including both program participants and nonparticipants.
3. Twenty-four hour dietary recall, socioeconomic, and demographic, information from both nonparticipants and participants with varying rates of program participating.
4. Stratified random sample procedures to ensure representation of both rural and urban Title VII programs nationwide.

Until conclusive results are available, caution must be exercised in deriving conclusions from studies with nonexperimental designs, particularly those done in local programs if the intent is to determine the relationship of research findings to the Title VII program nationally. While the data from local studies may provide invaluable facts from the standpoint of short-term decision making, particularly at the local level, they cannot be interpreted as providing definitive statements concerning the quantitative impact of the national Title VII program on the health, nutritional status, and social isolation of elderly participants. They can, however, identify areas of potential Title VII impact.

One of the most hazardous results of deriving broad national conclusions from local studies is that they can falsely raise expectations of program impact and may therefore result in the development of unrealistic criteria of future program impact. In the long run, they could be detrimental to program viability. Therefore, while it may be politically necessary to provide policymakers with short-term evidence of program feasibility and impact, practitioners and researchers should attempt to maintain objectivity and perhaps even a conservative attitude in reviewing evaluation data.

Evaluating Title VII Impact on Diet and Related Behavior

The following discussion proposes the potential hazards of developing inappropriate criteria of program impact on dietary intake. It also provides some suggestions for realistic criteria of Title VII impact.

It is fully realized that dietary intake is but one of a multitude of factors that can affect the nutritional status of elderly individuals. (These factors are discussed in chapter 1.) Adequate nutritional status means far more than food alone or its consumption. As stated by the Panel on Nutrition of the White House Conference on Aging,[7] adequate nutrition means the "distribution, acceptability and utilization of information services, and facilities in the field of health, income, education, housing and transportation. It implies public and private sector responsibility for safeguarding the quality of foods and services and for guaranteeing the wholesomeness, the labeling, and economy of the nation's food supply. It entails protecting the aging and the aged of all economic levels from exploitation by unscrupulous commercial interests, food faddists, and medical quacks. Finally, it rests on research of the nutrition and aging interrelationships." Thus, it is clear that to focus on but one aspect of nutritional status, such as dietary intake, may be far too simplistic an approach. Nonetheless, the federal investment in the Title VII program has reached $0.5 billion annually and the central focus of this program is the provision of congregate meals. Therefore it seems important for practitioners and policymakers to examine the potential impact of the provision of a congregate or home-delivered meal on the dietary intake and adequacy of diet of elderly individuals.

Kohrs[8] stated that from 30 to 80% of the daily allowance was provided by a single Title VII meal, which suggests that as program participation increases from one day to seven days per week, from about 5 to 80% of weekly dietary allowances could be provided by Title VII meals. This would be true, regardless of the changes that may occur in the individual participant's diet-related behavior, as long as the Title VII meal was consumed completely. On the other hand, the overall impact of the Title VII meal on the quality of the individual's diet would vary with prior nutrient intake and changes occurring in diet-related behavior after participation. Titlve VII impact on the nutritional status of elderly participants would depend on their prior nutritional status, prior quality of the diet, and changes in dietary quality as well as individual health after participation.

Relative to dietary impact, assume that a given individual consumes a diet providing 70% of the RDA for a nutrient prior to participation. Assume also that about one-third of the weekly intake of this nutrient is consumed at the noonday meal and that this meal is replaced with Title VII meals. In addition, assume as stated in the legislative mandate, that the Title VII meal provides one-third the RDA. Table 6-1 illustrates the potential impact of the Title VII meal on weekly nutrient consumption by varying levels of program participation. One-day participation would increase the weekly nutrient intake from 70 to 71.3% of the RDA. Five-day attendance would increase nutrient consumption from 70 to 77% of the RDA. Daily participation would raise weekly nutrient intake to 79% of the RDA.

While there are a number of rigid assumptions in these theoretical calculations, they lead to two major conclusions: as the rate of program participation increases, the relative effect of the program on nutrient intake increases; and

Table 6-1
Theoretical Estimates of Dietary Intake among Title VII Participants by Rate of Program Participation and Prior Nutrient Intake[a]

Prior Intake % RDA[b]	Rate of Title VII Program Participation (days/week)		
	1 day	5 days	7 days
100	100.0	100.0	100.0
90	90.5	92.2	93.0
80	81.0	85.0	87.0
70	71.3	77.8	79.0
60	61.9	69.3	73.0
50	52.5	62.2	67.0
40	42.7	53.6	59.0
30	33.3	46.4	53.0
20	23.9	39.3	47.0
10	14.1	30.4	39.0

[a]Relative to the recommended dietary allowances. These figures are not based on actual calculation of changes in dietary intake over time after Title VII participation; rather they reflect potential impact of a Title VII meal that provides one-third the RDA on the weekly nutrient intake of Title VII participants when the Title VII meal substitutes for one-third the nutrients provided by the pre-Title VII participation diet.
[b]RDA figures from Recommended Dietary Allowances, 8th ed., 1974. Reproduced with the permission of the National Academy of Sciences.

among individuals with prior nutrient intake falling below the RDA, consumption of the Title VII meal alone will not result in nutrient intake that will be adequate relative to dietary standards. To raise dietary intake to a standard of adequacy among those whose intake prior to Title VII participation was inadequate, other changes in food purchasing, preparation, and consumption will be necessary.

These estimates suggest that if dietary quality relative to the RDA is used as a criterion of program evaluation, Title VII impact may not be adequately reflected in the data generated. Even participants may continue to have inadequate dietary intake relative to recommended intake, despite program participation. More appropriate criteria of program impact would be change in nutrient intake over time by program participant; change in nutritional status over time by program participant, for example, change in dollars expended for food, change in food preparation practices and methods, and change in nutritional knowledge. In the optimum situation the measurement of nutritional status, dietary intake, and nutrition knowledge or diet-related behavior would take place prior to participation as well as some time after exposure to the Title VII intervention.

Other Areas of Program Impact

In addition to the manner in which nutritional status and diet-related behavior may be affected by participation, a number of other potential effects and benefits of Title VII participation exist, including income subsidy, increased socialization and recreation, improved health status, improved morale, psychological well-being, and increased awareness and utilization of services. As with the nutrition-related areas of program impact, evaluation in these additional areas would optimally be examined in a longitudinal study.

Longitudinal research evaluations are often difficult to incorporate into program planning strategies as their cost may be considerable and, as a result, they may encounter resistance as they compete for limited funding. Program impact evaluation was one of the planning stages that was relegated to a low priority position in the initial Title VII program implementation strategy. The eventual data generated to support the legitimacy of the congregate meal program included the number of operating Title VII meal sites, the number of congregate and home-delivered meals provided to participants, and the number of persons served. While these statistics were easily generated from project area records, the data do not provide information concerning the areas in which program impact has been realized, the characteristics of those who were served, the awareness and patterns of utilization of congregate meals and supportive services, and the comparative costs and efficiency of service delivery schemes. The

Boston Title VII evaluation was designed to provide information for program
planning purposes.

Rationale of the Boston Evaluation

The Boston Title VII evaluation research is consistent with the legislative intent
of the Title VII program. Section 706(a) (PL 93-351) of the Title VII mandate
includes a specific provision for program evaluation. It states that "during any
fiscal year, funds shall be disbursed by the State Agency to recipients of grants
or contracts who (in addition to the provision of nutrition and fulfillment of
other requirements) agree . . . to provide an opportunity to evaluate the effectiveness, feasibility, and cost of each particular type of project."

Furthermore, Title VII legislation clearly stipulates a planning, technical,
advisory, and evaluation role to the local Area Agencies on Aging (AAA) that
oversee Title VII operations in state planning and service areas (PSA). In Boston,
the Commission on the Affairs of the Elderly is the designated AAA. The
commission recognized the need for an evaluation. Prior to this research, the
commission had not been involved in Title VII activities to any great extent,
despite its mandated advisory roles. Therefore to fulfill its roles and to involve
itself in Title VII implementation, it approved and supported the Boston evaluation of Title VII. The commission perceived the implementation of the study
as a means of increasing its knowledge of existing activities and an initial step in
a communication process with local nutrition projects.

In addition to the legislative and organizational justifications for the research, the more fundamental rationale arises from the extreme paucity of
evaluation information concerning the operational nature and significance of
this major elderly nutrition intervention. There is in progress a national longitudinal evaluation of the Title VII program but the results will not be forthcoming before 1980. Hitherto, a near-vacuum existed in evaluation literature
regarding the nutrition programs for the elderly. The research presented here is
one step in filling this gap. Hopefully it will be useful to nutrition program
decision makers and researchers in the field.

The research was conducted by the author in cooperation with the Commis-
sion on the Affairs of the Elderly, the AAA Subcommittee of the Mayor's
Elderly Advisory Council, and the Department of Elder Affairs (Massachusetts
State Office on Aging).

Study Objectives

Discussion of Research Goals

The goals of the research were twofold: to measure the achievement of federal
and local Title VII program goals in the Boston area, and to identify and analyze

by project area some key performance determinants of the degree of goal attainment. Achievement of these goals required the specification of research questions and the development of appropriate research design. To facilitate the discussion of the Boston Title VII evaluation in light of the program's multiple goals and program components described in chapter 2, a program process model is presented (figure 6-1). The model consists basically of inputs generating outputs that may produce effects that may in turn yield benefits.

Title VII goals specified at the federal, state, and local levels all differ relative to the step(s) of the process model to which they refer. The federal goals focus largely on the effects and potential benefits of Title VII participation: promotion of health, improved nutrition, reduced social isolation, and support of dignity and independent living in old age. At the general level the federal mandate specifies the forms of program outputs, for example, congregate and home-delivered meals; authorizes social services; and identifies the characteristics of the target program beneficiaries, for example, low-income and minority elderly. In the form specified, the federal goals may be thought of as qualitative rather than quantitative. They lack the clear, concise, specific, and measurable dimensions that appear in classical program objectives, which become the intended effects against which program operating activities are evaluated.

Local goals for the most part are also qualitative. However, in contrast to federal goals, their focus is program inputs (characteristics of staffing, allocation of funds between service components) and program outputs (Title VII mandated meals and supportive services).

State goals mimic both federal and local goals in their absence of quantitative terminology. As seen with the local goals, state goals focus on program inputs and outputs. However, they differ from local goals in that they relate to development of a national and coordinated state utilization of Title VII funds; statewide development of the program infrastructure; and development of a

Figure 6-1. Title VII Process Model

Program Goals	Program Inputs	Program Outputs	Effects	Benefits
Regulation	Food	Meals	Improved nutrient intake	Improved health and nutritional status
Legislative mandates	Funds	Transportation		Increased life span
	Staff	Outreach	Increased socialization	Improved psychological and social well-being
	Equipment	Information & referral	Increased availability of services	Maintenance of independent living
	Program consultants	Nutrition education	Savings	Increased life satisfaction
	Technical assistance	Counseling	Target group elderly served	
		Escort service		
		Shopping assistance		

communication process between local projects, State Offices on Aging, and the federal Title VII administration.

The contrast between federal, state, and local goals can also be analyzed in a different manner. The goals differ in their relative time dimensions. The federal goals are long-term in nature, specifying the intended benefits of program outputs and effects. The state and local goals are short-term in nature, specifying the means through which intended benefits are sought.

As suggested in chapter 5, achievement of the long-term federal goals is implied, but not necessarily guaranteed, by the achievement of short-term goals. Historically, it appears that implementation of short-term Title VII goals fulfilled short-term political motives of assuring program visibility and generating local, state, and federal support. At the same time, policy measures diverted attention away from long-term Title VII goals for health promotion and improved nutritional status.

The Boston Title VII evaluation focused on federal and local goals. State goals were excluded from the research to make the scope manageable and because the primary research focus, the Boston area, was only one of the Title VII operating regions in the Commonwealth of Massachusetts.

The Title VII program in Boston is operated by three separate and autonomous projects. Estimates of area-specific performance were derived. Comparisons were made to gain insight into the determinants of program performance. The area-specific data are only highlighted where applicable to the topic of discussion. For the most part, the data are summarized for the Boston Title VII program as a whole.

Research Questions

The following research goals were stated. To achieve the goals, corresponding research questions and strategies were developed.

Research Goal 1: To measure the achievement of federal and local Title VII program goals in the Boston area.

Research   To what extent is the Title VII program meeting the nutritional,
Question 1   health, and social service goals in the Boston area?

Approach   Quantify by area the degree of program impact on the health,
                dietary intake, and socialization of elderly participants.

Research   What is the prevalence of unmet needs for nutrition, health, and
Question 2   supportive services among project area participants.

Approach   Document the prevalence of unmet needs for nutrition, health, and
                supportive services among project area participants.

Research   To what extent are the target group elderly being served by the
Question 3   Title VII program in the Boston area?

Approach   Measure the extent of participation in the Title VII program in the
                Boston area.

                Compare the health, social, socioeconomic, and demographic
                characteristics of Boston Title VII participants to target group
                characteristics.

Research Goal 2: To identify and analyze by project area some key determinants of the degree of goal attainment.

Research   To what extent are the Title VII elderly participants aware of and
Question 4   utilizing services?

Approach   Determine participant awareness of supportive service by project
                area; measure by area the utilization rates of supportive services.

Research   Why do Title VII program participation rates vary among participants across project areas?
Question 5

Approach   Quantify differences in patterns of program participation among
                elderly individuals between project areas; determine factors underlying and precipitating participation behavior by project area.

Research   To what extent and why do meal and social service delivery costs
Question 6   and performance vary across project areas?

Approach   Compare cost and efficiency of delivering meals and supportive
                services of project areas.

The Boston Title VII evaluation was retrospective, though it was supported with prospective data to the extent that these data were available for selected areas of study. The retrospective approach has obvious weaknesses; nonetheless the research questions were selected because they could be validly answered in the context of this research design.

The data sources utilized in the preparation, presentation, and discussions which follow include in-depth personal interviews with a random probability sample of 175 Title VII congregate program participants; project area records, financial audits, and quarterly reports submitted to the Department of Elder Affairs (State Office on Aging); and other related research, particularly the statewide assessment of health care needs of the elderly in Massachusetts, for which the author served as a nutritionist consultant.

To determine the proportion of target groups served by the Title VII intervention, the current unmet needs for supportive services, awareness and utilization of services, determinants of program participation, and cost of services delivered, retrospective data are appropriate. To generate data concerning patterns of congregate meal participation, project site data on the frequency of program participation for a six-month period were reviewed and summarized. To generate data concerning the effects and benefits realized by program participants, the researchers relied on subjective data derived from individual participants. In addition, data were derived from the results of a statewide assessment of the health care needs of the elderly in Massachusetts.[9] This state survey ran concurrent with the collection of data for the Boston Title VII evaluation. To the extent possible, the interview schedules used in the Boston evaluation were designed to be identical to those used in the state survey such that the data generated could be used for comparison purposes. Because of the interview schedule design, comparisons between the following groups of elderly persons were possible: Title VII participants from separate and autonomous urban program project areas; and the Massachusetts elderly population, the vast majority of whom are not exposed to Title VII interventions or other congregate meal programs for the aged. The study samples in both the Massachusetts survey and the Boston Title VII evaluation were selected to provide probability estimates of their respective elderly populations.

The remainder of the book focuses on the results and discussion of findings in the Boston Title VII evaluation in relation to other pertinent research. The individual research questions are elaborated in chapter 7. The final chapter contains a summary discussion of the research.

Notes

1. Weiss, C.H.: *Evaluation Research Methods for Assessing Program Effectiveness*, Englewood Cliffs, N.J.: Prentice-Hall, 1972.

2. Howard, L.: "The National Title VII Evaluation Study," paper presented at the Annual American Dietetic Association Meetings, October 1977.

3. Kohrs, M.B.: "Influences of the Congregate Meal Program in Central Missouri on Dietary Practices and Nutritional Status of Participants," Jefferson City, Mo.: Lincoln University, Department of Agriculture and Natural Resources, Human Nutrition Program, August 1976a; Kohrs, M.B., et al.: "Contribution of the Nutrition Program for Older Americans to Nutritional Status," paper delivered at American Gerontological Society Meetings, New York City, 1976b; and Kohrs, M.B. "Nutrition Data from an 'Aging Program': Implications for Planning," paper presented at the Society for Nutrition Education Annual Meeting, Kansas City, Mo., 1976c.

4. Campbell, D.T., and Stanley, J.C.: *Experimental and Quasi-Experimental Designs for Research: Handbook of Research on Teaching*, Chicago, Il.: Rand McNally & Co., 1963.

5. Haffron, D., et al.: "Title VII Nutrition Program: Profiles of Non-Participants, Participants and Dropouts in a Midwestern Community," paper presented at the American Gerontological Society Annual Convention, October 1976.

6. U.S. Senate Select Committee on Nutrition and Human Needs: "Nutrition and the Elderly," 1974.

7. "Toward a National Policy on Aging," Proceedings of the 1971 White House Conference on Aging, Vol. 2, 1971.

8. Kohrs: "Congregate Meal Program"; Kohrs et al.: "Nutrition Program", and Kohrs: "Nutrition Data."

9. Branch, L.G.: "Understanding the Health and Social Service Needs of People over Age 65," Center for Survey Research, a facility of the University of Massachusetts and the Joint Center for Urban Studies of MIT and Harvard University, 1977.

7   Presentation and Discussion of Results

Introduction

This chapter presents the results and discussions relative to the following six research questions posed in chapter 3: to what extent is the Boston Title VII program meeting the nutritional, health, and social service program goals; what is the prevalence of unmet needs for nutrition, health, and supportive services among project area participants; to what extent are the target group elderly being served by the Title VII program in the Boston area; to what extent are the Title VII elderly participants aware of and utilizing available supportive services; why do Title VII program participation rates vary across project areas; and to what extent and why do meal and supportive service delivery costs and performance vary across project areas?

The research questions are discussed separately and sequentially. In chapter 8 an integrated summary and discussion of the data are presented and future areas of research are proposed.

Program Impact

Introduction

Since the appropriation of Title VII funds in the summer of 1973, the evaluation function has not been comprehensively completed nationwide. A national longitudinal evaluation has been implemented, but conclusive results of this study will not be available before 1980. Until the results appear, the primary source of data on the progress of the program toward goal achievement will be derived from local program evaluations and to some degree from the quarterly reports filed by each nutrition program with its State Office on Aging. The local program evaluations will be the primary source of information for ongoing nutrition program activities at the local levels.

Hitherto, no data were available on the degree to which programs in the Boston area were achieving the mandated Title VII program goals. This section presents program impact data and attempts to answer the following research question posed in the Title VII evaluation: to what extent are the Boston Title VII programs reaching the federally mandated program goals?

Methods

The data were derived from in-depth personal interviews with a random probability sample of participants who attended the program in one of three autonomous Title VII programs in the Boston area during 1976. These results are
compared with Title VII studies in other locations. The research methods were
elaborated in chapter 3.

Standardized interviews lasting up to 45 minutes were conducted by the
author and trained and experienced professional interviewers from the Survey
Research program, a Joint Center for Urban Studies of Massachusetts Institute
of Technology and Harvard University. Most questions related to program
impact were open-ended and coded after all interviewing took place. Data are
presented for each project area and for the Boston Title VII program as a whole.
Program estimates were derived from weighted responses from individuals in
each project area.

Results

Participants' Perceptions of Title VII Program Value: In response to the question—do you think the Title VII program is very, somewhat, or not very worthwhile—not surprisingly, nearly all the participants surveyed (85%) indicated that
the program was very worthwhile while only 7% reported it was somewhat
worthwhile (table 7-1). More revealing, however, were the reasons for considering the program worthwhile. These are summarized in the table and included
provision of a nutritious meal; an opportunity for increased socialization with
peers; increased social and recreational activities for elderly individuals; particularly those who are lonely and isolated; and indirect financial assistance. As
assessed by participants, 66% reported provision of a nutritious meal; some
25.2% socialization with peers; 27.6% increased social and recreational activities;
and 21.1% indirect financial assistance.

A small proportion (under 5%) indicated that the program also assisted in
improving overall morale and life satisfaction for participants. On the other
hand, a small proportion of individuals indicated that poor meals and use of the
program by elderly with fewer needs detracted from the program's overall value
to participants.

Reasons for Program Attendance: Across all participants (table 7-1), 69%
indicated that the socialization aspects were the primary determinants of attendance while 65% and 47% reported the nutritious meal and opportunity for
activities outside the home, respectively. Another 28% reported attendance
because of recreational and social entertainment, and 24% had an economic
incentive.

Table 7-1
Boston Title VII Participants' Perceptions of Program Value to Elderly, Goals, and Achievement of Goals

Program Value	Boston Title VII Program % Population (n = 174)
Program worth	
Very worthwhile	85.4
Somewhat worthwhile	6.7
Not very worthwhile	1.9
Don't know	6.0
Factors contributing to or detracting from program value[a]	
Provides nutritious meal	66.2
Increases socialization	25.2
Increases activities	27.6
Provides financial assistance	21.1
Improves morale	3.7
Other	1.1
Poor meals	4.5
Abused by less needy	3.7
Other	0.8
Don't know	4.5
Reasons for attendance[a]	
Socialization	68.5
Title VII meal	64.7
Activity outside the home	47.4
Costs less	24.4
Don't know	0.9
Other	12.2
Entertainment	27.6
Program goals[a]	
Increase aged's socialization	39.7
Provide nutritious meal	42.7
Improve health of aged through nutrition	38.8
Provide indirect monetary assistance	16.4
Provide entertainment	2.8
Improve life satisfaction	0.9
Serve the aged	4.3
Achieving purpose	
Yes	80.6
No	8.8
Don't know	10.6
Suggestions for improvement[a]	
Don't know	60.8
Satisfied	12.9
Offered suggestions	26.3
Menu selection & food preparation	12.0
Other[b]	14.3

[a]Multiple responses accepted.
[b]All others under 2.6%, respectively.

Participant-perceived Program Goals, Achievement, and Suggestions for Improvement: Program goals are summarized in table 7-1. Similar proportions of participants (39 to 43%) indicated that increased socialization among the aged, provision of the nutritious meal, and health promotion were the program goals. Another 16% reported that provision of indirect financial assistance was a program goal. Four-fifths of Boston Title VII participants concluded that the program was achieving its goals. About one-tenth were uncertain about goal achievement while 9% indicated that goals were not being met.

Though the majority of participants reported that the program was achieving its goals, only 13% were satisfied with the current program operating procedures. Some 61% were unable to articulate specific areas for program improvement while 26% offered suggestions. Improvement in menu selection and food preparation method was the most frequently reported suggestion, indicated by 12% of the participants. The remaining suggestions—improved transportation, reservation systems, outreach, and site atmosphere; and program expansion—were mentioned by fewer than 2.6% of participants.

Areas of Title VII Program Impact: The areas in which the participants report impact are summarized in table 7-2.

Financial Savings: Half of all participants indicated that they realized financial savings as a result of Title VII participation. The quantitative dimensions of monetary savings were not assessed.

Food Purchasing Behavior: Some 31% of all participants indicated that attendance at the program had a significant impact on their food purchasing behavior. For the most part, the aged who reported impact in this area noted that they reduced the amount of food purchased for home consumption. Despite program participation, however, 33 to 59% continued to reduce food expenditures as frequently as once a week to meet nonfood household expenses.

Food Consumption Behavior: About one-fourth of all participants indicated that the program had affected their own eating habits at home or in restaurants. The principal effect was a reduction in the amount of food consumed at home.

Food Preparation Behavior: Among all participants, 20.6% indicated that food preparation behavior was altered by participation. The primary impact of the program appeared to be on a reduction in the size of meals prepared at home, though a smaller proportion of participants (5.2%) indicated that they no longer prepared meals at home.

Socialization and Other Areas of Program Impact: The program also had impact on important nonsavings related to aspects of elderly individuals' lives, as seen in table 7-2. Some 53% of participants indicated that the program had an

Table 7–2
Areas of Title VII Impact

Area	Boston Title VII Program % Population (n = 174)
Financial impact	
Savings realized	50.1
No savings realized	36.6
Don't know	13.4
Food purchasing behavior	
No	67.9
Don't know	1.3
Yes	30.6
Buy less food	25.9
Better purchasing habits	0.9
Other	3.8
Reduce food expenditures despite Title VII participation	39.7
Food consumption behavior	
No	72.6
Don't know	3.2
Yes	24.2
Consume less food at home	12.5
Consume less food in restaurants	1.1
Switch to large noon meal	1.3
Other	9.0
Number of meals	
Increase number of meals	7.7
Decrease number of meals	8.3
Same number of meals	84.0
Food preparation practices	
No	77.2
Don't know	2.2
Yes	20.6
Reduce meal size	12.1
Don't cook	5.2
Other	3.4
Life changes[a]	
None	45.0
Don't know	1.9
Yes	53.0
Increased socialization	26.1
Improved morale	21.6
Increased social & recreational activities	21.6
Improved health	4.3
Improved diet	3.7
Other	9.5

[a]Multiple responses accepted.

impact on one or more aspects of their lives. About 26% found that they were meeting more and socializing more with their peers, and 22% reported that their morale had been uplifted, their outlook on life had improved, and their loneliness had decreased due to participation. Another 22% reported that they had increased their social and recreational activities outside their home. Overall, about 4% reported that their diet or health had improved as a result of program participation.

Factors related to increased socialization among the participants are summarized in table 7-3. Some 89% indicated that they ate with other peers at the congregate meal. Over half of participants in all three areas ate alone at home. Three-fourths indicated that they ate with the same group of persons when they attended the program. In addition, nearly all the participants reported they were comfortable with other participants and found the program staff friendly.

Beyond the fact that the Title VII meal encouraged elderly who otherwise ate alone at home to eat with others, it appeared that the program also stimulated new social activities and acquaintances outside the program. Some 47% of participants engaged in social and recreational activities outside the congregate program with peers whom they met there for the first time.

Table 7-3
Patterns of Socialization

Social Value	Boston Title VII Program % Population (n = 174)
Title VII program eating habits	
Alone	8.8
With others	88.6
Home eating habits	
Alone	58.8
With others	37.9
Eat with same persons at Title VII program	
Yes	74.2
No	18.7
Comfort with other Title VII participants	
Very comfortable	88.3
Somewhat comfortable	8.2
Not very comfortable	1.8
Perception of Title VII staff	
Very friendly	89.0
Somewhat friendly	4.5
Not very friendly, wouldn't return	3.1
Don't know	3.5
Socialization outside Title VII program	
Yes	47.2
No	49.4
Don't know	3.5

Determinants of Program Impact: The results of chi-square analyses between program impact variables and selected participant characteristics are summarized in table 7-4. The rate of program participation was found to have a significant positive relationship to Title VII impact on monetary savings, food purchasing behavior, and food preparation practices.

The proportion of the population that reported a positive program impact increased as the rate of program participation increased. Though the program impact on food consumption behavior was not significant, the data indicated that persons who attended the program more frequently were more likely to report program impact on food consumption behavior.

Satisfaction with the Title VII meal also had a significant positive association to impact on monetary savings, food purchasing behavior, and food preparation practices. It did not bear significant association with impact on food consumption behavior, though slightly more persons who were satisfied with the meal reported program impact on food consumption behavior.

Satisfaction with meals other than those consumed at the program site was related to program impact on savings and all aspects of diet-related behavior. Over twice as many persons who were dissatisfied with meals consumed outside the program indicated a positive impact on savings and diet-related behaviors. In addition, more persons who were not satisfied with their meals also reported an impact on nonfood aspects of their lives.

A significant relationship was found between therapeutic diet management and program impact on savings, and food purchasing, preparation, and consumption behavior. Persons with prescribed therapeutic diets (whether adhering to them or not) were more likely to report an impact on all areas of impact studied than those without therapeutic restrictions. Proportionately more persons who were adhering to their diets reported program impact in all aspects of food-related behavior while proportionately more persons not adhering to their diets indicated impact on savings and in other areas. Weekly food expenditures had a significant inverse relationship to impact on food purchasing; proportionately more who spent less on food per week reported more impact on food purchasing behavior. Financial food purchasing problems bore a significant inverse relationship to impact on savings and food purchasing and consumption. The same trend, though not significant, was found in other areas of impact.

Significantly more persons who lived alone realized financial and food purchasing benefits of participation. Similar trends were found in other diet-related areas while slightly more persons residing with others than their spouses perceived impact on other aspects of their lives.

Project area was significantly related to financial savings and other life changes; area Y participants were more likely to realize savings while area X participants were more likely to realize impact on life changes.

Food preparation problems had a significant association with impact on monetary savings and food preparation practices. Those with problems were more likely to realize impact on savings. Likewise, those with problems (particularly major problems) realized impact on food preparation behavior.

Table 7-4
Proportion of Persons Title VII Program Impact
in Specific Areas by Participant Characteristic

Participant Characteristic	Savings	Food Purchasing	Food Preparation	Food Consumption	Life Changes
Rate of Participation[a]					
1	37.2	26.2	16.5	19.7	34.1
2	56.6				51.5
3	58.2	38.0	27.2	34.6	54.0
4	63.0				45.5
	***[b]	*	*		
Satisfaction with Title VII Meals					
Unsatisfied	28.9	10.8	0.0	22.9	43.9
Satisfied	55.9	34.8	24.8	25.3	41.9
	**	**	***		
Satisfaction with non-Title VII meals					
Unsatisfied	88.4	64.7	55.3	43.7	60.5
Satisfied	48.0	27.3	16.8	23.2	41.1
	***	***	****	***	
Therapeutic diet					
Not on one	46.7	21.5	11.4	19.4	41.3
Prescribed, adhering	71.6	74.6	58.9	56.3	48.2
Prescribed, not adhering	88.4	65.1	55.8	44.2	60.5
	***	****	****	***	
Weekly food expenditures					
Under $15	69.8	41.4	29.1	39.5	37.8
$16–25	56.0	38.4	22.9	19.6	40.4
$26–35	43.9	25.5	24.9	29.0	61.6
$36+	48.4	16.2	7.5	11.0	31.3
	****	****			
Financial problems with food purchases					
Yes	62.6	39.7	24.3	34.2	49.7
No	41.6	25.8	19.1	20.2	37.6
	**	*		**	
Living situation					
Alone	55.7	40.1	28.6	29.8	44.2
With spouse	45.3	26.8	15.9	26.4	37.2
With others	38.5	7.7	3.8	9.0	46.2
	**	***			
Project area					
X	59.4	32.0	13.5	26.2	53.5
Y	63.1	38.2	28.0	32.7	39.6
Z	40.9	27.9	21.0	22.4	39.6
	***				*

Table 7-4 (Continued)

Participant Characteristic	Savings	Food Purchasing	Food Preparation	Food Consumption	Life Changes
Food preparation problems					
Big	57.7	32.5	52.8	32.5	37.4
Little	69.0	40.6	36.0	38.2	48.7
None	45.7	29.5	16.3	23.2	41.5
	**		**		

[a]Rate of Program Participation
  1 = 0-15 days per quarter;
  2 = 16-30 days per quarter;
  3 = 31-45 days per quarter;
  4 = 46 plus days per quarter.
 [b] * $.10 < p < .05$;
  ** $p < .05$;
  *** $p < .01$;
 **** $p < .001$.
   $n = 174$

Discussion

It would appear from the results of the Boston Title VII evaluation that program impact is greatest in the nondiet and direct physical health-related areas of participants' lives. One-half of participants realized financial savings due to their attendance at the program as well as significant life changes, primarily increased socialization. These findings are consistent with those of Postma[1] who studied Title VII participants in the Eugene-Springfield, Oregon, area and concluded that the major impact was on socialization and increased life satisfaction, and to a lesser extent on improved nutrition of the elderly. Hosowkawa et al.[2] also found that improved life statisfaction, increased socialization, and recreation were the more frequently participant-reported benefits of Title VII participation.

Quite strikingly different than other studies were the Boston Title VII results which indicated that under 5% of all program participants realized any improvement in their diet or health due to program attendance. Postma[3] suggested that 30.4% of participants found that their diets improved due to attendance. Hosowkawa et al.[4] found that about half of participants in the Central Missouri program had improved diets while 27% indicated that their health had improved due to participation.

Up to one-third of Boston Title VII participants indicated that changes had occurred in one or more aspects of their diet-related behavior as a result of

program attendance, including changes in food purchases, food preparation practices, and food consumption behavior. The primary effect appeared to be one of
substitution rather than actual diet or health improvement. In addition to substitution effects on food-related behavior, it appeared that in some cases, monetary savings were realized on food expenditures.

However, as indicated by the relatively higher proportion of participants
reporting savings (50.1%) compared to that reporting impact on food purchases
(30.6%), savings were also apparently realized in nonfood areas (possibly transportation, recreation, and other service areas). The financial dimensions of
impact were not examined in this evaluation and deserve attention in subsequent
research.

The low level impact on diet-related behavior relative to other areas was
related to a number of participant characteristics, including low rate of program
participation, satisfaction with non-Title VII meals, dissatisfaction with Title VII
meals, lack of therapeutic diet restrictions, lack of financial food purchasing
problems, living situation (among those living with others), and lack of food
preparation problems. It appears that those who are more likely to have problems related to diet management, that is, perhaps those with more need for
Title VII services, and those attending the program more frequently are more
likely to realize positive benefits of participation.

The finding that increasing frequency of program participation significantly
affected aspects of diet-related behavior was consistent with the findings of
Kohrs[5] who studied the dietary intake and nutritional status of Title VII participants and nonparticipants in Central Missouri. She concluded that mean intake
of many nutrients increased and nutritional status relative to many nutrients
improved as participation increased. Kohrs also reported that nutrient intake of
participants on days of program attendance were significantly better than their
diets on days they did not attend. The mean nutrient intake and nutritional
status of Missouri Title VII participants were better in many cases than nonparticipants. In addition to the direct impact on dietary intake and nutritional
status, Kohrs also found that participation appeared to eliminate significant
differences between sex, age, educational, and occupational strata relative to
dietary intake and nutritional status. These findings need further examination in
future research, particularly as diet improvement per se was not an area in which
program impact was prevalent among Boston Title VII participants.

Impact of the program on life changes, most notably socialization, was
related significantly to only one variable, project area. Proportionately more area
X participants realized impact on socialization. This finding was consistent with
the fact that proportionately more area X participants also perceived socialization as the primary program goal and suggests that the area X program may have
attracted persons with greater need for socialization than the other areas.[6]

Title VII impact on finances had a significant relationship to all participant
characteristics studied. Those more likely to report impact on savings were per-

sons who attended the program frequently, those who were unsatisfied with their diets and satisfied with the program meal, those adhering to their therapeutic diets, those who expended more per week on food, those with financial problems related to food purchases, and those with food preparation problems. Individuals who were more likely to have financial problems and those who attended the program frequently were therefore more likely to realize the benefits of participation on financial savings. Area Y participants realized more financial impact.

Conclusions

As was logical to expect, nearly all who participated in the Title VII congregate meal and other activities reported that the program is worthwhile. The primary determinants of program value to participants included the congregate meal, recreational and social activities, and indirect financial assistance. Participant-perceived program goals included provision of the meal, increased opportunities for socialization, and better health through improved nutrition. The majority of participants (81%) indicated that the program was achieving its goals. Nonetheless, 26% offered suggestions for program improvement, most frequently for menu improvement and food service changes.

The program had its greatest impact in financial, social, and recreational areas. Half of the participants indicated that the program had a significant impact on financial savings. About half also indicated that the program affected other aspects of their lives, including increased socialization, improved morale, and increased social and recreational activities. Less than one-third of all participants indicated that the program had a significant effect on any single aspect of diet-related behavior, including food-consumption, food purchasing practices, and food preparation methods. Less than 5% reported that the program had an impact on improved diet or health. Among those who realized impact on diet behavior, the effect was one of substitution. Because of attendance at the Title VII meal, food consumption at home or in restaurants decreased, and food purchasing and preparation for at-home food consumption was also reduced in some cases. The program also appeared to reverse the social behavior of food consumption in that the majority of participants indicated that they ate alone at home but consumed the Title VII meal with peers. Despite program participation, however, two-fifths of participants reported that as frequently as once a week they reduced their food expenditure to meet nonfood household expenses. Financial savings also appeared to be realized in nondiet areas, though the dimensions in specific areas were not quantified in this research.

The most consistent determinants of program impact included the rate of program participation, dissatisfaction with non-Title VII meals, satisfaction with the Title VII meals, therapeutic diet restrictions, and financial food purchasing

problems. A positive relationship was found between the rate of program participation and participant-perceived program impact on monetary savings, food
purchasing behavior, and food preparation practices. As participation rate increased so did the proportion of persons realizing impact in these areas. Satisfaction with meals other than those consumed at the program was inversely related
to program impact on monetary savings, food purchasing behavior, food preparation practices, and food consumption behavior. Individuals who reported dissatisfaction with non-Title VII meals were more likely to report impact in these
areas. Satisfaction with the meal was associated with a positive impact on
monetary savings, food purchasing, and food preparation practices. Persons who
adhered to their therapeutic diet prescriptions reported significantly more
impact on monetary savings, food preparation practices, and food consumption
behavior than those not adhering to their diets or those without therapeutic
restrictions. This appeared due to the assistance of the program in providing
meals that were suitable for some therapeutic diets. Those without therapeutic
restrictions were less likely to report impact on food preparation practices and
food consumption and more impact on savings than those not adhering to therapeutic diets. Persons with financial food purchasing problems were consistently
more likely to realize impact on monetary savings and food purchasing and
consumption behavior.

It was concluded that those with more frequent patterns of participation
and those with greater need for financial and dietary management assistance
realized significantly more impact on monetary savings, food preparation practices, food consumption, and food purchasing behavior, as well as on other
aspects of their lives, including socialization, recreation, and life satisfaction.

Current Unmet Needs for Services Among Boston Title VII Elderly

Introduction

The pervasive health, economic, and social needs of the aging in the United
States, and the inadequacies of the institutions and community-based services
which serve them have become increasingly visible and a source of public indig-
nation. As the number and proportion of persons aged 60 and older increase,
both the inequities and inefficiencies in our national system of care for the aged
will demand priority attention of the government, health care professionals, and
taxpayers.

As funding for programs for the aged increases, care must be taken to plan,
coordinate, and integrate human services, lest program fragmentation result in
deleterious effects on the delivery of services to the aging.[7] Assessment of needs

for health and social services is fundamental to the determination of the range and priority of services required to ameliorate problems of the aged.

Two general approaches for estimating the needs for health services for the aging exist.[8] The medical model of needs assessment holds that physical examinations are necessary to determine baseline health and need for supportive services. In contrast, the functional model of needs assessment is predicated on the concept that an individual's subjective assessment of disability, limitations in activities, or functional capacity are the best predictors of health status and need for services.[9]

Past estimates of physical health and need for services using the medical model have differed from subjective estimates by elderly persons. Differences may have resulted from low expectation of services,[10] personality or coping style,[11] adaptation to illness,[12] or optimisim/pessimism about health among the aging.[13] More recently researchers have resolved differences between the two approaches by producing reliable subjective survey methodologies which closely parallel the assessment of needs for services made by clinicians.[14]

Drawing on these methodologies, this section addresses one of five evaluation research questions that were posed: what are the current unmet needs for supportive services among Title VII participants? The section defines the needs for health and supportive services among Boston Title VII participants, compares the prevalence of needs among among the aged in Massachusetts,[15] and discusses the implications of these findings for Title VII program development.

Methods

The data were derived from in-depth interviews with a stratified random probability sample of 174 Title VII participants who attended the Boston congregate Title VII program during January to June 1976, and a random probability sample of 1,317 persons aged 65 and older in Massachusetts. The aged in Massachusetts were being studied as part of a longitudinal assessment of their health care needs, the latest segment of which the author served as a nutrition consultant. The results of the Massachusetts survey have been summarized.[16] Title VII participants were being studied concurrently as part of an evaluation of the program in the Boston area.

Title VII participants were categorized into one of four strata according to their average frequency of program participation during January to June 1976: (1) 0–15 days per quarter; (2) 16–30 days per quarter; (3) 31–45 days per quarter; and (4) 46+ days per quarter. The research sample was selected to ensure inclusion of participants for each strata in proportion to their number in the area-specific Title VII population. Participant responses were weighted to derive estimates for the program as a whole.

Standardized interviews were conducted by the author and professional interviewers from the Survey Research Program, a Joint Facility for Urban Studies of MIT and Harvard University. The interview schedules used in the Title VII evaluation were designed to be identical in a number of areas to the schedule used in the state assessment of needs among the aged[17] such that valid comparisons between the two data sets could be made.

Chi-square analyses and Fisher Exact Tests were conducted between socioeconomic, demographic, and other selected descriptive characteristics of the Title VII population and needs for individual supportive services according to the cross tabulation procedure described by Nie et al.[18] and Siegel.[19] The purpose of these analyses was to identify significant relationships between population parameters and the distribution of needs for services. The Friedman Two-way Analysis of Variance was used to test the hypothesis that the area Title VII study sample participants were drawn from the same population.[20]

Quantitative estimates of needs for individual supportive services were derived using operational definitions of needs, similar to those developed by Branch.[21] Using clinical criteria of needs for services, Branch had tested the reliability and validity of these operational definitions of need on a random sample of 206 aged and found that they paralleled clinical needs assessment determinations.[22] The operational definitions of needs incorporated two dimensions of potential problem areas: (1) the evaluative dimension, for example, do you feel you need assistance with food preparation? (2) the behavioral dimension, for example, do you completely adhere to your therapeutic diet, or are there times you buy less food in order to meet nonfood household expenses? All potential response profiles for the evaluative and behavioral dimensions were considered, ordered from greater to lesser self-sufficiency, and placed into four categories of need which were first described by Branch and Fowler:[23]

1. Need currently met and no apparent problem
2. Need currently met; potential problems apparent
3. Need may currently be unmet; potential problems apparent
4. Need currently unmet; current problems.

By using the operational definitions of need, it was possible to determine whether or not current problems existed, problems had been resolved in a stable manner, or potential needs for services existed among the Title VII participant population. A summary of the definitions of current unmet needs for supportive services is in table 7–5. The appendix details the operational definitions of needs for each supportive service.

Results

A comparison between the socioeconomic, demographic, and general health characteristics of Boston Title VII participants and persons aged 65 and older in Massachusetts is in table 7-6. The mean age of the Massachusetts sample was 74 while that of Boston Title VII participants was 72.6. Significantly more racial minorities and persons who lived alone participated in the Title VII program (6.8% and 59.2%, respectively) than were found in the Massachusetts elderly population (1.5% and 30.1%, respectively). The median annual income of Title VII participants was $3,500 and substantially lower than that of the Massachusetts' aged, $4,500. Proportionately more females than males were served by Title VII, 69% versus 31%, respectively. The Massachusetts' elderly population had 63% females and 37% males. Significantly more widowed, separated and divorced, and individuals who had never married attended Title VII (43.9%, 12.1%, and 14%, respectively) than were found in Massachusetts' elderly population (39%, 3%, 8%, respectively).

Concerning the health status of Title VII participants, 18% reported excellent health, 41% good health, 30% fair health, and 12% poor health. The proportion of Massachusetts' aged who reported excellent or good health was 17% and 42%, respectively; 32% reported fair health and 9% poor health. Nearly 59% of Title VII participants considered their own health better than their peers, 31% reported health similar to their peer group, and 11% considered their health worse than their peers. Some 57% of the Massachusetts' aged considered their health better than their peers, 34% reported health similar to peers, and 7% considered their health worse than their peer group. Significantly more of the Title VII aged (65%) had chronic illnesses than the Massachusetts' aged (45%).

About two-thirds of both Massachusetts' and Title VII aged had not seen a dentist in the last year and about a third had seen a dentist. On the other hand, 81% of both Massachusetts' and Title VII aged had seen a physician in the last year while 19% had not seen a physician.

Looking at functional capacity, about 90% of both Massachusetts' and Title VII aged were able to climb stairs. Over three-fourths of both groups were able to walk a half mile without assistance. Significantly fewer Title VII participants (50%) than Massachusetts' aged (62%) were able to do heavy work.

Furthermore, of the 29% of Title VII participants on prescribed therapeutic diets, 64% were not adhering to their diets and 18% did not understand the diet restrictions. Some 40% found the Title VII meals inappropriate for their special diet needs. In addition, 9.3% of Title VII participants reported dissatisfaction with non-Title VII meals.

The proportion of Title VII and Massachusetts' aged with current unmet needs for supportive services (need category 4) are in table 7-7. Significantly more Title VII participants (11.9%) had unmet needs for short-term emergency services than elderly in Massachusetts (1%). The proportion of Massachusetts' aged with unmet needs for transportation assistance (7%) exceeded that of Title VII participants (4.2%). The proportion of Title VII participants with unmet needs for shopping assistance (2.7%) exceeded that of the Massachusetts population (1%). Need for long-term emergency services in the Title VII population (4.9%), was significantly greater than that found in the Massachusetts aged (1%). Less than 1% of both Title VII and Massachusetts' aged had current unmet needs

Table 7-5
Operational Definitions of Current Unmet Needs for Supportive Services[a]

Short-term emergency services: No one to call in an emergency; has available telephone, lives alone, and rarely has visitors or visits others. Someone to call in emergency but no available telephone, lives alone, and rarely has visitors or visits others.

Long-term emergency services: No one to call if sick, lives alone, and has poor perceived health.

Socialization: No available opportunities for social interaction or recreation, no close friends or confidants, or perceived needs for counseling services (seven-item socialization index).

Transportation: Problem with transportation, perceived need for transportation services, rarely gets out of residence or only gets out in case of an emergency (homebound).

Food shopping: Problem with shopping, perceived need for shopping assistance, and shopping done by self or others.

Housekeeping: Very serious problem with housekeeping and perceived need for homemaker assistance.

Food preparation: Problem with food preparation, usual eating pattern is one or no regular meals a day, not adhering to therapeutic diet if one was prescribed, and unsatisfied with diet in general.

[a]Operational definitions adapted from Branch, L.G., "Understanding the Health and Social Service Needs of People over Age 65," Center for Survey Research, A Facility of the University of Massachusetts and the Joint Center for Urban Studies of MIT and Harvard University, 1977.

Table 7-6
Comparison between Boston Title VII Participants and Massachusetts Persons over Age 65: Socioeconomic, Demographic, and Health Characteristics

Characteristic	Massachusetts Persons over Age 65 (n = 1316)	Boston Title VII Participants (n = 174)	X^2 Level of Significance
	% Population		
Age			
Mean (X)	(74.0)	(72.6)	
65	0.0	17.8	
66-74	60.0	47.9	
75+	40.0	34.3	$214.33p < .001$
Race			
White	99.0	93.2	
Other	1.5	6.8	$18.55p < .001$
Sex			
Male	37.0	31.1	
Female	63.0	68.9	$2.29p < .10$
Income			
Median	($4,500)	($3,500)	
Marital status			
Married	50.0	29.4	
Widowed	39.0	43.9	
Separated/divorced	3.0	12.1	
Never married	8.0	14.6	$53.55p < .001$

Table 7-6 (Continued)

Characteristic	Massachusetts Persons over Age 65 (n = 1316)	Boston Title VII Participants (n = 174)	X^2 Level of Significance
Educational attainment			
8th grade	37.0	41.1	
1–3 years high school	22.0	20.1	
High school graduate	24.0	31.2	
Some college	17.0	7.6	$12.64p < .01$
Living situation			
Alone	30.1	59.2	
Spouse	38.8	23.7	
With family members	15.8	14.9	
With nonrelatives	15.3	2.2	$68.07p < .001$
Current health status			
Excellent	17.0	17.9	
Good	42.0	40.9	
Fair	32.0	29.7	
Poor	9.0	11.6	$1.42p < .5$
Health compared to peers			
Better	57.0	58.6	
Same, better than some, worse than others	34.0	30.9	
Worse	9.0	10.5	$0.66p > 0.75$
Current chronic disease			
Yes	60.0	65.2	
No	40.0	34.8	$25.12p < .001$
Utilization of dental & medical services			
Annual dental visits			
None	63.0	65.7	
One or more	37.0	34.3	$0.45p = .5$
Annual medical visits			
None	19.0	19.1	
One or more	81.0	80.9	$0.0p > .975$
Rosow functional health items— ability to perform activities of daily living			
Able to climb flight of stairs	91.0	88.0	$1.94p > .10$
Able to walk half mile	76.0	78.9	$0.58p > .5$
Able to do heavy work	62.0	50.3	$8.87p < .01$

In addition to these comparative descriptive characteristics, Title VII aged also had the following characteristics: 29.1% had therapeutic diet needs including in decreasing order of prevalence, needs for diabetic, modified sodium, modified fiber, low cholesterol, low saturated fat, weight reduction, and fat modification; 64.4% of those on diets were not adhering to them; 17.5% did not understand their diet restrictions; 45.9% found the Title VII meal inappropriate for their therapeutic needs; 20.6% reported diet preparation difficulties; and 9.3% reported dissatisfaction with non-Title VII meals.

[a]Source: Branch, L.G., "Understanding the Health and Social Service Needs of People over Age 65," Center for Survey Research, A Facility of the University of Massachusetts and the Joint Center for Urban Studies of MIT and Harvard University, 1977.

Table 7–7

Current Unmet Needs for Supportive Services Among Boston NPOA and Massachusetts Aged

Supportive Service	Total Boston Title VII Congregate Population		Total Massachusetts' Persons over 65 Years of Age[a]		X^2	p
	% Current Unmet Needs	n	% Current Unmet Needs	n		
Short-Term Emergency Services	11.9	(174)	1.0	(1299)	83.5	< .001
Transportation	4.2	(173)	7.0	(1290)	1.6	> .10
Shopping Assistance	2.7	(169)	1.0	(1302)	5.2	> .25
Long-Term Emergency Services	4.9	(172)	1.0	(1308)	20.1	< .001
Food Preparation Assistance	0.7	(172)	0.5	(1286)	1.4	> .25
Housekeeping Assistance	1.1	(174)	2.0	(1289)	0.4	> .50
Socialization	3.7	(172)	2.0	(1314)	1.2	> .25
Needs for Services						
0	80.1	(174)	80.0	(1317)		
1	3.3	(174)	14.0	(1317)		
2 or more	16.6	(174)	6.0	(1317)	35.5	< .001

[a]Source: Branch, L.G., "Understanding the Health and Social Service Needs of People over Age 65," Center for Survey Research, A Facility of the University of Massachusetts and the Joint Center for Urban Studies of MIT and Harvard University, 1977.

for food preparation assistance. Some 1% and 2% of Title VII and Massachusetts aged, respectively, had unmet needs for housekeeping assistance and 3.7% of Title VII and 2% of Massachusetts aged had needs for socialization. Four-fifths of both the Title VII and Massachusetts' aged had no current unmet needs for supportive services. Among those with needs for services, 3.3% of the Title VII participants had unmet needs for one service, compared with 14% of the Massachusetts' aged. On the other hand, 16.6% of Title VII participants and 6% of Massachusetts' aged had current unmet needs for two or more supportive services.

The pattern of needs for supportive services among the Massachusetts' and Title VII aged are in tables 7–8 and 7–9, respectively. Some 7% of the aged in Massachusetts had current needs for transportation services while less than 2%

had needs for the remaining services, including short-term and long-term emergency services, shopping and food preparation assistance, housekeeping services, and socialization. Some 12% of Title VII participants in Boston had needs for short-term emergency services, 5% for long-term emergency services; 4% for shopping assistance or transportation, and 1% or less for food preparation or housekeeping services. Looking at need categories 3 and 4 combined (uncertain need met, potential problem; and need unmet, current problem), significantly more Title VII participants (23%) than Massachusetts' aged (2%) had needs for short-term emergency services. Significantly more Title VII participants (13%) than Massachusetts' aged (5%) had needs for shopping assistance. Significantly more Title VII participants (46%) than Massachusetts' aged (12%) had needs for long-term emergency services, and significantly more Title VII (15%) than Massachusetts' aged (3.5%) had needs for food preparation assistance.

The perceived current needs for information and referral, counseling, and nutrition education among Title VII participants by project area and for the Boston Title VII participants are summarized in table 7-10. About 9%, 5%, and 7% of the Boston Title VII participants had current needs for information and referral, counseling, and nutrition education, respectively.

A summary of chi-square analyses between selected characteristics of the Title VII population and needs for supportive services is in table 7-11. Living situation (alone) and race (white) had a significant positive association with short-term emergency assistance needs. Age and sex (female) had a significant positive association with needs for transportation. Poor health, living situation (alone), race (white), and chronic conditions had a significant positive association with needs for long-term emergency assistance. Poor health, living situation (alone), and chronic conditions had a significant positive association with needs for one or more supportive services. Program participation did not bear a significant association with any of the supportive service needs.

A comparison between the proportion of persons living alone and in poor health with current unmet needs for services among the aged in Massachusetts and in the Boston Title VII population is in table 7-12.

Significantly more Title VII participants who lived alone (24%) than Massachusetts, aged (4%) had unmet needs for short-term emergency services. Significantly more Title VII participants who lived alone (8%) than aged in Massachusetts (2%) had unmet needs for long-term emergency services. Significantly more Title VII participants who were in poor health (44%) than Massachusetts' aged (5%) had unmet needs for long-term emergency services. Significantly fewer Title VII participants who were in poor health (5.6%) than Massachusetts' aged (32%) had unmet needs for transportation. Significantly more Title VII participants in poor health (29%) than Massachusetts' aged (2%) had unmet needs for short-term emergency services.

Table 7-8
Massachusetts' Persons over Age 65: Assessment of Needs for Supportive Services Using Operational Definitions of Need

Need Category	(n)	Need Met; No Apparent Problem	Need Met; Potential Problem	Uncertain Need Met; Potential Problem	Need Unmet; Current Problem
			Population %		
Short-term emergency assistance[a]	(1,299)	97	1	1	1.0
Transportation[b]	(1,290)	69	20	4	7.0
Shopping assistance[c]	(1,302)	86	9	4	1.0
Long-term emergency assistance[d]	(1,308)	79	9	11	1.0
Food preparation assistance[e]	(1,286)	86	10	3	0.5
Housekeeping assistance[f]	(1,289)	86	3	9	2.0
Socialization[g]	(1,314)	70	23	4	2.0

Source: Branch, L.B., "Understanding the Health and Social Service Needs of People over Age 65," Center for Survey Research, A Facility of the University of Massachusetts and the Joint Center for Urban Studies of MIT and Harvard University, 1977.

[a]Significant positive association between short-term emergency service needs and living alone; needs for multiple supportive services.

[b]Significant positive association between transportation need and poor health; age; living with children; and needs for multiple supportive services.

[c]Significant positive association between shopping assistance need and age; poor health; and needs for multiple supportive services.

[d]Significant positive association between long-term emergency assistance and living alone; poor health; and needs for multiple supportive services.

[e]Significant positive association between food preparation assistance and living alone or with children; needs for multiple supportive services; and poor health.

[f]Significant positive association between housekeeping needs and living alone and with children; and multiple needs for supportive services.

[g]Significant positive association between socialization needs and age; poor health; and multiple needs for supportive services.

Table 7-9
Boston Title VII Participants; Assessment of Needs for Supportive Services Using Operational Definitions of Need[a]

Need Category	(n)	Need Met; No Apparent Problem	Need Met; Potential Problem	Uncertain Need Met; Potential Problem	Need Unmet; Current Problem	Chi-square Analyses Comparing Title VII & Massachusetts' Aged-pooled Categories Tables 27, 27A	
				Population %		X^2	p
Short-term emergency assistance	(174)	72.8	4.8	10.6	11.9	143.6	<.001
Transportation	(173)	55.7	31.7	8.4	4.2	0.7	NS[b]
Shopping assistance	(170)	65.3	23.4	8.7	2.7	9.8	<.01
Long-term emergency assistance	(172)	42.7	10.9	41.5	4.9	130.8	<.001
Food preparation assistance	(174)	59.4	25.4	14.5	0.7	47.9	<.001
Housekeeping assistance	(174)	74.5	15.8	8.7	1.1	0.3	NS[b]
Socialization	(174)	51.2	43.8	1.3	3.7	0.1	NS[b]

[a]Estimates of need based on weighted area-specific statistics.
[b]Not significant

Table 7–10
Perceived Needs for Supportive Services Among Title VII Participants

Need Category	Boston Title VII Program % Population
Information & Referral	9.4
Counseling	5.4
Nutrition education	6.7

Discussion

The socioeconomic and demographic characteristics of Boston Title VII participants differed markedly from those of the Massachusetts' aged in that the Title VII program attracted proportionately more blacks; females; persons with low incomes; persons who were widowed, separated, or divorced; and persons who lived alone than found among the aged in Massachusetts. Across all Title VII participants, perceived health, health relative to peers, and functional capacity were similar to that of the Massachusetts' aged, though the ability to perform heavy household work was diminished among Title VII participants.

Branch[24] indicated that needs for supportive services among the aged in Massachusetts were related to needs for multiple supportive services, living alone or with children, poor health, or old age (see footnotes in table 7-8). Given the significantly greater proportion of persons living alone and having multiple needs for supportive services among Title VII participants, one would have expected the greater potential unmet needs for short-term and long-term emergency and food preparation services found among Title VII participants in this evaluation. As could also be expected, proportionately more Title VII participants had unmet needs for shopping assistance, due to the greater proportion of Title VII participants relative to Massachusetts elderly with multiple needs for supportive services. Needs for multiple services in the Massachusetts aging population were related to poor health, being a racial minority, being widowed or never married, living alone or with children, low income, and older age. Title VII participants were somewhat younger than Massachusetts' aged and did not report proportionately poorer health. Nonetheless, Title VII population had proportionately more blacks, persons who were widowed or never married, persons who lived alone or with children, and persons with low incomes. Therefore the Title VII program attracted persons at greater risk of supportive services; this fact was supported by the greater prevalence of single as well as multiple needs for services among Title VII relative to Massachusetts' aged.

Table 7-11
Current Unmet Needs for Supportive Services among Boston Title VII Participants by Strata Using Operational Definitions of Need

Characteristics of Population	n	Short-term Emergency Assistance	Transportation	Shopping Assistance	Long-term Emergency Assistance	Food Preparation Assistance	Housekeeping Assistance	Socialization	1 or More Supportive Service Needs
Age									
< 70	62	16.8	0.6	0.6	2.3	0.0	2.3	4.6	19.1
≥ 70	109	11.0	6.1	0.7	6.8	1.1	0.4	2.6	19.2
		NS	*	NS	NS	NS	NS	NS	NS
Health									
Good-Excellent	108	11.1	1.1	0.7	0.0	0.0	0.4	3.3	14.1
Fair-Poor	64	19.0	8.4	0.5	12.1	1.6	2.1	4.2	29.0
		NS	NS	NS	**	NS	NS	NS	**
Living situation									
Alone	105	24.0	5.4	1.3	8.7	1.1	1.6	5.4	31.1
Others	65	0.0	2.7	0.0	0.0	0.0	0.5	1.6	4.3
		***	NS	NS	**	NS	NS	NS	***
Sex									
Male	58	12.9	0.7	0.0	6.4	2.1	0.7	5.0	22.2
Female	115	14.7	5.9	1.1	4.5	0.0	1.3	3.3	19.1
		NS	*	NS	NS	NS	NS	NS	NS
Race									
White	155	14.9	3.9	0.6	5.2	0.7	1.2	3.4	20.1
Black	118	3.2	9.6	3.2	3.2	0.0	0.0	9.6	19.1
		***	NS	NS	**	NS	NS	NS	**
Chronic conditions									
0	64	8.7	3.7	0.0	0.0	0.0	0.0	0.0	9.3
1+	110	16.9	4.3	1.0	7.6	1.0	1.7	5.6	25.5
		NS	NS	NS	*	NS	NS	NS	**
Rate Title VII participation									
0–15 days	77	14.6	3.7	0.8	4.1	1.1	0.0	4.9	19.8
16+ days	97	13.3	4.6	0.5	6.1	0.0	2.6	2.0	19.9
		NS	NS	NS	NS	NS	NS	NS	NS

$*p < .05$
$**p < .01$
NS not significant

Table 7-12
Current Unmet Needs for Services among Massachusetts' Aged and Boston Title VII Participants Who Live Alone and Have Poor Health

Supportive Service Category	Living Situation: Alone		Perceived Health: Poor	
	Massachusetts' Aged (n = 388-396)	Boston Title VII Participants (n = 105)	Massachusetts' Aged (n = 107-111)	Boston Title VII Participants (n = 21)
		% Unmet Needs for Services		
Short-term emergency assistance	4.0	24.0 ***a	2.0	29.3 ***
Transportation	7.0	5.4	32.0	5.6 ***
Shopping assistance	1.0	1.3	0.0	1.9
Long-term emergency assistance	2.0	8.7 ***	5.0	44.0 ***
Food preparation assistance	1.0	1.1	2.0	5.6
Housekeeping assistance	3.0	16.0	9.0	7.6
Socialization	4.0	5.4	11.0	5.6

Source: L.G. Branch, "Understanding the Health and Social Service Needs of People over Age 65," Center for Survey Research, 1977.
[a]$p < .001$ ***

Of those services studied, short-term and long-term emergency and house-keeping/homemaker services are not mandated under the Title VII program legislation. Potential needs for these services are prevalent among Title VII participants in Boston and could be considered in the expansion of supportive services in the future.

Using the estimated proportion of participants with current unmet needs for supportive services, about 500 Boston Title VII participants (20%) have current needs for one or more services. About half of these persons have needs for long-term and short-term emergency services, suggesting a need to include them in the list of services provided by Title VII as well as closer coordination with the Visiting Nurses Association and the Title III Home Care Corporations. Both long-term and short-term emergency services are critical in the maintenance of independent living for the elderly.

The relatively low perceived needs for nutrition education and counseling among Title VII participants also suggests that expansion of these services is not warranted at this time. However, the documented health care needs, prevalence of chronic illness, and special diet needs, as well as the living situations[25] suggest needs may be underestimated and that there services need expansion.

The relatively low current unmet needs for the remaining services among the current Title VII participants suggest that in the short-runs service provision will not require substantial expansion. However, in order that the provision of services maintain pace with the changing need for these services as participants' profiles of need change, the changing status of Title VII participants relative to their needs for these services could be monitored on a regular basis.

Conclusions

The Title VII program appears to attract elderly individuals who are at greater risk of needs for some supportive services, particularly individuals who live alone, racial minorities, those with lower incomes, the widowed or those who never married, and persons with multiple supportive service needs. Overall, the current level of unmet needs for supportive services among Boston Title VII participants is low, implying that substantial expansion of the current level of supportive service activities would not be needed at this time. However, to meet the current needs for services and to institute the Management Information System described in chapter 8 will require considerable expansion of supportive services.

Short-term and long-term emergency assistance were the supportive service categories in which the greatest current unmet needs and potential needs for services (categories 3 and 4) existed. This suggested that Title VII services could be expanded to include these categories and that closer coordination was needed between Title VII programs, the Visiting Nurse's Association (VNA), and Home Care Corporations. The VNA and Home Care Corporations currently have limited capacity to provide short-term and long-term emergency assistance.

To maintain ongoing service delivery in line with the changing needs for supportive services among Title VII participants, ongoing monitoring of the changing status of participants should be accomplished by the Title VII project areas with assistance of the Area Agency on Aging.

Delivery of Services to Target Group Elderly

Introduction

Census data are a source of pertinent socioeconomic and demographic characteristics of the aging population to whom Title VII and supportive services may be delivered. The census data may be useful in two critical areas of nutrition program planning and implementation. First, on the planning side, the data can be used to identify the location and descriptive characteristics of target groups within defined geographic areas. In addition, census statistics can provide reference parameters that may be useful in program evaluations. The evaluation research question addressed in the section is: to what extent are the target group elderly served by the Boston Title VII Nutrition program?

Results

Program Participation: A comparison between Title VII participation statistics from available site records January to June 1976 and the number of persons served the last day of June 1976 is presented in table 7-13. Available site records suggest that project reports overestimate the number of persons actually served by from one-third to 2.2 times. Nonetheless, examination of the number of persons served on the last day in the quarter suggests that as many as 30% of participants may not become part of the record system in the short run. Site records were used in this research.

Population Characteristics: Table 7-14 summarizes the age distribution data for persons 60 years of age and older for the City of Boston as a whole. Of the city's total population, 17.6% (n = 112,215) are 60 or older. The proportion of the total city population 60 to 64 years of age is 4.8% (n = 30,708) 65 to 74 is 7.7% (n = 49,257), and 75 or over is 5 (n = 32,750). A summary of the characteristics of Boston residents aged 60+ is found in table 7-15. A total of 112,215

Table 7-13
Comparison of Title VII Participation Data from Available Project Records and Boston Project Area Quarterly Report Figures January–June 1976[a]

Available Project Records Total Title VII Congregate Participants Jan.-June 1976		Total Reported Unduplicated Congregate Persons Jan.-June 1976	No. Persons Served on Last Day June 1976
Area X	521	691	532
Area Y	620	1,700	819
Area Z	1,369	3,047	2,050
	2,510	5,438	3,401

[a]Discrepancies in data may arise due to inadequate reporting procedures or maintenance of files on inactive participants, or both.

Table 7-14
Number and Proportion of Population Aged 60+, Boston

Age	City Total	
	%	n
60–64	4.8	30,708
65–74	7.7	49,257
75	5.0	32,250
% total city population 60+	17.6	112,215

Source: Derived from data given in: U.S. Department of Commerce, Bureau of Census, "1970 Census of Population and Housing, Boston, Massachusetts, Standard Metropolitan Statistical Area."

Table 7-15
Target Group Characteristics of Boston Title VII Project Area Residents Aged 60+

Project Area	Total Area Population Aged 60	% Boston Population Aged 60	Persons Aged 60 with Incomes below Poverty	Minority Individuals Aged 60	% Boston Elderly with Incomes below Poverty	% Boston Elderly Minorities
Total	112,215	100	22,441	21,683	20.0	19.0

Source: Derived from data in U.S. Department of Commerce, Bureau of Census, 1970 Census of the Population and Housing, Boston, Massachusetts, Standard Metropolitan Statistical Area.

elderly reside within the city and are eligible for Title VII program services. Of these, 21,683 are minorities and 22,441 have incomes below poverty, characteristics which designate them as target groups for Title VII intervention.

Title VII Program Participants: The socioeconomic and demographic characteristics of the Boston Title VII Nutrition program congregate participants are in tables 7–16 and 7–17.

Table 7–16
Boston Title VII Elderly Congregate Nutrition Program Participants

| | Participants, % | |
Demographics	Male	Female
Age distribution		
< 60	–	2.2
60–64	1.1	8.1
65–74	16.1	37.1
⩾ 75	13.5	21.1
Total	31.6	68.4
Mean age	72.6	
	% Males and Females	
Marital status		
Single	14.7	
Married	29.3	
Separated or divorced	12.0	
Widowed	44.0	
Educational level, years		
1–7	16.7	
8	22.7	
9–11	20.3	
12	31.4	
Over 12	8.9	
Residence		
Type: private	66.6	
public, including elderly	33.4	
Length: mean (years)	30.8	
Under 10	30.0	
Over 10	70.0	
Living situation		
Alone	59.1	
With spouse only	23.9	
With family members	14.9	
With nonrelatives	2.2	
Race		
White	93.2	
Black	6.8	
Birthplace/parentage (US)		
United States/United States	23.1	
United States/foreign	42.5	
Foreign/foreign	34.4	

Ethnic background	
Irish	31.5
Jewish	12.4
Italian	11.5
Black American	6.7
French	4.9
Irish/English	4.0
Lithuanian	3.8
English	3.8
German	2.9
Other	18.6
Presence of chronic conditions	
No	34.2
Yes	65.8
Health	
Excellent	18.0
Good	41.3
Fair	29.0
Poor	11.7
Functional capacity	
Cannot work at all	5.7
Limited	48.0
Unlimited	46.3
Therapeutic diet	
Yes	28.3
No	71.7
Complete adherence to special diet	
Yes	11.5
No	17.9
Not on one	71.7
Understanding diet	
Very well	21.3
Fairly well	2.6
Not very well	2.0
Not on one	71.7
Don't know	2.4

Age: The mean age of persons served by the Title VII program in Boston was 72.6. Overall, 2.2% of those served were under 60 years of age; 8.1% were 60 to 64; 37.7% were 64 to 75; and 21.1% were over 75.

Sex: Proportionately more elderly females than males were receiving Title VII services in Boston; 68.4% versus 31.6% of the total population served, respectively.

Marital Status: Widowed persons comprised 44% and married elderly 29.3% of those served in Boston. In addition, 14.7% of the participants never married and 12% were divorced or separated.

Table 7–17
Boston Title VII Congregate Nutrition Program Participants

	Participants, %	
Economics	*Male*	*Female*
Annual income (Q163)		
(respondent-spouse)		
< $3,000	21.1	25.9
$3,000–$5,000	46.3	63.5
$6,000–$9,000	22.0	8.4
⩾ $10,000	10.6	2.3
Refused to respond	16.8	
Mean income	$4,214	
Median income	$3,500	
Mean weekly food expenditures (Q161, Q162)		
Grocery stores	$22.32	
Restaurant	$3.04	
(excludes contributions to Title VII meals)		
	% Males and Females	
Work Status (Q52)		
Retired or not working	83.0	
Working	17.0	

	Income Below Poverty	Income 125% Poverty
Population Characteristic	*% Title VII Congregate Population*	
Age (Q41)		
Under 60	0.0	0.0
60–64	25.0	36.4
65–74	12.6	37.4
⩾ 75	27.6	57.7
	**a	**
Sex (Q44)		
Male 0	19.7	37.0
Female 1	19.8	48.2
Health status (Q1)		
Excellent	32.4	43.8
Good	17.1	38.8
Fair	12.3	46.6
Poor	22.9	55.6
	**	
No. of chronic conditions		
0	25.7	38.5
1	25.5	46.8
⩾ 2	10.0	47.7
	***	
Living situation		
Alone	15.4	41.0
Spouse only	14.8	30.3
Family member	44.5	82.6
Nonrelative	29.4	58.8
	***	***

Table 7–17 (Continued)

Project area		
X	32.5	46.0
Y	34.2	47.7
Z	8.7	42.1
Total	19.6	44.2

[a]** $p < .01$; *** $p < .001$

Educational Background: Persons with less than eighth grade education comprised 16.7% of those served in Boston Title VII programs. About two-fifths (22.7%) had eighth to eleventh grade education; 30.5% had high school degrees; and 9.6% had at least some college.

Housing and Living Situation: Type of residence—over half of the participants (66.6%) owned or rented their own homes or apartments. About one-third (33.4%) lived in public housing, particularly housing designed for the elderly. The average length of residence in a neighborhood was over 31 years. Some 30% of the population had migrated from other neighborhoods in the past 10 years. Household composition—the majority of Title VII participants (59.1%) lived alone. About one-fifth (23.9%) lived with spouses, 14.9% lived with other individuals, and 2.2% lived with nonrelatives.

Racial Background: Whites comprised 93.2% of those served by the Title VII program in Boston, and blacks accounted for 6.8%. No persons of other racial characteristics were served. (The Title VII site serving the Chinese-American community was excluded from the sample due to lack of participant records.)

Birthplace—Ethnic Origin: About 43% of participants in all three project areas are first-generation Americans with foreign parentage; 34% were born overseas; and 23% were second-generation Americans. Elderly with diverse ethnic origins were served in the Boston Title VII program, though 32% were Irish, 12% Jewish or Italian, 8% black, and under 5% other ethnic origins.

Health and Diet Needs: Some 66% of Title VII participants had chronic conditions. Over half of the Boston participants (59%) considered their health good to excellent; whereas 6% could not work at all due to poor health. While 28% of Boston participants had been prescribed therapeutic diets, only 11% were adhering to their diets, and about 5% did not understand the diet prescriptions.

Income and Expenditures: The medium annual income of Title VII participants and their spouses was $3,500 (table 7–17). The participants spent an average of about $22 per week on food, or about one-third their weekly income; and about $3 per week in restaurants.

Work Status: Some 83% of those served were retired and not working; 17% were retired and working part-time for pay or volunteer services (table 7-17).

Poverty: The proportion of persons whose income fell below the Bureau of Census poverty level and the near-poor (incomes 125% the poverty level) are found by selected population characteristics in table 7-17. One-fifth of all Boston Title VII participants (19.6%) had incomes below poverty and 44% at or below 125% the poverty level ($2,572 for one person living alone or with nonrelatives; $3,232 for two persons, head of house 65 or older.) Chi-square analyses indicated significant associations between poverty and all variables studied with the exception of sex. A greater proportion of participants who were older, in excellent health, with fewer chronic conditions, or lived with relatives other than their spouses had incomes below poverty. Proportionately more older and female participants and those residing with their families had incomes at or below 125% the poverty level.

Comparison between Elderly Residing in Boston and Those Served by Title VII Program: Comparisons are made between estimated aging population characteristics from census data and characteristics of the aged served by the Boston Title VII program in table 7-18. At most, 5% of the aging population in any socioeconomic or demographic strata were served by the Title VII program. In the City of Boston, about 2% of aged females and males or elderly poor were served. Some 25% of whites and less than 1% of the city's minority elderly were served by the program.

Discussion

Ongoing Title VII program monitoring, which is accomplished by the State and Area Agencies on Aging, is dependent upon the availability of valid and reliable project area statistics. It is also essential that the same set of program data is collected in a uniform manner across all areas such that interprogram comparisons and performance appraisals can be completed. It was clear that at the time of this evaluation, no uniform method of reporting program statistics had been implemented throughout the Boston Title VII project areas. Project area quarterly reports to the Department of Elder Affairs appeared to overestimate service statistics by a minimum of one-third and up to two times the available statistics from Title VII meal site records. In addition, comparisons between meal site participation records and the number of meals served on the last day of June 1976 (table 7-13) indicated that up to one-third of participants in the short run

Table 7-18
Delivery of Title VII Services to Boston's Aging Population

Population Characteristics	Estimated City Population 60 Years	Estimated Title VII Participants Jan.-June, 1976	Participation Rate (% of Population)
Males (age)			
60–64	13,000	28	0.4
65–74	19,271	419	2.3
75	11,513	339	2.8
Females (age)			
60–64	17,708	203	0.9
65–74	22,987	931	3.1
75	20,737	530	2.5
Total	112,216	2,450	2.2
Poverty			
60–64	4,595	48	1.1
65	17,862	429	2.4
Total	22,467	477	2.1
Race[a]			
White	90,222	2,339	2.6
Other	21,867	171	0.8
Black	7,135	171	2.4
Spanish	209	0	0.0

[a]Estimates of black and Spanish elderly populations were derived from census tract with 400 black or Spanish persons of all ages.

may not become a part of the program participant information systems. If errors such as these occur chronically throughout the operating period (and there are strong indications that they do in fact exist), they will create large discrepancies between available operating data, quarterly reports, and actual service delivery levels. Therefore the socioeconomic, demographic, and descriptive characteristics given in quarterly reports must be considered unreliable for monitoring and evaluative purposes at this time. Consequently, actual congregate meal site records must be reviewed to provide summary estimates of program service delivery.

This evaluation indicated that 2.2% of the Boston elderly population and the same proportion of the city's aged poor were served by the Title VII program between January and June 1976. Less than 1% (This figure may be slightly deflated due to the exclusion of the Title VII meal site serving the China-American community. It was excluded because of inadequate participant records.) of the city's total minorities, 2.4% of the city's black elderly, and about twice as many female as male aged were served. Less than 5% of the project area aged within any of the socioeconomic or demographic strata were served.

A major determinant of this level of service delivery was the general low level of funding for the delivery of Title VII congregate meal and supportive services to the aged. The Title VII program nationally is designed to serve only about 2% of the aged. Nonetheless, Title VII legislation designates both minority and elderly poor as targets for intervention. At the same time, the legislation specifically states that income eligibility criteria or means tests cannot be used to restrict Title VII participation in any way. This creates a dilemma for program administrators who must determine appropriate allocation of scarce resources to the aged in their project area.

In the Boston area, low-income elderly were served in proportion to their concentration in the city but minorities were underserved relative to their concentration. Nonetheless, their overall low level of participation, particularly in light of their specification as target groups, suggests the need to concentrate outreach efforts to encourage and maintain participation by a greater number of those with low incomes and from racial minority groups. Census data suggest that the elderly poor are found throughout all Boston Title VII project areas, yet they are concentrated within certain census tracts.[26] Outreach efforts could be concentrated in these census tracts.

Conclusions

The Boston Title VII program attracted predominantly female, low to moderate income, white aged who resided in public housing or alone. A total of 2.2% of the city's elderly were served between January and June 1976. Elderly females and males were served in proportion to their concentration in the population aged 60+ and accounted for 68% and 32% of those served, respectively. Some 2.2% of the city's elderly poor were served, indicating that they were served to a somewhat greater extent than their relative concentration in the community.

Less than 1% of the city's total minority elderly were served by the Title VII program and 1% or less of the minorities in each of the three project areas were served. Minorities were served to a lesser extent than their number in the total population and area populations would dictate.

The low participation of low-income and minority individuals in the Boston Title VII program could in part be explained by the Title VII policy which restricts application of any means or income tests to exclude participation by any group of elderly individuals. Since all elderly are technically eligible for Title VII participation, this creates a dilemma for the administrator who tries to concentrate services within a particular substrata of the elderly population. Low participation by low-income and minority elderly in Boston indicated a need to concentrate future outreach efforts on these individuals. Outreach efforts could be guided by census data which designates the location of target group elderly within project area neighborhoods and census tracts.

Current program participant information systems were inadequate to support ongoing Title VII program monitoring and evaluation activities in the Boston area. To ensure ongoing documentation of program service delivery statistics, to facilitate development of valid and reliable profiles of Title VII program participants, and to enable State and Area Agencies on Aging to carry out monitoring and appraisal activities, a uniform method of collecting and reporting participant and program operating information is needed throughout all Title VII operating areas.

Awareness and Utilization of Services Among Title VII Participants

Introduction

This section focuses on the following program evaluation question: to what extent are Title VII participants aware of and utilizing available supportive social services?

Results

Utilization of Services: The proportion of participants utilizing the program and community-based health and social services for the Boston Title VII program is summarized in table 7-19. The median number of medical visits among participants was three per year while the median number of annual dental visits was less than one. Some 66% of participants had not seen a dentist in the last year. About one in five participants had received Title VII transportation service and shopping assistance. Some 14.1% and 12.5% had received nutrition education and home-delivered meals, respectively. In addition, 5.3% and 7.7% of participants had received information and referral or counseling services through the program, respectively.

Regarding non-Title VII social services, none of the participants had received speech therapy during the last year; 4.2% had received rehabilitative therapy. About 10% had received professional counseling or housekeeping assistance and 6.4% home nursing services. Some 2.2% had received the assistance of a home health aide. In all, 2.4% had arranged services with the assistance of a neighborhood Home Care Corporation.

Awareness of Services: Title VII participants for the most part do not hear of or arrange non-Title VII supportive services through the program. The level of awareness of Title VII and community services among participants are sum-

Table 7-19

Utilization of Available Community and Health Services by
Title VII Elderly Congregate Nutrition Program Participants[a]

Service	% of Participants
Medical care	
Median no. annual physician visits	3.0
Dental care	
Median no. annual dental visits	0.0
% no dental visits	66.0
	% of Participants
Community services	
Speech therapy	0.0
Rehabilitative therapy	4.2
Counseling	10.3
Home nursing	6.3
Home health aides	2.2
Housekeeping/chore service	9.8
Title VII Services	
Transportation	22.0
Shopping assistance	20.2
Information and referral	5.3
Counseling	7.7
Nutrition education	14.1
Home-delivered meals	12.5

[a]Data were collected from a random probability sample of Boston Title VII
participants.

marized in table 7-20. The level of awareness of services among participants
varies across project areas. More area X participants are aware of transportation
and shopping assistance while area Y participants are generally more aware of
the remaining services, including information and referral, counseling, nutrition
education, and home-delivered meals. Overall, 71% of participants are aware of
home-delivered meals; 67% of transportation services; 67% of shopping assistance; 32% of counseling services; 31% of nutrition education activities; and
27% of information and referral services available through the program.

At least three in five of the participants were aware of the five benefits
available through the Social Security System, including retirement, disability,
and survivor benefits; medicare; and supplemental security income; 35.2% were
aware of Home Care Corporations and their services.

Factors Affecting Utilization and Awareness of Services: Chi-square analyses
indicated that only two variables, perceived health and race, had any significant

Table 7-20

Boston Title VII Elderly Congregate Nutrition Program Participants

Knowledge of Services	% of Participants
Supportive services	
Transportation	66.6
Shopping assistance	54.8
Home-delivered meals	70.6
Information & referral	27.1
Counseling	31.7
Nutrition education	30.6
Home Care Corporations (HCC)	
Knowledge of HCC	35.2
No knowledge of HCC	64.8
Past use of HCC	2.4
No past use of HCC	97.6
Awareness of Social Security benefits	
Retirement benefits	83.2
Disability benefits	61.2
Survivor benefits	62.2
Medicare	73.7
Supplemental security income	64.4
Use of Title VII program for *service knowledge source*[a]	
Speech therapy	0.0/0.0
Rehabilitative services	0.0/0.0
Counseling	0.9/0.9
Home nursing	1.3/0.4
Home-delivered meals	7.1/7.1
Home-health aides	0.2/0.2
Housekeeping chore service	0.9/0.9

[a]Figures should be interpreted in the following manner; first figure refers to proportion of population hearing of the service through the Title VII program; second figure refers to arranging service through the program, that is, 1.3/0.4 indicates that 1.3% of participants heard of the service through the program and 0.4% arranged the service through the program.

impact on utilization of individual supportive services. Home-delivered meals were more likely to be used by those in poorest health and minority individuals.

Chi-square analyses indicated that awareness of services was not affected by any of the variables studied, including perceived health, age, sex, race, birthplace, chronic conditions, need for services, income, or educational attainment. When the effect of awareness of services was controlled, some of these variables had an impact on perceived need for services. Among those aware of transportation services, individuals living alone perceived a need for service at some time to a greater extent than persons living with others. No single variable had a significant impact on needs for services among those who were unaware of transportation service availability. Among those aware of shopping assistance, persons with multiple chronic conditions were more likely to perceive need for shopping assistance than those without multiple chronic conditions. No single variable affected perceived need for shopping assistance among those who were unaware of available shopping assistance.

Among those aware of counseling services, the older the person the more likely was the perceptive need for counseling. No variable affected perceived need for service among those unaware of counseling services. Among those aware of homemaker services, individuals with multiple chronic conditions were more likely to report need for homemakers than those without chronic conditions. No single variable had a significant impact on perceived need for services among those not aware of homemaker availability.

Discussion

Knowledge of service availability and sophistication have been proposed as preconditions to recognition of a need for a supportive service. Linder[27] showed that those with higher incomes and educational attainment use medical services to a greater extent than those with lower incomes and educational attainment, particularly the preventive medical measures. His data suggest that those with higher educational attainment may perceive a greater need for services and therefore utilize services to a greater extent than those with lesser educational attainment; those with higher incomes can afford services. Studies in the field of mental health support the theory that knowledge about concepts, such as mental illness, are prerequisites to self-assessment of need for services. Fowler and McCalla[28] concluded from a study on the aged in Boston that knowledge about the existence of a service is not the result of the need for service and searching services out, rather that knowledge of services is a precondition for recognizing needs for services. They also found that those to whom it was most important to deliver services—the poor, immigrants, the very old, and those in poor health— were least likely to know of services.

This study of the Boston Title VII program participants does not suggest the same interrelationship between awareness and utilization or perceived needs for services among the aged. Rather, those with lower incomes or less educational attainment, minorities, and persons in poor health did not utilize most services to a lesser extent nor were they less aware that these services were available through the Title VII program or other community-based sources. Among those aware of services, persons in need appeared to utilize services to a greater extent suggesting that indeed the need for services was the motivation to search out services.

Nonetheless, if in fact those in greatest need are most isolated, unaware of services, and unable to get services because of environmental or physical/psychological barriers, the Title VII program appears to reduce or eliminate the effects of these barriers among Title VII participants.

Conclusions

Awareness of three Title VII services—transportation, shopping assistance, and home-delivered meals—were high among all participants as well as Social Security benefits. At least three-fourths of participants were aware of these available services. In contrast, only one-third of participants were aware of information and referral, counseling, or nutrition education services available through the program. In addition, only 35.2% and 24.5% of participants were aware of Home Care Corporations or the availability of homemaker services through Home Care Corporations, respectively. Less than one-fifth of participants had utilized available Title VII and community services for the elderly. Income, educational attainment, racial, and health characteristics did not appear to act as barriers to utilization or awareness of services among the participants. Need for services appears to be the primary motivation in seeking services. The program eliminates any financial barriers to obtaining the following services in the community at large: home-delivered meals, nutrition education, transportation, shopping assistance, counseling, and information and referral services. Furthermore, participation in the program appears to increase knowledge of the availability of supportive services, particularly persons most in need of and least aware of services, that is, the poor, the very old, immigrants, and elderly in poor health.

Determinants of Program Participation

Introduction

Program participation has been examined in only a few of the available Title VII program research studies. Haffron et al.[29] surveyed participants, nonparticipants, and program dropouts in the Winnebago County, Illinois, area to determine the extent to which target group elderly individuals were being served by the program. They concluded that program participants did exhibit characteristics that would suggest greater need for Title VII services: lower incomes, more transportation needs, more feelings of loneliness, and more frequent periods of confusion. Postma[30] examined the characteristics of 125 participants in the Eugene-Springfield, Oregon, Title VII program and concluded that participants perceived themselves as self-sufficient and consider the program as "(1) a fortunate and convenient opportunity for at least one balanced meal a day at a cost they can afford, and (2) a chance for fellowship." His findings also indicated that participants were more apt to have lower incomes, to be unmarried, and live alone than the elderly population as a whole and for the most part considered their diets adequate. Overall, 56% indicated that conflicting activities and other recreational programs prevented more frequent program participation.

More extensive data on the nutritional status, dietary intake, and perceptions of program participants and nonparticipants were collected by Kohrs[31] in the Central Missouri Title VII program. The author found significant differences between the dietary intake and nutritional status of participants and nonparticipants. The results suggested that the congregate meal appeared to have a positive impact on dietary intake; from 30 to 80% of the daily nutrient intake was contributed by the Title VII meal among those participating in the program. In addition, diets more frequently met the recommended nutrient intake[32] and relatively better nutritional status was found among those who attended the program with greater frequency.

Theoretical estimates of potential program impact on dietary intake and income relative to program participation rate can be calculated. Assuming the Title VII meal provides a minimum of one-third of the recommended dietary allowance,[33] the minimum contribution of the meal to the weekly RDA for persons 55 years and over ranges from 5 to 33% as the rate of program participation increases from one day to seven days per week. Likewise, assuming that the average food expenditure among aged persons is about $28 per week,[34] the potential monetary value of the Title VII meal increases from $1 to $7 per week as program participation increases. While confirmation of the quantitative dimensions of Title VII impact on dietary intake and income over time will await future research endeavors, the data suggest the potential value of the program to its participants increases as program participation increases.[35] This concept is critical in light of national estimates which indicate that the average frequency of participation in the program is once in every seven to ten days.[36] Furthermore, participation dropout rates may be as high as 50% per year.[37]

This section of the Boston Title VII evaluation presents the determinants of program participation behavior among congregate nutrition program elderly in response to the following research question posed in chapter 6: why do participation rates vary among Title VII participations across project areas?

Methods

All data used in these analyses were derived from in-depth personal interviews with a stratified random probability sample of 175 Boston participants. Title VII congregate nutrition site records were reviewed and all Boston congregate participants were placed in one of four strata according to their average frequency of program participation during January to June 1976: (1) 0–15 days per quarter; (2) 16–30 days per quarter; (3) 31–45 days per quarter; and (4) 46+ days per quarter. Participants were randomly selected for inclusion in the study in proportion to their number in the Title VII Boston project area participant populations.

Because of the relevance of area-specific data to these analyses, data are presented for each project area and for the Boston Title VII program as a whole. The latter were derived from weighted area-specific participant interview data.

Results

Program Participation Rate: Aspects of program participation behavior are in table 7-21. About one in four (26.5%) Boston Title VII participants attended the congregate meal program three or more days a week; 28.4% (combining the 16-30 day and 31-45 day per quarter categories) attended the congregate program less than once a week. Some 78% of participants had attended the program

Table 7-21
Boston Title VII Program Elderly Participation Behavior

	Area X	Area Y	Area Z	Total
		% of Population		
Participation behavior				
Rate category				
0–15 days/quarter	54.1	60.0	40.4	48.1
16–30 days/quarter	16.3	13.9	13.7	14.3
31–45 days/quarter	10.0	10.8	17.2	14.1
46+ days/quarter	19.6	15.3	28.7	26.5
First day of program attendance				
Within last month	0.0	0.0	0.0	0.0
1–3 months ago	3.4	5.1	3.6	5.7
4–6 months ago	3.4	5.1	8.9	7.1
6–12 months ago	13.8	5.1	10.7	9.9
12 or more months ago	79.3	84.7	76.8	77.9
Attendance companionship				
Came alone	55.2	65.5	51.8	55.0
Came with spouse	15.5	18.6	7.1	10.0
Came with other elderly companion	19.0	19.0	28.6	25.2
Other	10.3	6.9	12.5	9.8
Companion still coming	88.5	61.1	76.0	77.2
Companion no longer coming	11.5	38.9	24.0	22.8

for the past 12 months. Half of the participants had initially attended alone whereas the remainder had attended with a spouse or friend. For the most part, these companions were still attending the program.

Participant-perceived Determinants of Program Participation: The variables defined by participants as determinants of their own program participation are summarized in table 7-22. Three major variables appeared to draw elderly from the community into program activities. In all three Boston Title VII project areas, the primary reported reasons for attendance included opportunities for socialization and peer group interaction; the congregate meal; and social and recreational activities outside the home. The order of importance of these variables differs somewhat across areas. In area Y the meal is the primary drawing factor, attracting 71.2% of participants; followed by socialization (47.6%); and social and recreational activities outside the home (40.7%). In areas X and Z socialization is the most important participant-perceived determinant of program participation, reported by 72.4% and 64.9%, respectively, though the congregate meal is mentioned by 63.8% and 60.0%, respectively. Two other variables that acted as incentives to participation, albeit to a lesser extent to all areas, are lower cost of the meal and selected individual recreational or social activities.

On the other hand, one primary variable was reported as a reason for reduced program participation (table 7-23); from 30 to 60% indicated that conflicting social and recreational activities prevented more frequent program attendance. Poor health was reported by 10 to 36.6% within project areas. From 7.3 to 20% reported that poor Title VII meal quality reduced their attendance, and 10 to 13.3% that the meal was inappropriate for their therapeutic diets. Transportation problems were less frequently reported deterrents, mentioned by 3.3 to 15%. Some 3% of participants in area Y and 23.3% of the aged attending Title VII meals in area X indicated that difficulties encountered during interaction with peers reduced their participation. The program was inconvenient for 13% of participants.

Table 7-22
Factors Motivating Title VII Attendance

Factors	Area X	Area Y	Area Z	Total
		(percent)		
Title VII meal	63.8	71.2	51.9	60.0
Entertainment, activities	32.8	22.0	26.3	27.5
Socialization, to meet peers	72.4	47.6	64.9	63.8
To get out of house	56.9	40.7	50.9	47.9
Costs less	19.0	27.1	28.6	24.1
Meal & entertainment	20.7	16.7	10.5	12.1
Entertainment & socialization	24.1	15.3	19.3	19.9
Socialization & meal	48.3	33.9	35.1	37.1
Socialization & to get out	44.8	27.1	43.9	38.5

Table 7-23
Factors Reducing Title VII Program Participation

Factors	Area X	Area Y	Area Z	Total
		(percent)		
Poor health	10.0	23.3	36.6	31.2
Conflicting activities	60.0	30.0	48.8	51.2
Poor Title VII meal quality	20.0	13.3	7.3	11.3
Inappropriate Title VII meal	10.0	13.3	12.2	12.3
Transportation problems	3.3	3.3	14.6	13.3
Uncomfortable with peers	23.3	3.3	0.0	4.0
Inconvenient	6.7	13.3	12.2	13.0

Regression Analyses: The following discussion describes the methodology and derived results.

Methods: In addition to participant-perceived determinants of program participation, multiple regression analyses following the procedures of Kim and Kohout[38] were used to define the relationship between the rate of program participation (dependent variable) and a set of independent interview-derived variables that were organized into one of the following variable blocks:

Block 1 Selected demographic characteristics of participants

Block 2 Variables unrelated to demographic characteristics or program impact, such as satisfaction with Title VII meal

Block 3 Impact variables

These variable blocks were determined through a series of analyses described below.

Factor analyses using the principal-component method with orthogonal varimax rotations described by Kim[39] were used to test underlying relationships between 35 independent variables thought to be related to program participation rate, exclusive of those related to demographics, need for supportive services, and program impact. The results of these analyses were unimpressive; the original variable list was not reduced to any great extent into a smaller subset of independent factors.

The 35 variables used in the factor analyses as well as demographic, need for services, and impact variables were then cross tabulated with program participation rate (four categories of participation as defined below). Dichotomous variables with highly skewed distributions, that is, those which provide little information that could be used to discriminate members of the population were excluded.

Three stages of regression analyses were then performed. In the first stage, stepwise multiple regressions were run with 26 independent variables against the dependent variable, rate of program participation. Participation was defined in terms of fours levels of participation 0-15 days per quarter; 16-30 days per quarter; 31-45 days per quarter; and 46+ days per quarter. Separate analyses were made for each Title VII project area and for the total sample.

Variable blocks were considered in a predetermined order (demographic variables, variables unrelated to other variable blocks, for example, satisfaction with the Title VII meal, and impact variables). Individual variables were entered stepwise into the regression if they met two criteria—specification of an acceptable F ratio ($F \lessdot 2.5$) and the total number of variables in the regression equation ($n \gtrdot 20$). As the F ratios for the variables not in the regression changed with subsequent entry of variables at each step of the regression, variables from higher-order variable blocks were considered for entry in the equation before variables from lower-order blocks, according to the statistical criteria for variable consideration. (A discussion of the stepwise variable block regression design is in Nie.et al.[40]

The first-stage regressions reduced the initial variable list to 18 variables, exclusive of the need for service variables. Second-stage regressions then proceeded with the same participation rate category specifications in the dependent variable. At this time the F ratio and variable number criteria were not used. Variable blocks were entered in a predetermined order (blocks 1 to 3 in table 7-25) using the simple regression procedure also described by Nie et al.[41] In the third-stage regression, only those variables with insignificant F ratios were included. Again the variable block sequential entry and simple regression procedures were used.

Results: The summary results for these hierarchical regressions of participation rate appear in tables 7-24, 7-25, and 7-26. The regression equation at the stage of entering and demographic variables alone (step 1) was not significant in any of the project areas. Steps 2 and 3 regressions were significant in areas Y and Z and for the sample as a whole. The addition of step 2 variables produced a significant improvement in the regressions in areas Y and Z and in the sample as a whole. The addition of step 3 variables produced a significant improvement in the regression in areas Z alone.

The unreduced and reduced list of determinants of program participation appear in tables 7-25 and 7-26. The determinants of program participation varied across project areas. In area X satisfaction with the Title VII meal quality was positively related to program participation rate; perception of conflicting activities acted as deterrents to program participation. More frequent participants were more likely to be satisfied with meal quality and less likely to have conflicting social and recreational activities.

In area Y more frequent participants were more likely to be foreign-born elderly without perceived counseling needs for conflicting social or recreational

Table 7-24

Summary of Significance Tests for Stepwise Regression Analyses
of Participation Rate Using Four Categories of Participation[a]

Project Area[b]	R^2	ΔR^2	F	Degrees of Freedom	Significance
Area X					
Step 1	.038		0.452	4/46	$p > .25$
		.038	0.452	4/46	$p > .25$
Step 2	.395		1.393	16/34	$p > .10$
		.357	1.679	12/34	$p > .10$
Step 3	.446		1.424	18/32	$p > .10$
		.051	1.453	2/32	$p > .10$
Area Y					
Step 1	.184		2.419	4/43	$p > .05$
		.184	2.419	4/43	$p > .05$
Step 2	.656		3.700	16/31	$p < .005$
		.472	3.552	12/31	$p < .005$
Step 3	.687		3.539	18/29	$p < .005$
		.031	1.430	2/29	$p > .25$
Area Z					
Step 1	.183		2.123	4/38	$p > .10$
		.183	2.123	4/38	$p > .10$
Step 2	.665		3.230	16/26	$p < .005$
		.482	3.124	12/26	$p < .005$
Step 3	.758		3.947	18/24	$p < .005$
Sum areas					
Step 1	.047		1.703	4/137	$p > .10$
		.047	1.703	4/137	$p > .10$
Step 2	.255		2.675	16/125	$p < .005$
		.208	2.905	12/125	$p < .005$
Step 3	.266		2.477	18/123	$p < .005$
		.011	0.919	2/123	$p > .25$

[a]Unreduced variable list.

[b]Step 1 variables include demographic variables: living situation, sex, birth origin, work
status; step 2 variables include: comfort with peers, satisfaction with Title VII meal, similarity of Title VII ahd home-prepared meals, information and referral needs, counseling needs,
nutrition education needs, distance to site, availability of special diets, appetite, perceived
conflicting activities, perceived poor Title VII meals, perceived inappropriate Title VII
meals; step 3 variables include impact variables: monetary savings, persistent financial food
pruchasing problems.

activities as well as those who lived close to the meal sites. Other frequenters
were those who found the quality of the meal high, Title VII meals appropriate
for therapeutic diets, and a monetary impact of the program.

In area Z frequent participants were American-born who were comfortable
interacting with their peers, perceived Title VII and their home-prepared meals
as similar, had good appetites, and had no financial food purchasing problems.

Across all project areas, the determinants of program participation included
living situation, comfort with peers, distance to site, perceived conflicting social

Table 7-25
Regression Equations Examining Determinants of Title VII Participation[a]

Variables	Area X Beta	Area X F	Area Y Beta	Area Y F	Area Z Beta	Area Z F	Sum Areas Beta	Sum Areas F
Demographic								
Living situation (1 = alone; 2, 3, 4 = other)	-.09	0.34	-.16	1.90	-.09	0.42	-.17	4.47
Sex (1 = female; 0 = male)	.00	0.00	-.21	2.32	.34	4.55	.06	0.47
Birth origin (1 = US; -1 = foreign)	-.07	0.16	-.42	7.99	.25	3.62	.01	0.04
Work status (1 = not working; 5 = working)	.09	0.25	.03	0.05	-.20	2.16	-.02	0.04
Other								
Comfort with peers (1 = very; 2 = some; 3 = not very)	.02	0.02	.19	2.55	-.73	26.19	-.16	3.38
Satisfaction with Title VII meal (1 = yes; 0 = no)	.32	3.68	-.27	2.83	.43	4.07	.11	1.31
Similarity of Title VII and home meals	-.05	0.09	.16	1.01	.28	3.96	.04	0.26
Perceived information & referral needs	-.06	0.09	-.09	0.46	.19	1.75	.01	0.22
Perceived counseling needs (1 = yes; 0 = no)	-.08	0.14	-.37	4.72	.05	0.16	-.04	0.18
Perceived nutrition education needs	-.20	1.55	-.22	2.66	-.37	5.34	-.19	4.72
Distance to site in blocks	-.10	0.42	-.23	2.85	.01	0.01	-.07	0.73
Availability of therapeutic diets	.14	1.05	.12	0.86	-.00	0.00	.15	3.23
Appetite (1 = fair or poor; 2 = good, excellent)	-.02	0.01	.14	1.37	.60	11.5	.11	1.72
Deterrents to frequent program participation								
Conflicting activities (1 = yes; 0 = no)	-.34	3.07	-.27	4.59	-.13	0.79	-.20	4.80
Poor Title VII meals (1 = yes; 0 = no)	.14	0.71	-.27	3.97	.33	2.55	-.04	0.21
Inappropriate Title VII meals (1 = yes; 0 = no)	-.03	0.04	-.47	8.66	.03	0.04	-.15	2.85
Impact								
Monetary savings (1 = yes; 1 = no)	.10	0.41	.19	2.31	-.19	1.38	.10	1.39
Persistent financial food purchasing problems (-1 = yes; 1 = no)	-.27	2.53	-.06	0.25	.36	6.29	-.04	0.24
R^2; F	.466, 1.43		.687, 3.54		.747, 3.95		.266, 2.48	
Multiple R	.667		.829		.865		.516	
Degrees of freedom	18/32		18/29		18/24		18/123	
Individual variable degrees of freedom	1/32		1/29		1/24		1/123	
Significance levels								
p < .05	4.15		4.18		4.26		3.92	
p < .01	7.50		7.56		7.82		6.84	
p < .1	2.87		2.89		2.93		2.71	

[a]Participation categories: (1) = 0–15 days/quarter; (2) = 16–30 days/quarter; (3) = 31–45 days/quarter; (4) = 46+ days/quarter; [b](1, 2 = yes; -1 = no); [c](1 = yes; 0 = no); [d](1 = yes; 0 = no); [e](1 = yes; 0 = no).

Table 7-26
Regression Equations Examining Determinants of Title VII Participation[a]-Reduced Variable List

Variables	Area X Beta	Area X F	Area Y Beta	Area Y F	Area Z Beta	Area Z F	Sum Areas Beta	Sum Areas F
Demographic								
Living situation (1 = alone; 2, 3, 4 = other)			-.16	2.11	.10	0.69	-.14	3.59
Sex (1 = female; 0 = male)			-.20	2.48	-.31	7.39		
Birth origin (1 = US born; -1 = foreign)			.33	6.47	-.03	0.08		
Work status (1 = not working; 5 = working)								
Other								
Comfort with peers (1 = very; 2 = some; 3 = not)	.32	7.91	.10	0.92	-.53	21.51	-.17	5.65
Satisfied with Title VII meals (1 = yes; 0 = no)			-.16	1.26	.20	1.64	.09	1.45
Similarity of Title VII and home meals (1, 2 = yes; -1 = no)					.30	5.18		
Perceived information & referral needs (1 = yes; 0 = no)					.19	2.70		
Perceived counseling needs (1 = yes; 0 = no)			-.41	9.82				
Perceived nutrition education needs (1 = yes; 0 = no)	-.10	0.68	-.19	2.40	-.16	2.05	-.13	2.98
Distance to site (in blocks)			-.39	12.06				
Availability of special diets (1 = yes; 0 = no)							.17	5.40
Appetite (1 = fair, poor; 2 = good, excellent)					.49	15.58	.12	2.45
Deterrents to frequent program participation								
Conflicting activities (1 = yes; 0 = no)	-.38	9.57	-.26	5.29			-.23	9.92
Poor Title VII meal quality (1 = yes; 0 = no)			-.34	7.69	.31	5.53		
Inappropriate Title VII meals (1 = yes; 0 = no)			-.37	7.71			-.16	4.81
Impact								
Monetary savings (1 = yes; 0 = no)			.20	3.45	-.02	0.03	.14	3.12
Persistent financial food purchasing problems (-1 = yes; 1 = no)					.29	5.87		
R^2; F	(.32, 6.19)		(.62, 4.90)		(.63, 5.17)		(.26, 5.78)	
Multiple R	.56		.80		.79		.51	
Degrees of freedom	(4, 53)		(13, 37)		(12, 38)		(9, 145)	
Individual variable degrees of freedom	1/53		1/37		1/38		1/145	

[a]Participation categories: (1) = 0-15 days/quarter; (2) = 16-30 days/quarter; (3) 31-45 days/quarter; (4) 46+ days/quarter.

or recreational activities or inappropriateness of the Title VII meal, and perceived financial impact of the program. Frequent participants were more likely to live alone, feel comfortable with peers, live close to the meal sites, be free of conflicting social and recreational activities, find the meals appropriate for therapeutic diets, and perceive a financial impact of the program.

Discussion

The Boston Title VII evaluation suggests that program participation is a complex phenomenon affected by a number of factors, primarily those unrelated to demographic or program impact variables. The proportion of variance in participation explained by the "other variable" block, including such variables as conflicting social and recreational activities and satisfaction with the Title VII meal, was 41 to 49% across all project areas, indicating the significant effect of these variables on variance explained. Because of the different variables accounting for the greatest independent effect on program participation (high beta values and F tests) within project areas, the total percent of variance in participation explained in the sample as a whole was reduced, as was the percent of variance explained by the other variable block. This suggests that attempts to intervene on participation behavior will require area-specific intervention strategies.

Looking with project areas, a number of variables amenable to intervention can be defined which have significant and substantial independent effects on program participation. In area X these are the Title VII meal quality and existence of conflicting social and recreational activities which deter more frequent program attendance. In area Y these variables include conflicting activities, Title VII meal quality, and appropriateness of the meal for therapeutic diet needs. In area Z they include similarities between the Title VII meal and home food consumption patterns (cultural/ethnic food habits) as well as peer group interaction. In all three areas, while the meal is an issue in program participation behavior, the determining factors in participation rate appear to differ. In area X it is general meal satisfaction; in area Y it is appropriateness of the meal for therapeutic diet needs and general meal quality; in area Z it appears to be related to cultural ethnic food practices. In both area X and Y conflicting social and recreational activities appear to deter more frequent participation. In area Z, on the other hand, discomfort with peers acts as a deterrent to program participation.

The issue of diet and meal quality may be treated by considering the appropriateness of the Title VII meal for therapeutic diet restrictions, consideration of the provision of special diets, and provision of cultural/ethnic foods periodically in all three project areas. The therapeutic diet production for the Boston Title VII program could possibly be managed by the centralized project-operated kitchen in area Y. Participant suggestions could be elicited to determine preferred menu selections. The issue of conflicting social and recreational activities may best be handled by giving priority to those without conflicting social obligations (see chapter 8). Furthermore, peer group interaction may be handled by initial escort of new Title VII participants to meal sites. It would also seem worthwhile to train site personnel in the management of participant crises should they occur at the site level. This could prevent a conflict or crisis from disrupting the meal program environment or peer group interaction.

Giving priority to the delivery of Title VII meal services to those without conflicting social and recreational activities would introduce a new theory into the delivery strategy. It could be facilitated by some form of initial triage and referral system. This system could identify, through interview, persons with the greatest risk of nutritional problems (criteria and triage are discussed in chapter 8), direct them to the congregate meal, and provide the supportive service needed to maintain services for them on a regular basis, such as transportation, home-delivered meals, or escort services. Persons with nonnutritional problems or interested in other activities could be directed to those activities alone. Then to the extent that meals were available, all persons participating in the various Title VII activities could receive meals. This system would give priority to those in greatest need. It would attempt to define separate and specific needs for health, nutrition, and supportive services for the aged, then direct persons with needs to those specific services and provide the means for continued service delivery. This concept is similar to the case assessment concept employed in the delivery of Title III homemaker and home health aide services.

To the extent that the Title VII program serves a unique population, particularly those living close to the congregate meal sites or in housing which also has a congregate meal site, it is not known whether the elderly served are in fact those with the greatest need for services. Therefore the screening and triage system would optimally be tied to a screening of the needs for services among elderly in the community. Chapter 8 elaborates on the development and implementation of a triage and referral system.

Conclusions

Program participation behavior is a complex phenomenon which is of great concern for the following reasons: only 56% of Boston Title VII participants attend the congregate meal program as often as once a week, thereby reducing the potential impact of the program on dietary intake, nutritional status, and financial savings; the dropout rate among participants appears to reach as high as 50% annually; and the rate of program participation appears to be closely associated with program impact.

The determinants of program participation vary across project areas suggesting that efforts to mitigate erratic program participation behavior will require area-specific intervention strategies. Variables that appear to have significant independent effects on rate of program participation include the quality of the Title VII meal, the appropriateness of the meal for therapeutic dietary intervention, the similarity between Title VII meals and home-prepared meals, conflicting social and recreational activities, and comfort of participants interacting with peers.

It is concluded that Title VII menus should be reviewed for their appropriateness with regard to therapeutic diets, that the provision of therapeutic diets be considered, and that cultural/ethnic foods be offered periodically. To facilitate peer group interaction, escort services should probably be expanded and congregate meal site staff should be trained by professionals to manage participants' crises as they occur at the site. Furthermore, a triage and referral system is proposed to attempt to give priorities to the delivery of congregate meal and supportive services to those in greatest need, thereby making optimum use of scarce resources.

Program Operating Features

Introduction

This section focuses on the following program evaluation question: to what extent and why do meal and supportive service delivery costs vary across Boston Title VII project areas?

Methods

Data Sources: All data used in these analyses were derived from fiscal data appearing in project area quarterly reports for fiscal year 1976. Fiscal year data were used to derive comparative meal delivery costs between Boston Title VII project areas while the July to September 1976 operating quarter statistics were used to derive comparative supportive service delivery costs. The use of July to September 1976 data for supportive service comparisons resulted because of widely varying definitions for "unit of supportive service" delivered across project areas in other operating quarters. In the July to September quarter a "unit of service" was the unduplicated number of persons to whom supportive services were delivered. The reported fiscal data, unlike the participant data in some project areas, seemed reliable. Reported fiscal data paralleled annual financial audits closely.

Definition of Terms: Several indexes were used to measure the level of program service delivery and to relate that to resources deployed by each project area in delivering the mandates Title VII services. These include:

1. Number of meals served = m_i
2. Cost/meal served = aB_i/m_i
3. Number of unduplicated persons receiving supportive services = s_i
4. Cost/unit of supportive service delivered = cB_i/s_i

For this study, these indexes were defined as:

m_i = total number of meals served in fiscal year 1976 in a project area

a = proportion of the total budget (B_i) allocated to meal costs

B_i = total budget, where i = fiscal year 1976

s_i = total number of persons to whom social services were delivered July to September 1976; unduplicated person count

c_i = proportion of the total budget (B_i) allocated to supportive services July to September 1976

It would have been preferable to derive separate statistics for the home-delivered meal component and individual supportive services. At the time of this research, however, the project area records did not contain information concerning costs of delivering congregate versus home-delivered meals or costs of delivering individual supportive services.

Results

Program Expenses: The fiscal year 1976 Title VII budgets, Title VII spending, and operating expenses by program operating component and project area are in table 7-27. Title VII funds make up from 65 to 78% of the project areas' total elderly nutrition program budgets. The remainder of program operating budgets is derived from income through community resources, donations for Title VII meals, in-kind resources, federal non-Title VII funds, and interest on savings (see footnote in table 7-27). Administrative expenses account for 10 to 23% of the operating budgets and capital expenditures for up to 13% of total budgets. Supportive service expenditures are 14 to 26% of total operating budgets and meal expenses are 55.2 to 61.2% of the 1976 program operating budgets.

Table 7-27
Fiscal Year 1976 Title VII Program Budget and Expenditure by Operating Component[a]

Area	Total Program Expenditures FY[b] 1976	Title VII Expenditures FY 1976	Percent of 1976 Expenditures				
			Title VII Funds	Administrative	Supportive Services	Meal Expenses	Capital Investment
X	236,701	170,757	72.2	18.7	26.0	55.2	0.0
Y	337,107	262,570	77.9	23.0	14.2	60.2	2.5
Z	579,461	374,748	64.7	10.2	16.0	61.2	12.6

[a]Boston Title VII project areas.

[b]FY - fiscal year.

Sources: [c] Audit, submitted to area X and Department of Elder Affairs, Jan. 14, 1977. In addition to $170,757 Title VII funds, area X had income from participant contributions for meals ($25,700); in-kind resources ($38,613); and interest ($1,630). Title VII funding contains $18,099 in carry-over funds from FY 1975.

[d]Fiscal year 1976 summary report, submitted to Department of Elder Affairs, Oct. 21, 1976. In addition to $262,560 Title VII funds, area Y had income from participant contributions for meals ($48,000); in-kind resources ($25,337).

[e]Fiscal year 1976 summary report, submitted to Department of Elder Affairs, Oct. 28, 1976. In addition to $374,748 Title VII funds, area Z had income from participant contributions for meals ($70,060); in-kind resources ($133,107); and commodity credit ($1,546). Title VII funding contains $2,090 in carry-over funds from FY 1975.

Cost/Meal Index: Title VII project area meal delivery statistics are summarized in table 7-28. Total meal expenses (aB_i) vary across project areas. Area Y expenses are 55% higher than in area X; area Z expenses are 76% greater than in area Y and 173% greater than in area X. The number of meals served increases from 285 meals per day in area X to 536 meals per day in area Y and 976 meals per day in area Z. The total number of meals served in area Y was 1.9 times that served in area X; the total number of meals served in area Z was 1.8 times that served in area Y and 3.4 times that served in area X. The number of congregate meal sites increased from 8 sites in area X to 13 and 16 sites in areas Y and Z, respectively. Home-delivered meals made up 8.3%, 13.5%, and 16% of the meals served in areas X, Y, and Z, respectively.

The total fiscal year 1976 meal costs (aB_i), the number of meals served (m_i), and the cost per meal index (aB_i/m_i) by project area are summarized in table 7-29. The average cost per meal in area X is $1.85 which represents a cost

Table 7-28
Boston Title VII Project Area Operating Characteristics[a]

Area	Meal Expense	Meals/ Day	Total Meals	Congregate Meals	Home- Delivered Meals	Sites
X	$130,670[b]	285	70,802	64,957	5,845	8
Y	203,044[c]	536	103,308	89,311	13,994	13
Z	356,317[d]	976	229,466	192,751	36,715	16

[a]Fiscal year 1976.

[b]Contains: food costs, $76,682.85 and $2,975.32 USDA commodity credit; salaries and labor, $27,398.70; and miscellaneous expenses related to meals, $28,564.19. Source: Audit submitted to area X and Department of Elder Affairs, Jan. 14, 1977.

[c]Contains: food costs, $70,141; salaries and labor, $86,313; and miscellaneous expenses (nonedibles), $46,590. Source: FY 1976 summary report submitted to Department of Elder Affairs, Oct. 21, 1976.

[d]Contains: food costs, $241,127 and USDA commodity credit, $1,546; salaries and labor, $107,451; and miscellaneous expenses, $6,193. Source: FY 1976 summary report submitted to Department of Elder Affairs, Oct. 28, 1976.

Table 7-29
Cost per meal Index by Title VII Project Area

Area	Total Meals Costs [a]1976 (aB_i)	No. of Meals Served FY 1976 (m_i)	Cost/Meal Index (aB_i/m_i)
X	$130,670	70,802	$1.85
Y	203,044	103,308	1.97
Z	356,317	229,466	1.55

[a]FY = fiscal year.

that is 6.1% less than the cost per meal in area Y ($1.97) and 19% higher than the meal cost in area Z ($1.55).

Cost/Unit of Supportive Service Index: The duplicated numbers of persons to whom individual supportive services were delivered by project area are in table 7-30. The differences across project areas in units of services delivered are not so much related to the distribution of various types of services as to the total number of supportive services delivered. Across all but the transportation category, area X delivers substantially more units of each service than the other areas. Area Z delivers 1.3 times the number of transportation service units as area X.

The fiscal year 1976 and July to September 1976 supportive services expenditures (c_iB_i), the units of supportive services delivered (s_i), and the cost per unit of service delivered (c_iB_i/s_i) are summarized by project area in table 7-31. The cost per unit varies from $0.65 in area X to $1.57 per unit in area Z and $8.80 per unit in area Y. Unit costs are 2.5 times greater in area Z than in area X while those in area Y are 14 times greater than in area X.

Discussion

Comparative Meal Costs: The distribution of Title VII funds across the three Boston Title VII project areas had the single greatest impact on the level of meal service delivery within project areas. For the most part, Title VII funds are the sole source of resources for the preparation and purchase of meals served in the congregate sites or delivered to home-bound elderly. Therefore total number of meals served parallels available resources, those getting more funds producing more meals. Title VII funding also influences the cost per meal index, but the operating features of meal service delivery in each project area have to be examined more closely to determine the other components of comparative meal costs.

Looking first at the type of meal served, home-delivered meals account for varying proportions of the meals served in area X (8.3%), area Y (13.5%), and area Z (16%). The remaining meals are served in congregate meal sites. Though site records do not reflect the comparative costs of home-delivered meals versus congregate meals, the former are more costly because of additional manpower, equipment, and transportation, to package and deliver meals to residences. The relative average costs of home-delivered meals versus congregate meals nationally are $2.50 and $1.50, respectively.[42]

Looking next at the method of preparation, area Y operates and maintains a centralized kitchen where all meals are prepared, except a small number of kosher meals served daily. Areas X and Z purchase Title VII meals from private food caterers. Because of the large volume of meals prepared by the commercial

Table 7-30
Duplicated Number of Persons to Whom Supportive Services Were Delivered in Boston Title VII Project Areas, July–September 1976

Area	Total	Information & Referral	Outreach	Transportation	Escort	Shopping Assistance	Nutrition Education	Recreation	Counseling
						Supportive Service Category			
X	29,106	2,768	933	7,050	5,795	1,440	2,460	7,360	1,150
Y	1,635	135	50	766	30	117	12	375	150
Z	17,888	210	195	9,172	899	983	78	6,255	94

Source: 1976 quarterly report submitted to Department of Elder Affairs.

Table 7-31

Cost per Unit Supportive Service Delivered[a]

Area	Supportive Service Expenditures FY[b] 1976	Supportive Service Allocation July–Sept. 1976 $(c_i B_i)$	Unduplicated Persons Delivered Services July–Sept. 1976 (s_i)	Cost/Unit Supportive Service Delivered $(c_i B_i / s_i)$
X	$61,735	$18,575	29,106	$0.64
Y	47,941	14,382	1,635	8.80
Z	92,030	28,000	17,888	1.57

[a]Boston Title VII project areas.

[b]FY = fiscal year

caterer relative to the centralized kitchen operated in area Y, the caterer can realize an economy of scale which can be passed on to the project area in the form of a lower cost per meal. These economies are reflected in the lower salary and labor costs, and miscellaneous expenses per meal served in areas X and Z. Salary costs per meal were $0.39 in area X, $0.97 in area Y, and $0.47 in area Z. Miscellaneous expenses per meal were $0.40 in area X, $0.45 in area Y, and $0.03 in area Z. On the other hand, raw food costs were $1.08 per meal in area X, $0.68 per meal in area Y, and $1.05 per meal in area Z. The caterer's profit margin did not appear as separate line items in the quarterly reporting scheme and appears to be factored into the raw food costs, resulting in higher caterer raw food costs despite the large volume of meals served. Higher labor and salary and miscellaneous costs per meal in area Y are reflected in a comparison between areas X and Y. The total meal costs in area Y are 55% higher than in area X while the number of meals produced are only 46% higher. On the other hand, area Y is able to produce half the meals served in area Z for less than 43% of the cost. Area X and area Z differences reflect higher raw food costs and profit margins of the caterer that are utilized in area Z. They suggest that the operation of a centralized kitchen may have a comparative cost advantage over the catered meal, particularly if operated efficiently so economies of scale can be realized. If the centralized kitchen at the project level or at the caterer level is operated below capacity, costs per meal served may increase dramatically.

Another cost consideration is that the use of a caterer offers an advantage of minimal fixed capital investment for meal preparation and delivery. Equipment for congregate meal service is the only primary outlay for a project area using a caterer. Certainly areas using either caterer or centralized kitchen will have additional transportation and delivery costs as well as packaging costs for home-delivered meals. These costs per meal should not vary greatly across areas unless distance to elderly residences differs markedly. This could occur when comparing rural and urban programs.

Beyond the meal cost considerations, other features illustrate the comparative advantage of a centralized project-operated kitchen. First, the kitchen may provide jobs for persons in the community. Second, and far more fundamental to the health and nutrition goals of the program, operation of a centralized kitchen facilitates making rapid changes in menu selections in light of program participant suggestions; preparing meals for holidays and special occasions, and providing therapeutic diets at little or no extra cost per meal. These factors all require negotiation of a contract with the caterer and may be particularly difficult to accomplish if they are desired within an ongoing contract period.

Comparative Supportive Service Delivery Costs: Unlike the total number of meals served, allocation and expenditure for supportive services do not appear to be primary determinants of total number of units of supportive services delivered. Supportive service expenditures in area X are 29% higher than in area Y, yet area X delivers 14 times the number of supportive services that area Y does. Area X's expenditures for supportive services are 66% of area Z's, yet area X delivers 1.6 times the number of supportive services that area Z does. Certainly the availability of Title VII funds is fundamental to the ability to delivery supportive services. Efficient utilization of funds and staff time and service monitoring are even more critical in the Boston Title VII programs. These latter features appear to be the primary determinants of cost differences per unit of supportive service delivered in the Boston area. Area X and to a somewhat lesser extent the staff in area Z are attempting to make maximum use of area-operated vehicles for transportation, shopping assistance, and recreational activities. In addition, the purpose of all area X incoming telephone calls are monitored to identify information and referral service delivery. Area X program participants have been informed of available services and have been encouraged to use them. Specific outreach campaigns have been implemented to area X and community nutrition specialists have given nutrition education. In addition, the supportive service coordinator in area X monitors supportive service activities daily.

The somewhat less efficient delivery of services in area Z relative to area X arises from less effective use of staff, resources, and vehicles. Specific monitoring of phone calls to document information and referral service delivery was not done at the time of this research. Specific outreach campaigns had not been implemented and counseling services had not been developed. Furthermore, community nutrition specialists were not being used to as great an extent as in area X to provide nutrition education. Reasons for low escort service statistics relative to high transportation service delivery suggests that area Z may have underreported escort service figures.

The lower operating level for supportive services in area Y is in small part due to the lower expenditures for these services. Though a supportive service coordinator develops and coordinates the service delivery plan and monitors supportive service delivery, the complex administrative structure of the Title VII program makes area Y supportive service monitoring difficult. The area Y program is administered by a community agency which concurrently operated many other community programs. Personnel and resources of the community agency are shared among the programs. Elderly persons who attend the program may also participate in other agency activities and contact a variety of the agency's staff. At the time of this research area Y had apparently not ferreted out a solution to the complex task of allocating service delivery statistics to the various programs. Therefore service delivery statistics may have underreported the actual units of supportive service delivered.

Operating Cost Conclusions

Meal Delivery: Utilization of a private caterer for provision of the Title VII meal offers advantages of low fixed capital investments on food preparation and delivery by the project area, economies of scale reflected in lower cost per meal, lower salaries and labor costs, and lower miscellaneous costs per meal. A centralized kitchen operated by the Title VII area has the advantages of rapid menu change according to client evaluation of meals, ease of holiday and weekend preparation of meals, therapeutic diet provision at little or no extra cost per meal, and relative cost advantage if operated at capacity. Raw food costs per meal may be lower if using a centralized area-operated kitchen because of profit margins added to these costs by the caterer.

The larger volume of meals served in area Z allowed for economies of scale, low miscellaneous costs per meal, and an overall lowest cost per meal served. Miscellaneous expenses in area X drove the cost per meal higher than in area Z, though the other components of meal costs (raw food, salaries and labor, commodity credit) were more similar. Higher meal costs in area Y resulted from higher salaries and labor costs per meal and higher miscellaneous costs per meal.

Supportive Services: The size of expenditures on supportive services is fundamental to their availability but is not the major determinant of the comparative volume of these services delivered to Title VII participants across project areas. Efficient staff and resource utilization and close documentation of service delivery were more important for differences in delivery statistics. Despite larger appropriations for supportive services in area Z, it delivered only about 40% of the total supportive services given by area X and yet had a budget 1.5 times the size of area X's. Supportive service delivery in area Y was well below the other two project areas. The greater level of service delivery in area X resulted from continuous use of vehicles for transportation, shopping assistance, and escort services; implementation of outreach campaigns; monitoring of telephone calls for information and referral service delivery; use of community resources for nutrition education; informing participants of available services and encouraging their use; development of a variety of recreational activities; and close coordination and monitoring of these activities by the supportive services coordinator.

Additional Comment: A meal cost per person index could have been developed using statistics on the number of persons served Title VII meals. This figure is frequently reported among the figures released by the Administration on Aging. Index figures were not included in this analysis since they neglect the issue of program participation rate which has been shown to be related to program impact on dietary intake, nutritional status, diet-related behavior, monetary savings, and other aspects of elderly persons' lives, including socialization, life satisfaction, and recreation.[43] The total number of persons served can be inflated due to erratic program participation, program dropout and turnover, and inaccurate reporting. If such is the case, inflated participation figures will erroneously suggest the relative service delivery efficiency of one program or program delivery scheme over another. Clearly, comparisons of relative program costs and efficiency must be tied to both subjective and objective measures of program impact.

Perhaps more appropriate indicators would not only reflect the rate of program participation but would be readily available from project data. Two potential indicators could be considered: meals per participant served index or the proportion of participants falling into high frequency of participation categories. The first indicator ties frequency of participation to meals delivery in one index. As the size of the index increases, the number of meals served to an elderly individual in a given time frame also increases. The latter indicator does not tie participation frequency to the meal but indicates what proportion of participants fall into various levels of program participation. The four categories of participation that were used in quarterly reports could be utilized for this index (category 1 = 0-15 days participation per operating quarter; category 2 = 16-30 days participation per operating quarter; category 3 = 31-45 days participation per operating quarter; and category 4 = 46+ days participation per operating quarter).

Research conclusions are examined in the final chapter. The implications of the Boston Title VII evaluation relative to the design of congregate nutrition interventions for the aged are stated. In addition, the future nutrition research needs as they pertain to the elderly are discussed.

Notes

1. Postma, J.S.: "The Characteristics and Needs of the Eugene-Springfield Elderly Nutrition Congregate Meals Program Participants and Their Perceptions of the Program's Effects and Operation," doctoral dissertation, University of Oregon, 1974.

2. Hosowkawa, M.C., et al.: "Central Missouri Nutrition Assessment Project," 1975; and idem: "Nutrition Project Assessment," Central Missouri AAA, 1976.

3. Postma: "Eugene-Springfield Program."

4. Hosokawa et al.: "Central Missouri Nutrition Project"; and idem: "Nutrition Project Assessment."

5. Kohrs, M.B.: "Influences of the Congregate Meal Program in Central Missouri on Dietary Practices and Nutritional Status of Participants," Jefferson City, Mo.: Lincoln University, Department of Agriculture and Natural Resources, Human Nutrition Research Program, August 1976a; Kohrs, M.B., et al.: "Contribution of the Nutrition Program for Older Americans to Nutritional Status," paper delivered at American Gerontological Society Meetings, New York City, 1976b; and Kohrs, M.B.: "Nutrition Data from an 'Aging Program': Implications for Planning," paper presented at the Society for Nutrition Education Annual Meeting, Kansas City, Mo., 1976c.

6. Posner, B.: "Evaluation of the Title VII Nutrition Program for Older Americans," thesis submitted in partial fulfillment of requirements for the degree of Doctor of Public Health in nutrition, 1978.

7. Hardman, A.P., and Bringewatt, R.J.: "Program Integration: An Approach Using Titles III and VII of the Older Americans Act and Title XX of the Social Security Act," paper presented at the Gerontological Society 30th Annual Scientific Meeting, Nov. 18-22, 1977.

8. Shanas, E.: "The Health Status of Older People Cross-National Implications," *A.J.P.H.* 64:261-64, 1974.

9. Haber, L.D.: "Identifying the Disabled: Concepts and Methods in the Measurement of Disability," *Soc. Sec. Bull.* 30:17-34, 1967; Katz, S., et al.: "Progress in the Development of the Index of ADL," *The Gerontologist* (Spring) 1970; and Lawton, M.P.: "The Functional Assessment of Elderly People," *J. Am. Ger. Soc.*, vol. 19, 1971.

10. Shanas: "Health Status of Older People"; and idem: "Measuring the Home Health Needs of the Aged in Five Counties," *J. Ger.* 26:37-40, 1974.

11. Havinghurst, R.J.: "A Social-psychological Perspective on Aging," *Gerontologist* 8:67-71, 1968.

12. Ibid; and Kuhlen, R.G.: "Aging and Life Adjustment," in *Handbook of Aging and the Individual*, ed. J.E. Birren, Chicago: University of Chicago Press, 1959.

13. Maddox, G.L.: "Self-assessment of Health Status—A Longitudinal Study of Selected Elderly Subjects," *J. Chron. Dis.* 17:449-60, 1964.

14. Katz et al.: "Index of ADL"; Branch, L.G.: "Understanding the Health and Social Service Needs of People over 65," Center for Survey Research, a facility of the University of Massachusetts and the Joint Center for Urban Studies of MIT and Harvard University, 1977; and Branch, L.G., and Fowler,

F.J.: "The Health Care Needs of the Elderly and Chronically Disabled in Massachusetts," Survey Research Program, a Joint Facility of the University of Massachusetts/Boston and the Joint Center for Urban Studies of MIT and Harvard, March 1975.

15. Branch: "Health Care Needs."

16. Branch: "Health and Social Service Needs."

17. Ibid.

18. Nie, N.H., et al.: *Statistical Packages for the Social Sciences*, 2d ed., New York: McGraw Hill Book Co., 1970.

19. Siegel, S.: *Non-Parametric Statistics for the Behavioral Sciences*, New York: McGraw Hill Book Co., 1956.

20. Ibid.

21. Branch: "Health and Social Service Needs."

22. Ibid.

23. Branch: "Health Care Needs."

24. Branch: "Health and Social Service Needs."

25. Posner: "Evaluation."

26. Ibid.

27. Linder, F.E.: "The Health of the American People," *Sci. Am.* 214, June 1966.

28. Fowler, F.J., and McCalla, M.E.: "Need and Utilization of Services among the Aged in Greater Boston, AoA," 1969.

29. Haffron, D., et al.: "Title VII Nutrition Program: Profiles of Nonparticipants, Participants and Dropouts in a Midwestern Community," paper presented at the American Gerontological Society Annual Convention, October 1976.

30. Postma: "Eugene-Springfield Program."

31. Kohrs: "Congregate Meal program"; Kohrs et al.: "Nutrition Program"; and Kohrs: "Nutrition Data."

32. National Academy of Sciences, Food and Nutrition Board: *Recommended Dietary Allowances*, 8th ed., Washington, D.C., 1974.

33. Ibid.

34. Branch: "Health and Social Services."

35. Kohrs: "Congregate Meal Program"; Kohrs et al.: "Nutrition Program"; Kohrs: "Nutrition Data"; and Posner: "Title VII Nutrition Program."

36. Watkin, D.M.: Personal communication, 1978.

37. Haffron et al.: "Title VII Nutrition Program."

38. Kim, J. and Kohout, F.J.: "Multiple Regression Analysis: Subprogram Regression." *Statistical Packages for the Social Sciences*, 2nd edition. New York: McGraw Hill Book Company, 1970.

39. Kim, J.: "Factor Analyses," in *Statistical Packages for the Social Sciences*, 2d ed., New York: McGraw Hill Book Co., 1970.

40. Nie et al.: *Statistical Packages for the Social Sciences*.

41. Ibid.

42. Region I AoA: Personal communication, 1978.

43. Kohrs: "Congregate Meal Program"; Kohrs et al.: "Nutrition Program"; and Kohrs: "Nutrition Data."

Summary of Conclusions, Intervention Design Implications, and Future Research Needs

Introduction

The purpose of this chapter is threefold: to discuss the historical development of the Title VII legislation and its subsequent impact on the program's implementation; to summarize the findings of the Boston Title VII program evaluation and discuss their implications for future Title VII programming; and to identify some of the key research needs relative to the aging, health, and nutrition triad.

This is not a synopsis of the entire research project; rather, it emphasizes federal policies which have affected all levels of Title VII program development, the major program design features generated from this research, and future research needs.

Title VII Historical Development Summary

The Title VII Nutrition Program for the Aged (NPOA) was launched in response to the growing awareness of and concern for the nutritional needs of the aged[1] and to the specific recommendations of the White House Conference on Aging,[2] the White House Conference on Food, Nutrition, and Health,[3] the Administration on Aging,[4] and the President's Task Force on Aging.[5] These expert groups called for the development of congregate and home-delivered food delivery systems whereby nutritious meals could be distributed to the aged and through which supportive social and health services could be provided to older Americans. They also urged the development of technical and financial aid programs to assist local groups and community agencies in providing services to the elderly.

The Title VII program was not the first attempt to intervene on the nutritional and health status of elderly individuals. The commodity food distribution and food stamp programs, which had been instituted during the 1960s and operated by the U.S. Department of Agriculture, had become available to the aged. It was recognized, however, that these programs, while serving some aged, were inadequate in meeting the unique needs of specific groups of elderly, including those who were more socially isolated, the chronically disabled, and the very poor.[6] As a result, in 1968 Congress authorized $2 million annually for a three-year nutrition research and demonstration project under Title IV of the Older Americans Act of 1965. The R&D programs were carried out in 23 individual settings and in nine research projects through 1971 under the direction of the Administration on Aging. The purpose of these programs was to study alternative approaches to meals and supportive service delivery to the aged in congregate community settings.

A comprehensive quantitative evaluation of these programs was never accomplished. Nonetheless, it was concluded that congregate meals were both feasible and well-received community-based mechanisms for delivery of services to the aged.[7] Limited data on the characteristics of congregate meal program participants suggested that Title IV programs attracted elderly persons with potential nutritional problems, particularly those with low incomes and minority individuals. In addition, it was evident that nutrition and related problems, including inadequate diet, lack of nutritional knowledge, poor health, social isolation, limited access to transportation, social and rehabilitative services, and leisure activities existed among those served. The severity of these problems seemed to be reduced by participation in the congregate meal program.[8]

Despite the lack of quantitative evaluation of the Title IV programs, their popularity among program participants and in the public at large was so overwhelming that efforts to discontinue them in 1971 were futile.[9] They were continued with emergency funds appropriated by Congress in 1971 and 1972. The Title IV experience succeeded in providing momentum behind the passage of legislation to expand the congregate nutrition program nationwide.

In 1971 the Title VII amendment[10] was attached to the Older Americans Act of 1965 to establish the Nutrition Program for Older Americans (NPOA). The statute was signed into law by the president on March 22, 1972.

Unfortunately, the 1972 actions of the 92d Congress resulted in a stalemate since appropriation of Title VII funds was vetoed in April 1972 along with the entire fiscal year 1973 Labor-DHEW Appropriation Bill. The 93d Congress passed amendments to an appropriation bill in 1973 which was again threatened by veto, this time, because riders attached to the appropriation bill required a halt to the bombing in Cambodia. In mid-June, a compromise was reached to end the bombing on August 15, 1973. Therefore at the very end of fiscal year 1973, the president signed a bill providing $100 million Title VII appropriation, precisely at the end of the year for which it had been originally intended. Immediately, Congress and the president signed a continuing resolution for extention of the 1973 funding levels to fiscal year 1974. The Department of Health, Education and Welfare adopted a forward funding scheme under which only $100 million of the potential $200 million could be used in fiscal year 1974 to implement the Title VII program in all 56 U.S. jurisdictions.

Thus the Title VII program was born in 1973. It was at this time that the complex task was instituted to implement NPOA in line with the rules and regulations that had been published in 1972.[11]

While the spirit and intent of the Title VII legislation were evident in the regulations, minor changes had occurred during their drafting which ultimately had major influences on the focus and implementation strategy of Title VII nationally. All references to professional medical, health, and nutrition person-nel were removed from drafts of the regulations. This left the task of determin-ing the qualification requirements of Title VII administrative and operating staff, advisory personnel, and project advisory councils to the State Agencies on Aging. Though quite subtle, these changes, in concert with subsequent contro-versial decisions, diverted program philosophy and activities away from the Title VII health goals stated in the original legislative mandate.

Subsequent to the 1973 authorization of the Title VII implementation funding, two key decisions helped to shift the program's focus farther away from its health and supportive service components toward an almost singular concentration on the meals delivery component. As of July 1973, all Title VII programs were required to become operational on the first day of their budget year and fully operational to the level approved in their grant application by 90 days. This decision was modified in September 1973 by a moratorium on the implementation of Title VII supportive service implementation for 90 days and up to 180 days with the consent of the Commissioner on Aging if justified by the state. These moves were deliberately made to speed implementation of the readily quantifiable program output, viz., number of meals served daily; provide local, state, and national visibility; and assure utilization of appropriated Title VII funds.[12] The net result was a rapidly expanding number of meal sites, meals, and total number of elderly served.

The price paid for rapid implementation of the Title VII program, however, was lesser participation by target group beneficiaries, including the disabled, isolated, those with transportation problems, the poorest of the poor, very old, and minorities;[13] greater reliance on meal service vendors; and lesser reliance on project-operated kitchens for home-delivered and congregate meals.[14] Lackoff[15] concluded that these decisions led to a deviation from the long-term Title VII program goals related to health and nutrition to satisfy the short-term political motives for program visibility.

Recognizing the need for a redirection of Title VII policy, the Senate Select Committee on Nutrition and Human Needs reviewed the program and recom-mended[16] that "the time has come to broaden the reach and responsiveness of the Title VII program ... to act on recommendations that have been ignored." The committee proposed the following activities which could lead to greater program goal realization: program evaluation, development of the Title VII supportive service component, allocation of administrative monies to cover expenses, assurance of elderly individuals' rights, outreach to low-income and minority elderly, and more direct interaction between program staff and elderly participants.

Since the last quarter of 1975 onward, additional emphasis has been placed on the improvement of staffing supportive services so that all Title VII sites could have adequate personnel. Meal service capacity has been increased to assist particularly those sites which had been rationing meals. The nutrient standard method of menu planning and monitoring[17] was implemented to attempt to reduce the number of meals served by commercial food management firms and to increase the number of project-operated meal service facilities. Furthermore, a national longitudinal evaluation of the program was begun.

Therefore many of the Senate Select Committee recommendations relative to the program have been considered and swifty incorporated into program operating policy. The responsiveness of the program to these recommendations has been impressive. The program's reach and quantitative dimensions are likewise impressive.

As of the first quarter of fiscal year 1978, a total of 1,074 Title VII Nutrition projects and 9,732 nutrition sites were operating in all 50 states and 6 U.S. territories. Total program participation had reached 1.5 million elderly persons of whom 66% were estimated to be low-income and 22.5% minority individuals. About 14% of all participants were black, 4% were Spanish, and 2% were American Indians. The average daily number of meals served was 477,133, including 83% that were congregate meals and 17% that were home delivered. About 41% of the meals were prepared in project-operated central kitchens, while the remaining 59% were prepared by food management firms. Meals were delivered in a number of settings, including senior centers (25% of total nutrition sites), religious facilities (25%), public housing (14%), schools (5%), restaurants (3%), and other locations (28%). Most meal sites (83%) were providing meals five days a week, although 3% of sites were serving meals six or seven days a week. The Title VII program employed 22,024 paid staff, of whom 32% were aged 60+ and 27% were minorities. Some 127,200 volunteers were also providing services to the Title VII program. About $60 million in federal Title VII funds were expended in the first quarter of fiscal year 1978. In addition, $3.3 million in USDA commodity foods were used; the remaining $18.5 million in Title VII costs were derived from nonfederal sources, including in-kind contributions from community agencies and voluntary participants contribution for meals.

Since 1973 the program budget has more than doubled in size and is expected to more than triple by 1980. Its growth in numbers and firm placement in the community documents the program's successful achievement of short-term goals for growth and visibility. Nonetheless, the continuing adverse impact of early Title VII policy has been recently documented by the U.S. General Accounting Office (GAO). In February 1978 the GAO published a report[18] that was a review of the Title VII program at federal, state, and local levels conducted from September 1976 to December 1977. The GAO reviewed policies and interviewed representatives from the Department of Health, Education and Welfare (grants administration officials), the Administration on Aging (agency officials), and the U.S. Department of Agriculture (officials versed in the provision of federal commodities to the Title VII programs). In addition, representatives of three regional offices (regions III, V, and VIII), five state agencies (Maryland, Ohio, Michigan, Missouri, Iowa), and six Title VII grantees were interviewed.

On the one hand, the GAO concluded that the nutrition program sites were "clean and exhibited pleasant atmospheres." The meals "appeared to be wholesome and appetizing . . . Many sites were operating at capacity and providing an array of supportive services. On the other hand, the GAO noted "certain administrative problems which, if corrected, could lead to improvement in the administration of the nutrition program."[19] The primary observed administrative weakness was the unreliability and limited utility of program performance data. It was noted that AoA progress reports were never intended to serve as management tools. Confusion appeared to exist, however, concerning the purpose of the program performance report and the opportunities available to State Agencies on Aging to structure their own information systems to meet their needs.[20] The dilemma appeared to exist for a number of reasons, including limits imposed by the Office of Management and Budget on the type of data that could be collected by AoA for national Title VII summaries, unclear translation and communication of Title VII management information policies to the states, and low priority placed on adequate reporting procedures.

The result was the completion of program performance reports and national summaries that had limited usefulness and reliability. The reports were inadequate as management tools and could not be used to measure state progress toward Title VII goals.[21] Therefore the management capabilities of the states, HEW regional offices, and the Administration on Aging were severely limited.

Moving from administrative and management problems to Title VII progress in achieving health and nutrition goals, Watkin,[22] former medical director of NPOA, also recently concluded that the opportunity to develop the Title VII program's position as the vanguard of national health efforts related to the aged had not been accomplished, was only now at hand, and must be consolidated. Watkin stressed that efforts to improve the health and nutritional status of the aged must be implemented with knowledge of the following well in hand: the interrelationship between the aging process, nutrition, and various modes of health care delivery; the Title VII program's impact to date; and potential directions for future program planning.

Data relevant to future Title VII planning could have been provided by a national Title VII management information system[23] and periodic NPOA evaluations. Unfortunately a management information system had never been implemented and AoA progress reports were limited to data primarily concerning program growth and estimates of participant characteristics.[24] Conclusive results of the national Title VII evaluation will not be available until 1980.[25] For these reasons, data which are essential for the ongoing development and revision of Title VII operating policy cannot be generated systematically from the states.[26]

Until a management information system is in operation and valid national data are available, program planning information must be derived from local program evaluations. To the extent that the knowledge produced by local studies can be generalized (and there is strong evidence to suggest that this is true), information relevant to Title VII programming nationally will be available.

The remainder of the chapter concentrates on the results and implications of the Boston Title VII program relative to future program planning and future research needs in the aging, health, and nutrition triad.

It will become evident as the data are presented that the results of the Boston Title VII evaluation confirm many of the conclusions drawn by the GAO in its study of the Title VII program from 1976 to 1977. The similarity between the conclusions lends support to serious consideration of the results and conclusions of the Boston Title VII evaluation by regional and national Title VII planners and administrators, state administrators, and local practitioners.

Boston Title VII Program Evaluation

Goals and Methods

The goals of the Boston Title VII program evaluation were to measure the achievement of federal and local Title VII program goals in the Boston area; and identify and analyze some of the key performance determinants of the degree of goal attainment.

Achievement of these goals required the specification of the following six research questions: to what extent is the Title VII program meeting the nutritional, health, and supportive service goals in the Boston area; what is the prevalence of unmet needs for nutrition, health, and supportive services among project area participants; to what extent are the target group elderly being served by the Boston Title VII program; to what extent are Title VII participants aware of and utilizing available supportive services; why do rates of program participation vary across participants; and to what extent and why do meal and supportive service costs and performance vary across project areas?

The fundamental rationale behind asking these questions was to provide answers to questions critical to area Title VII program planning and in so doing fill a void in the available local data.

The data were derived from a number of sources: in-depth personal interviews with a random probability sample of 174 Title VII congregate nutrition program participants; project area records, financial audits, and quarterly reports submitted to the Department of Elder Affairs (State Office on Aging); and other related research, particularly the statewide assessment of health care needs of the elderly in Massachusetts,[27] to which the author served as a nutritionist consultant and other Title VII studies.

Research Conclusions and Implications for Planning

Program Impact: The goal of evaluation research is to measure intended and unintended effects of an intervention against its stated goals as a means of improving program decision making and planning. Evaluation provides a critical component in nutrition programming whereby information about intervention outcome and effects is generated and channeled into ongoing program planning activities (see chapter 6).

The goals of the Title VII Nutrition Program for Older Americans were stated in the original legislation:[28] (1) to provide persons aged 60 years and older and their spouses regardless of age, particularly those with low-incomes and minorities, with low-cost, nutritionally sound meals in strategically located settings ... where they can obtain other social and rehabilitative services; (2) to promote better health among the older segment of the population through improved nutrition; (3) to reduce the social isolation of old age; and (4) to offer older Americans an opportunity to live out their remaining years in dignity.

Of interest in the Title VII program are program operating goals which have been stated at the state and local levels. These goals include reference to program design features and operating strategy but do not specifically indicate how the application of these features will result in federal Title VII goal achievement. Since federal goal achievement is implied but not ensured by state and local goal achievement, the federal goals became the criteria of program impact studied in the Boston Title VII evaluation. In addition, the local design features were studied to attempt to define determinants of program outcome and effects.

The results of the Boston Title VII program evaluation indicated that indeed the program had popularity and support among its participants. Nearly all participants found that the program was worthwhile and that it provided a variety of much needed services to the aged, including nutritious meals, opportunities for increased socialization with peers, and increased recreational activities outside the home. Relative to program impact in specific areas, however, it was clear that the proportion of participants who realized positive benefits from participation was variable across potential areas of program impact and generally lower in the health and nutrition-related areas. It appeared that program impact was greatest in the financial, social, and recreational areas; about half of the participants indicated that they had realized financial savings and experienced life changes as a result of program attendance, primarily increased social interaction and recreation with peers and improved morale. (The extent of monetary savings was not quantified.) In contrast, 31% of all participants reported changes in food purchasing behavior due to participation; about 25% reported an impact of the program on food consumption behavior, and about 20% indicated that their meal preparation practices at home had changed as a result of program participation. Among those who had realized an impact on food purchasing, most were reducing the purchase of food for home consumption. Likewise, those experiencing an effect of participation on food preparation behavior indicated that they were preparing fewer meals and a smaller amount of food for consumption at home. Those reporting an impact of the program on food consumption behavior also indicated that they were reducing consumption of food at home and in restaurants. Therefore the primary effect of the Title VII meal on diet-related behavior appeared to be one of substitution, that is, it replaced meals otherwise consumed at home or in restaurants.

Despite Title VII preparation, 40% of participants reported that as frequently as once a month they reduced their expenditure on food to meet non-food household expenses. This indicated that financial constraints persisted among the participants and could become potential barriers to adequate food and nutrition intake. Furthermore, less than 5% of participants specifically reported that improved health and dietary intake were changes affected by Title VII attendance.

Determinants of Program Impact: Lower levels of program impact on diet-related behavior relative to the impact realized in the financial, social, and recreational areas were associated with a number of critical factors, including erratic program participation behavior, dissatisfaction with the meal, lack of therapeutic diet management problems, weekly expenditures for food, living situation, food preparation problems, and dissatisfaction with diet. Those with therapeutic diet management problems, that is, not adhering to therapeutic regimens, experiencing problems with food preparation, and dissatisfied with their diets; those living alone; those expending less for food each week; and those attending the program frequently were more likely to realize an impact of the program on diet-related behavior.

The most consistent determinants of program impact in all areas included rate of program participation, dissatisfaction with non-Title VII meals, satisfaction with Title VII meals, therapeutic diet restrictions, and financial food purchasing problems.

As frequency of participation rose, the proportion of participants who realized impact on savings, food purchasing, and preparation behavior also increased. Satisfaction with meals other than those consumed at the program was inversely related to program impact on monetary savings, food purchasing behavior, food preparation practices, and food consumption behavior. Individuals reporting dissatisfaction with their diets in general were more likely to report an impact of the program in these areas. Satisfaction with the Title VII meal was positively related to program impact on monetary savings, food purchasing, and food preparation. Persons adhering to therapeutic diets reported significantly more impact of the program on monetary savings, food preparation practices, and food consumption behavior than those not adhering to or without therapeutic diet prescriptions. This appeared due to the assistance of Title VII in providing meals that were suitable for some therapeutic diets. Persons spending more per week on food were less likely to report impact on monetary savings and food purchasing behavior; those with persistent financial food purchasing problems were more likely to realize savings and impact on food purchasing and consumption behavior.

It is concluded that those with profiles of greater needs for financial and dietary management assistance, that is, those who reported dissatisfaction with their diets in general, those not adhering to their therapeutic diet regimes, those with food preparation problems, those living alone, and, in addition, those who attended the program more frequently realized the benefits of participation more frequently. Conversely, those with profiles that would suggest less apparent problems with diet and, in particular, those with erratic patterns of program participation were less likely to realize program benefits.

There is widespread support of this significant federal nutrition intervention among Boston Title VII participants. Nonetheless, progression toward program goal achievement has been hindered. Erratic program participation and variety of other factors related to satisfaction with diet in general, ability to manage one's diet, and dissatisfaction with Title VII meals were associated with reduced program impact. Drawing persons at greater risk of nutritional problems, that is, those who were living alone and those with food management and financial problems, was positively related to program impact. Title VII services were not directed solely at persons with these characteristics; therefore potential program impact was lowered.

The Boston Title VII evaluation indicated that program impact was primarily on savings and socialization of the aged rather than health and nutrition. These findings were consistent with those of other Title VII studies.[29] The association found between rate of program participation and Title VII impact on diet-related behavior has also been emphasized by Postma.[30] Furthermore, Kohrs[31] found that improvement in dietary intake and nutritional status among the elderly was related to the frequency of Title VII participation. The dietary intake and nutritional status of participants was frequently significantly better than nonparticipants. The dietary intake and nutritional status of more frequent program participants was significantly better than persons who attended less frequently.[32]

The attraction of elderly persons with greatest needs for health and nutrition services and continued service delivery to these persons will be a primary issue in the achievement of Title VII program goals. To attract those in greatest need, community outreach and screening activities will have to be tied to on-going service delivery. As has been emphasized by the GAO in its study of Title VII from 1976 to 1977,[33] outreach and supportive service activities have been hindered in the past because of Title VII policy which shifted program implementation focus to meals delivery as well as recent emphasis on achieving program operating levels. It appears that continued unplanned delivery of meals as well as supportive services will be detrimental to the realization of Title VII federal goals for improved health and nutritional status among the aged. It may also result in continued lower participation by "some potential participants in need of the program including the disabled, the isolated, those without transportation, the poorest of the poor, the very old, and elderly members of minority groups."[34] The following section presents a possible solution to the problem: the triage and referral system.

Program Improvement: This centers on an evaluation of services and how best to deliver them to those in greatest need.

Assessment of Needs for Services: A redirection of thinking in the area of meal and supportive service delivery could bring the program back in line with its long-term health and nutrition goals. Program planning could begin with a general assessment of the needs for services among aged in the community. Table 8-1 presents some of the possible criteria for identifying the elderly with greatest needs for services. The data have been divided into two categories: socioeconomic and demographic characteristics of the elderly and physical and psychological health, nutrition, and related needs.

The socioeconomic and demographic data are usually readily accessible from census statistics, police precinct data, housing authorities, or agencies serving the aged. These data could be used by Title VII personnel to determine the residence and concentration of elderly persons in their community by age strata, sex, and family composition. Persons with specific characteristics, for example, low-income and minority elders, could also be located. Neighborhoods with larger proportions of widowed persons and elderly living in public housing or group quarters could be identified. Once these data were gathered, the characteristics of the aged and neighborhoods within project areas could be evaluated against target group criteria and current program service delivery statistics. The purpose of these analyses would be to identify the geographic locations and groups of aged on whom future program outreach and service delivery could be concentrated.

The physical and psychological health, nutrition, and related needs data are not often so accessible as the socioeconomic and demographic characteristics of the population. Detailed health and nutrition assessments are not needed for preliminary determination of a population's needs for services. Vital health statistics, which are readily available, can give Title VII practitioners and administrators a general appreciation of the range of problems encountered by the elderly as well as trends within the aging population, such as life expectancy, growth of the population, major diseases and functional capacity, or use of health services. These data may suffice to begin planning the mix of supportive services.

Subsequent to the identification of possible target group aged, outreach campaigns into the community could be instituted by the programs or Area Agencies on Aging to inform the aged of available services and to encourage their participation. The required supportive services, such as transportation or escort, could be provided to facilitate participation by the otherwise homebound or those with debilitating chronic disease.

Once the aged are drawn into the program, each individual could then receive an in-depth confidential interview and assessment of needs for services conducted by trained staff. The data collected at initial interview could serve two major purposes: determination of the individual's needs for specific Title VII services and provision of baseline data on the characteristics of program participants. The data collected at the initial interview could include socio-

Table 8-1
Elderly Nutrition Program Planning: Requirements for Problem Diagnosis and Target Group Identification at the Micro Level

Socioeconomic & demographic characteristics of elderly

Data source: Census, police precinct data,
   elderly community service agencies

Data Needs	Potential target group criteria
Number of elderly	High % aged
Age distribution	> 60 years, high % very old
Sex	Females, males, living alone; female head of households
Marital status	Particularly widowed individuals
Education level	< eighth grade
Ethnic composition Location and size of minority elderly group	Minority groups, high %
Income Number below poverty	< Poverty index
Housing	Low-income public or elderly housing, rooming and boarding houses
Housing composition	Elderly living alone, elderly female head of households
Migration	New elderly residents

Physical and psychological health, nutrition, & related needs

Data source: Health departments, community hospitals, universities,
   literature review, community service agencies

Data needs	Potential target group criteria
Vital and health statistics	Prevalent chronic disease, frequent hospitalization
Food consumption patterns	Ethnic practices, avoidance behavior
Dietary surveys	Low, excessive, unbalanced intake
Anthropometric clinical & biochemical studies[a]	Muscle wasting, impaired biological utilization, deficiencies, special dietary needs
Social & psychological characteristics[a]	Isolated, lonely elderly; low life satisfaction; vulnerability; high crime
Health & needs assessement surveys	Poor health, prevalent chronic disease, current unmet or potential need for services

[a]Multivariate, multiple regression analysis of nutritional status with socioeconomic and demographic variables by substrata (i.e., rural versus urban, high versus low income, white versus other races) can assist in clarifying determinants of inadequate intake and suboptimal nutritional status.

economic and demographic data, health, diet, nutritional status, and supportive service needs assessment. (The latter is discussed in the subsequent section.) The primary value of adding the detailed health, diet, and nutrition assessments at the initial interview is that they can assist in identifying persons with greater risk or current unmet problems, and persons with such unique needs as the diabetics who require therapeutic diets. In addition, they can provide baseline data that are critical in longitudinal program evaluations. (The disadvantages of adding these data are that they can be costly, time consuming, and require skilled personnel for collection. Nonetheless, their value to program practitioners and administrators far outweigh their limitations, particularly when implementing services and evaluating program impact.)

Subsequent to an assessment of needs for services, elderly individuals could be matched with appropriate services, including those needed to ensure supportive service delivery. Matching clients with appropriate services could provide assurance that those in greatest need were actually obtaining services.

Relative to the congregate meal, persons in greatest need for it could be identified in the initial interview, directed to the congregate meal program, and given the supportive services needed to maintain continuous service delivery, including transportation, escort, and home-delivered meals if necessary. Persons with nonnutritional needs could be directed to those services or recreational activities alone. Then to the extent that adequate meals were available, more persons could be given meals.

Triage and Referral: The system described above is known as triage and referral; in such a system priority is given to the delivery of services to those in greatest need. In the context of the Title VII program, a triage and referral system would attempt to define the separate and specific needs for health, nutrition, and supportive services among the aged, direct those with current needs to appropriate services, and then provide the means for continued service delivery.

Triage and referral would be a new concept for the program. A similar system is currently being used, however, for the delivery of community-based homemaker and home health aide services under Titles III of the Older Americans Act of 1965. Supportive service personnel in these programs take referrals from hospitals, community agencies, and families. To summarize, they assess a potential client's needs for services, make appropriate arrangement for services, and periodically evaluate the client's changing needs for services or recovery. While implementation of a triage and referral system would require modification of the current Title VII delivery mechanism, this system has been successfully implemented within other community-based programs for the aged.

Given the current limitations in funding for program meals and supportive services, the very limited number of elderly to whom services can be provided, and the limited impact realized to date on health and nutrition among participants, a triage and referral system seems to warrant serious consideration and implementation. It could also be an initial step in the program becoming the leader in national community-based health delivery efforts for the aging.

A fundamental issue in the establishment of a triage and referral system is the development of criteria to assess current needs for supportive services among the aging and to evaluate the impact of service delivery over time. Assessment of needs for health, nutrition, and social services is critical in determining the necessary mix of services to serve the aged and direct those with current unmet needs to appropriate services. Assessment of program impact is necessary to determine the ongoing change in needs for services among aging clients and to provide the basis for program impact assessment (evaluation).

The following section addresses the issue of assessing needs for services among the aged and quantifies the current unmet needs for services among the Boston Title VII participants. The needs of participants relative to those of the aged in Massachusetts are discussed. In addition, the possible flow of Title VII clients through the triage and referral system and program evaluation is discussed in greater detail.

Needs for and Delivery of Supportive Services among Boston Title VII and Massachusetts' Aged: Two major approaches to the problem of estimating needs for health and supportive services among the aged have been proposed: the medical model of needs assessment and the functional model. The medical model favors physical examinations to determine baseline service needs. In contrast, the functional model is predicated on the concept that an individual's subjective assessment of disability or limitations in activity are the best indicators of health status and needs for services.

Recent research has produced functional definitions of needs for services which closely parallel the clinical assessment of need.[35] The operational definitions of need first described by Branch and Fowler[36] make it possible to determine whether or not current needs for a variety of supportive services or potential problems exist. Using the operational definitions in table 7-5 (elaborated in the appendix) the needs for short-term and long-term emergency services, socialization, transportation, food shopping and preparation, and housekeeping assistance were assessed among Boston Title VII nutrition program participants. These results were compared with assessment of needs for these services in the population aged 65 and older in Massachusetts.[37]

The results of the Boston Title VII study indicated that 20% of program participants had current unmet needs for one or more of the supportive services studied; 16.6% of participants had multiple unmet needs for services (two or more services). The area of greatest unmet need was short-term emergency service, which is not currently listed in the Title VII legislative mandate. (Need for this service implied that the elderly person was isolated and no one was available to help in case of emergency.) Some 12% of participants had unmet needs for short-term emergency service while less than 5% had unmet needs for the remaining services. In contrast, 20% of the aged in Massachusetts had current needs for one or more supportive services and only 6% had multiple service needs. The greatest service need was transportation assistance; 7% of the Massachusetts aged population had unmet needs for this service, while less than 2% had current needs for the remaining services.

The data suggested that, on the one hand, the Title VII program attracted those with greater needs for services. On the other hand, needs for selected services persisted despite program participation. This was in part due to the fact that some supportive services (short-term and long-term emergency assistance and homemaker services) were not mandated by Title VII. Needs also persisted because of the general underdevelopment of supportive services, as discussed in chapter 7.

Title VII services could be logically expanded to include short-term emergency assistance since this was one area in which current unmet needs for services among participants was great. The general low unmet needs for other services suggested that extensive growth of current services was not necessary at this time. This seemed true despite low operating levels of supportive services in some project areas. To the extent that the mix of elderly served congregate meals and other supportive services changed, expansion of the supportive service component may be warranted. However if a triage and referral system were instituted to give priority to the delivery of services to the aged in greatest need, extensive support service expansion would be needed. The introduction of a triage and referral system itself would require an initial increase in outreach screening, information, and referral capacity. To the extent that new participants and current needs for services were identified, expansion of other services would also be required. Obviously, the implementation of a triage and referral system would take place in the context of ongoing Title VII operations. Outreach and screening might begin with current program participants to make sure that the program had information on the characteristics and needs of current participants and that they were receiving needed services. Then as this process was accomplished, within the current program outreach and additional service activities could be directed outside the program.

Measurement of Program Output and Impact: Measurement of program output is critical for program management and evaluation purposes. The following supportive service information would be useful in a management information system: the number of unduplicated elderly persons served by supportive service category; the units of supportive service delivered (units defined in a uniform manner across program); and the itemized costs of service delivery (salaries, overhead, vehicles, etc.) by source of income (federal Title VII, federal other, in-kind community, volunteers, participant contribution).

For program impact evaluation, measurement of outcomes as well as benefits realized through supportive service delivery would be needed. The proportion of persons whose problems had been resolved because of supportive service delivery would be an appropriate index of benefits for some services (information and referral, recreation). For other services such as the congregate meal, emergency assistance, counseling, nutrition education, and transportation, assessment of participant change in need over time would be required to quantify program impact.

For both management and evaluation, a continuum of supportive service delivery could be conceptualized as seen in figure 8-1. The management information system expands on the triage and referral concept by adding the actual service delivery phase, impact evaluation, and data needed to maintain program

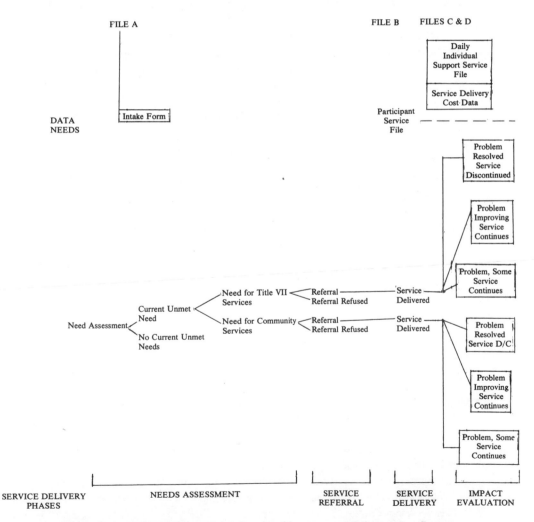

Figure 8-1. Title VII Supportive Service Management Information System

records. The congregate meal could be added to the list of supportive services since in the context of a triage and referral system, the meal would be only one of the potential services that could be delivered to the participant.

Service delivery has four phases: needs assessment, referral to supportive services, service delivery, and evaluation. Four data sets would be needed to record the process: initial interviews (file A); participant service records (file B); daily supportive service records (file C); and supportive service costs (file D, which include congregate and home-delivered meals and records of participant contributions for meals).

A potential Title VII participant could proceed through all service phases and thereby be recorded in all files of the management information system. Assessment of needs for service could take place, as previously described, during initial screening. At this time file A is opened.

Those with current needs for services would proceed to the next phase, service referral, and the participant service record could be opened (file B). If the participant accepted referral, he or she would then move on to the next phase, service delivery. The participant service record (continuation of file B) would be completed on an ongoing basis to monitor service delivery to individuals. As change in status relative to needs for services occurred, this would be documented in the participant record and retrieved subsequently for program impact evaluation.

Two concurrent reporting schemes could be kept to quantify the inputs (costs) and outputs (services delivered) for each supportive service (see figure 8-1). Supportive service delivery records (file C) could indicate the daily number of services delivered and the unduplicated number of persons served. Records could also be kept on the costs (file D) of delivering services (salaries, overhead, etc.) as well as the sources of income (Title VII funds, in-kind volunteer donations, volunteer time, participant donations).

This system is complex relative to the current methods of record keeping in some Title VII programs. It requires uniform data collected by identical methods across programs to be an effective management and evaluation tool. However, as the GAO noted in its recent study of the Title VII program,[38] a management information system could assist the programs, the states, HEW regional offices, and the Administration on Aging in improving their administrative capacity and thereby enhance the delivery of services to the aged. The development and implementation of a management information system deserves serious consideration. Once developed, priority could be placed on its implementation, including the provision of training and technical assistance to Title VII projects in instituting the system.

In addition to measures of program output that could be generated from a management information system, another variable can be utilized: the extent to which target group elderly from the surrounding communities are being served by Title VII. This issue, relative to the Boston Title VII, is discussed in the subsequent section.

Delivery of Services to Target Group Elderly: The Title VII mandate identifies persons with low incomes and minority elderly as targets for intervention. The legislative mandate, however, also specifically states that under no circumstances can an elderly individual be denied services for any reason. Furthermore, early program emphasis on meal service and recent program emphasis on reaching operating capacity have diverted attention from outreach and target group identification efforts.[39] These areas of program focus have created a dilemma for the administrator who must determine how scarce Title VII resources must be utilized in his or her community. As the GAO has noted,[40] the net result in many cases has been lower participation by some target group elderly, including the disabled, the isolated, those without transportation, the poorest of the poor, the very old, and elderly members of minority groups.

The Boston Title VII evaluation indicated that about 2% of the city's aged and about the same proportion of the city's aging poor were served by the program between January and June 1976. Less that 1% of the city's minorities were served and about twice as many elderly females as males. Men and women 60+ were served in proportion to their concentration in the community. The elderly poor and minorities were also served in proportion to their concentrations in Boston. Both the poor and minorities were underserved in a program sense, however, given their specific identifications in the legislative mandate as target groups for Title VII intervention.

Low participation of target group elderly is in part reflective of program policy which prohibits projects from restricting services to elderly with specific characteristics. The development of a triage and referral system could help alleviate this problem if persons in greatest need were directed to Title VII and available community services.

A triage and referral system also has the potential of providing baseline data on the characteristics of the elderly served. To the extent that a management information system was developed, the patterns by which participants' problems developed or resolved over time could be described and the costs and benefits of the program could be quantified.

The following section examines the issue of awareness of services among participants. Awareness is a critical determinant of utilization of available services by all aged. Awareness is particularly important since no Title VII triage and referral system has been developed or implemented to direct those in greatest need for services. The extent to which Boston Title VII participants were aware of community-based services and to what extent the Title VII program served as the basis of referral to other services were examined in the Boston evaluation.

Awareness and Utilization of Services among Title VII Participants: Knowledge and sophistication have been proposed as preconditions to recognition of a need for supportive service. Those with higher incomes and educational attainment have been found to utilize service to a greater extent than those with lower incomes and educational attainment, particularly the preventive services.[41] In a study of Boston elderly Fowler and McCalla[42] concluded that knowledge of a service was not the result of a perceived need for the service and searching it out, rather that knowledge of a service is a precondition for even recognizing the need for a service. They also found that those to whom it was most important to deliver services—the poor, immigrants, the very old, and those in poorer health—were least informed about service availability.

The Boston Title VII study indicated that the same interrelationship between awareness and utilization of services or perceived needs for services among the aged does not exist. Rather, those with lower incomes, minorities, those with lesser educational attainment, and those in poorer health were not utilizing services to a lesser extent nor were they less well informed about service availability. Among those who were aware of services, those in need appeared to utilize the services to a greater extent suggesting that indeed the need for services acts as the motivator in searching out services.

Title VII participants were well aware of transportation, shopping assistance, home-delivered meals, and Social Security benefits. Participants were less well informed of information and referral services, counseling, nutrition education, and Home Care Corporations or homemaker services.

Less than one-fifth of the participants utilized any of the available services for the elderly in the community or through the program. Title VII did not appear to be a major source of referral of participants to services available to the aged through other community agencies. On the other hand, the program limits, by its very nature, financial barriers to the receipt of transportation, home-delivered meals, nutrition education, shopping assistance, counseling, and information and referral services. In addition, if elderly who are in greatest need for services are in fact least aware of these services as Fowler suggests,[43] Title VII reverses this apparent lack of awareness of services among its participants.

Despite the fact that an individual is aware of a service, barriers to the utilization of the service (financial, physical, language) may inhibit the delivery of service to those in need or many influence continuous service delivery. The latter issue is discussed in the next section relative to the congregate meal delivery.

Determinants of Program Participation: Program participation has been researched in only a few available Title VII studies. Nonetheless, it appears that program impact is closely tied to frequency of program participation. As Kohrs indicated,[44] program participation influenced dietary intake and nutritional status of elderly individuals. Furthermore, more frequent program participants were more likely to consume diets which met the recommended levels of intake,[45] and to have fewer cases of inadequate nutritional status. Haffron[45] documented erratic program participation and levels of dropouts which reach as high as 50% annually. The results of the Boston Title VII evaluation indicated that frequency of program participation had a significant positive association with impact on financial savings, food consumption, and food preparation behavior among program participants. Less than 44% of Boston participants attended the program as often as once a week. Erratic program participation also decreased the likelihood of impact in the Boston area.

National figures suggested that the average rate of participation in the program is once every seven to ten days.[47] Erratic program participation is a reality which deserves further investigation throughout the Title VII program nationally.

A complex set of variables was found to affect the rate of program participation among Boston participants. Determinants of program participation were also found to vary considerably across project areas. This indicated that efforts to mitigate erratic participation behavior would require area-specific endeavors. Variables found to have a significant impact on the rate of program participation included the quality of the meal, the appropriateness of the meal for therapeutic diet needs, conflicting social and recreational activities, comfort with peers, perceived program impact on savings, and persistent financial food purchasing problems. The rate of program participation was reduced by poor-quality meals, perceived inappropriateness of the meal for therapeutic diets, dissimilarities between the meal and customary foods, conflicting social and recreational activities, discomfort with peers, lack of perceived impact of the program on financial savings, and lack of financial food purchasing problems.

It was concluded that the Title VII menus should be reviewed for their appropriateness for therapeutic diets, that the provision of therapeutic diets be considered, and that cultural/ethnic menus be offered periodically. To facilitate peer group interaction, escort services could be expanded and congregate meal site staff trained to manage participant crises as they occur. Furthermore, triage and referral and ongoing assessment of participants' changing needs for services were viewed as means of providing continuous services to those in greatest need and reducing erratic participation.

Reports on the rate of program participation was dropped from the national program summary in 1975. Rate of participant dropout was never reported. These variables seem critical in evaluating the delivery of services to the aged and should be introduced into the quarterly reporting scheme. Their purpose should be emphasized, however. For example, low dropout is desirable only if it can be shown that participants who continue to use services are in need of the services. It is conceivable that persons may need services, like the congregate meal, for only a short period of time. Under these circumstances, program dropout (perhaps retirement or improvement in participant status would be more appropriate terms) would be desirable and indicative of benefits realized by participation. By the same token, high rates of congregate meal participation by those in greatest need is desirable. Therefore, program impact as well as reasons for dropout or low levels of participation should be documented to provide data for meaningful interpretation of program participation rate and dropout (retirement).

In the next part of the Boston Title VII evaluation, program design features and the relative costs of delivering congregate meals and supportive services are discussed. Comparative costs and service output are one way of examining the interrelationship between program inputs and outputs. The importance of analyzing the interplay between these variables rests in the ultimate determination of the relative merits of alternative methods of providing services. These data provide information relative to future program planning and attempt to maximize effective and efficient service delivery.

Program Operating Costs: The Boston Title VII evaluation indicated that the cost per meal served across project areas was $1.55 to $1.97 and the cost per unit of supportive service delivered ranged from $0.64 to $8.80. The differences between project areas relative to meal cost delivery stemmed from the comparative costs of operating a centralized kitchen at the project area level and the use of private food management firms. Salary and labor costs were higher in the area utilizing the centralized kitchen. The lower salary and labor costs of the food management firms were due to economies of scale in operating a kitchen that prepares a large volume of meals. It appeared that while the management firms were able to realize and pass on cost advantages of the large-scale meal production to the projects, the same advantages were not realized in the raw food cost area. Raw food costs per meal for the food management firms were higher than the project using a central kitchen. This is in part due to the fact that food management firms have historically avoided the use of USDA commodity foods available to projects due to the extensive paperwork and other inconveniences associated with such use.[48] In addition, the management firms' profit margins were factored into the costs in this area.

The conclusions drawn from this analysis were that if the project-operated centralized kitchen produced meals up to its current capacity, it too could realize an economy of scale and make meal production very cost advantageous. Furthermore, the operation of a project area central kitchen could provide additional advantages of rapid menu changes in accordance with participant suggestions, ease of holiday and weekend meal preparation, therapeutic diet provision at minimal extra cost to the project areas, elimination of the profit incentives, and maximum use of USDA commodities.

Looking at the comparative cost of delivering supportive services, the total allocation of funds to supportive service delivery was not the major limiting factor. Rather, efficient use of staff and other resources and close documentation of service delivery were more important determinants of cost differences. The greatest level of supportive service output and cost effectiveness resulted from continuous use of vehicles for transportation, shopping assistance, and escort services; implementation of community outreach programs; telephone monitoring to identify information and referral activities; use of community resources for nutrition education; informing participants of available service through meal site information schemes; development of a variety of recreational and social activities outside the congregate meal; and close monitoring and coordination of supportive service delivery through a coordinator.

Comparative cost indexes in the congregate meal and supportive service delivery areas have the potential of becoming a continuous method of program monitoring. As the GAO noted,[49] the states could do a better job of monitoring and managing the Title VII program if they had better data on project performance. These data could also assist the AoA and HEW regional offices in identifying program problems and areas in which they could provide technical assistance.

Valid and reliable comparisons across project areas depend on the continuous collection of data in a uniform manner in each program. As of December 1977, revisions of the format of the quarterly report had been implemented eight times and a ninth revision was being considered. Furthermore, states were given flexibility in determining the type of data they collected. The result has been data which have limited reliability and value in determining program performance.

Meal cost delivery statistics would be improved if their reporting format differentiated the type of meal service (central kitchen, food management firm, or separate caterer), congregate or home-delivered costs and delivery statistics, and clearly identified and uniformly defined meal service inputs (raw food costs, labor and salaries, profit margin, participant meal contributions, storage, packaging, transportation, use and value of USDA commodities).

Supportive service delivery statistics would be more meaningful if they included the costs (labor, fuel, vehicles, etc.) and outputs (total units of service delivered, unduplicated numbers of persons served) for each supportive service. Supportive service delivery statistics would also ideally include the status of participants relative to their need for supportive services and stage in the service system (need for service identified, participant referred to service needed, participant receiving service, participant no longer receiving service, need no longer exists). The design of the management information system has been presented.

Until such time as a triage and referral scheme and program management information are implemented, two surrogate indicators of program impact could be introduced for program monitoring: a meal per participant served index (total meals delivered divided by the total number of persons served); and the proportion of participants (percent of total participants) falling into the high frequency of participation category (46+ days per quarter). Both indexes would provide somewhat similar data in a slightly different format. The first index would tie the frequency of program participation to the meal delivery statistics in one index. As the size of the index increased, the number of meals served per person would increase. The latter index does not tie meal and participant data together.

Nonetheless, as the proportion of persons in the high frequency of participation category increase, the index implies that meal service to a stable and consistent group of participants is being achieved.

In the short run these statistics could provide a basis for comparison programs and perhaps identify those programs with erratic patterns of program participation. In the long run, for reasons mentioned previously, these statistics would ideally be tied to data on the determinants of program dropout (retirement) or turnover.

An average meal or supportive service cost per person index was rejected for short-term monitoring for a number of reasons. These figures can be misleadingly inflated by erratic program participation and dropout rates which drive participation figures higher. In fact, reporting the number of persons served without tying these figures to a combination of cost, impact, and benefit data bypasses the issue of service quality and program operating efficiency and effectiveness. Reporting only gross figures as is currently the procedure nationally provides no data beneficial for short-term or long-term program planning. Therefore more meaningful statistics and indexes such as those described seem desirable for future reporting, program planning, and evaluation purposes.

Obviously, the cost per meal and unit of supportive services delivered would be desirable for comparing various modes of service delivery across programs. The current mode of collecting cost, other input, and output data varies to such an extent across programs that these figures are not meaningful in most cases. This would be rectified with the development and implementation nationally of a uniform program management information system.

Summary of the Nutrition Needs of Boston Title VII Participants: The nutrition needs of Boston Title VII participants are summarized in table 8-2. (See chapter 1 for a discussion of the factors that influence nutrition needs of the elderly.) Looking at the host factors which impact on the nutritional status of the aged, it can be seen that chronic disease and disability are major problems of participants. Nearly two-thirds of the participants have chronic diseases and are therefore limited in functional capacity to some extent. Some 28.1% of participants had therapeutic dietary restrictions. In addition, 64% of those with prescribed therapeutic diets did not adhere to their regimens, though 82% understood the need for adherence and the principles of diet management.

Examining dietary factors, 46% of participants reported that the meal was not appropriate for their therapeutic diet. Inappropriateness of the meal was related to erratic program participation. Some 21% reported problems related to food preparation and 9.3% indicated they were dissatisfied with their meals other than those consumed at the program.

Environmental factors also had important implications for the nutritional status of participants. Financial problems continued to impair the food purchasing among participants despite documented impact of the program in this

Table 8–2
Summary of Nutrition Needs of Title VII Participants

Diet Factors	Host Factors	Environmental Factors
46% of Title VII participants who require special indicate the Title VII meals are inappropriate for their therapeutic needs.	Prevalence of disease-related special needs is 28.1% among participants; decreasing order of prevalence are needs for:	40% of participants reduce food purchases monthly to meet nonfood household expenses.
21% of participants report food preparation difficulties.	Diabetic Modified sodium Modified fiber Cholesterol & saturated fat Weight reduction Fat-modified diets	Title VII current funding limits service to 2.2% of Boston's total elderly, 2.1% of Boston's poor, and 0.8% of elderly minorities.
9.3% of participants report dissatisfaction with non-Title VII meals.	64% of those on physician-prescribed diets report they do not understand dietary restrictions.	Current unmet needs for services: short-term emergency services, 11.8%; long-term services, 4.9%; transportation, 4.2%; socialization, 3.7%; shopping assistance, 1.1%; food preparation assistance, 0.7%; needs for one service, 3.3%; multiple service needs (2+ needs), 16.6%.
	Prevalence of chronic diseases is 65.2%; prevalence of limited functional capacity is 53.2%.	

area. Some 40% of participants indicated frequent need (once a month) to reduce food purchases to meet nonfood household expenses. In addition, limitations on Title VII funding resulted in 2% of Boston's total aged, low-income, and less than 1% of the minority elderly being served by the program. Low-income and minority elderly were underserved since they were identified targets for Title VII intervention. Unmet needs for individual supportive services were generally low among participants (under 12% for any specific service). Nonetheless, about one-fifth of all participants had need for one or more services.

Clearly diet, host, and environmental factors have the potential of adversely affecting dietary intake, nutritional status, and health of participants and the aged in the Boston population. It is also clear that the program can realize substantial impact on monetary savings, socialization, and recreation among the aged, and to a lesser extent on the diet-related behavior of participants.

In the future, planning and research activities will have to search for methods of improving program impact, particularly in the nutrition and health areas, such that long-term program planning and federal goals can be realized. The program's meal delivery scheme and supportive service delivery mechanism has the potential of becoming the leading force in coordinating the community-based delivery of health and related services to the aged. The ability of the current delivery scheme to realize impact on the health, diet-related, and social needs of the aged has been limited to some extent and methods of improving the administration, management, and impact of the program have been presented. In the final section future research needs relative to the nutrition, health, and aging triad are presented.

Future Research Needs

Introduction

Watkin[50] summarized the central dilemma facing researchers in gerontology:

> Aging, nutrition and the continuum of health care are three agglomerates forming a triad whose integrity is the essence underlying human aspirations for long, successful and happy lives.

> Concern about the components of the triad is widespread. Concern about the integral triad is less widespread, largely because proponents of any one component have little knowledge of the ingredients of the other two and little understanding of the complex reciprocal dependencies among all three.

If progress is to be made on slowing the aging process and enhancing the quality of life for the aged, far more basic and applied research into the nutrition, health, and aging will be needed. Research is also needed to explore the most advantageous modes of applying the knowledge gained from this research to specific programs for the aged as well as life-style changes among all age groups. The last issue is raised since aging, health, and nutrition research cannot afford to focus only on the older age groups. Aging is a continuous process that occurs from conception to death. Many of the biological changes and habits associated with the chronic diseases and disability in old age begin very early in life. Therefore knowledge gained by research into the process of aging will perhaps be best applied if integrated into prevention programs among all age groups, particularly the young.

Research priorities in health, nutrition, and aging have recently been summarized and discussed by the Senate Committee on Aging.[51] They fall into the following three categories: biomedical research, behavioral sciences, and human services and their delivery.

Biomedical Research

Biomedical research would cover the mechanisms of aging as well as the interaction between aging and environmental influences. The National Institute on Aging described the first area as consisting of everything from molecular genetics to clinical aspects of disease in the aged. The second area consisted of the study of factors which influence aging, such as diet, host, and environmental factors described in chapter 1. The research approaches utilized range from basic research to the application of knowledge. Priorities listed in the National Institute on Aging were cell-structure, biochemistry, genetics, physiology; normal physiological changes with age; immunological changes with age; clinical diagnostics—definition of normal standards by age; disease and aging interrelationships; organic brain disorders; and changing nutrient requirements and metabolism with age.

Behavioral and Social Research

Behavioral and social service research needs and priorities are influenced by the rapidly growing and diverse group of persons now in the older age strata. This research aims to understand the process of adapting to aging and the factors that influence decreased and improved quality of life in old age. It searches for fundamental determinants of a satisfying independent life with advancing years, determinants which may be important in social policy.

Relative to the behavioral and social sciences, the National Institute on Aging proposed the following priorities: reduction and prevention of dependency; income maintenance; age discrimination and employment: the retirement process; life expectancy and the aged personality; social competence and social integration; the aged and their families; mortality rates: men versus women; social experiments; psychological and psychiatric interrelationships; and government policy and the aged.

Human Service and Delivery Research

Research in human services and delivery systems is stimulated by the need for an effective network of facilities, programs, and services to enable survival during short-term crises and meet long-term needs. Research in these areas aims to increase efficiency, effectiveness, range of services, and their delivery to the aged. Priorities listed by the National Institute on Aging included: medical care; home care; mental health care; nutrition services; housing services; institutional care; reimbursement for services; transportation and communication services; legislated social services; supportive services; medicare; and comprehensive services.

Title VII Nutrition Program Research

Specific to the Title VII Nutrition Program for Older Americans, research in the realm of nutrition program planning can be categorized as: needs assessment, participant profiles, program efficiency, and program impact.

Review of the nutrition literature on the nutritional status of the elderly leads to the conclusion that little of a precise or scientific nature is available concerning the nutrient requirements of aged individuals. Collection of a data base in this area has been hindered by methodological weaknesses in currently utilized dietary assessment techniques as well as the relative neglect of the aged in clinical and biochemical assessments of nutrient requirements. Definitions of nutrient requirements are needed for basic understanding of the process of aging and for determining nutritional guidelines for intervention programs and biochemical and clinical standards to assess the nutritional status of the individual. Research on the reliability and validity of dietary assessment methodologies would assist in determining their utility when used with older persons. New methodologies for deriving quantitative and qualitative assessments of dietary intake are needed to facilitate monitoring changes in food consumption behavior.

The physical, psychological, and social aspects of aging have been only partially defined. It is also unclear why some persons opt not to participate in social intervention programs like the Title VII program, some continue to participate over time, and others drop out of program activities. Determinants of dropout behavior and potential barriers to program participation among nonparticipants would assist in developing program outreach and supportive service efforts.

There are many methods for assessing the efficiency with which program services are delivered. The research deficit, relative to the Title VII program, is primarily in the lack of application of these techniques to ongoing program monitoring and evaluation. Use of available techniques in a scientific manner could improve the quality of information available about the program and could also assist in improving the program's ability to monitor itself. If data on program performance are collected in a uniform manner across project areas, they can be used as a base to compare effectiveness of alternative delivery schemes. Both types of data would be useful in defining and selecting intervention strategies from existing alternative planning methodologies.

Reliable and valid indicators of program impact on the physical and psychological health and social well-being of the elderly should be employed in longitudinal evaluations of Title VII benefits and effects on program participants. The relative impact of alternative delivery strategies should also be defined. This implies the incorporation of prospective monitoring procedures into intervention schemes and the development of long-term longitudinal impact evaluations.

Closing Note

There is no doubt that the Nutrition Program for Older Americans (NPOA) has developed community visibility and widespread support among its 1.5 million participants. This is a major accomplishment and deserves recognition. Program growth to date and projections for future growth are likewise impressive. Since 1973, the investment in NPOA has more than doubled and is expected to triple by 1980. Federal, state, and local funding currently totals $500 million. This figure demonstrates the firm current and future commitment of persons at all levels of government as well as in the community to the delivery of community-based nutrition and supportive services to the aged.

Title VII impact on several aspects of the participants' lives are also noteworthy. Program impact has been greatest on financial savings, improved socialization, and enhanced morale and life satisfaction among participants. Most studies of the program to date and the Boston Title VII evaluation point to these areas as the major ones of impact. The effects of Title VII on savings, socialization, morale, and life satisfaction are of course critical in the maintenance of independent living of the aged and attack two of the most prevalent problems among the aging population: poverty and social isolation.

Contrary to the consistent impact of the program on savings, socialization, morale, and life satisfaction, however, impact in three other areas (improved health, nutrition, and diet-related behavior) has been more variable. This is a concern for three reasons: health and nutritional problems are pervasive among the aged; improved health and nutrition are primary long-term Title VII goals; and only a very small proportion of the legislatively defined Title VII aged participates in the program.

Lower levels of program impact in these areas appear to arise for a number of reasons. The overall frequency of program participation appears to be low and the annual rate of participant dropout appears to be high. On the average, participants attend the congregate meal once every seven to ten days.[52] Dropout may reach as high as 50% per year.[53] In addition to these factors, target group elderly have been underserved relative to their concentration in the community. Furthermore, supportive service delivery has been low relative to meal delivery. Other problems also seem to exist, including variable quality and appropriateness of meals, difficulties encountered interacting with peers, and conflicting activities competing for participants' time.

Each of these problems can reduce the likelihood of Title VII impact. In addition, it is conceivable that inadequate record-keeping systems have reduced the ability of the program to provide data on its effectiveness or efficiency.[54]

There is a shared responsibility for the current status of the program. All levels of government and many private community organizations and individuals have been instrumental in generating the strong support, determined program growth, and resultant impact on savings, socialization, morale, and life satisfaction among the aged. The redirection of Title VII activities away from the delivery of health and supportive services, while influenced primarily by federal activities away from the delivery of health and supportive services, while influenced primarily by federal activities, was perpetuated at all levels of program administration and operation.

Now is the time to address future directions the Title VII program could take. Program policymakers and practitioners must develop the dialog whereby the program's role in improving the health and nutritional status of the aged can be discussed. Evaluation of current services and impact to date in light of the long-term program goals for improved health and nutrition among the aged warrant close consideration; that is, if the program is to become a focal point of delivering community-based services to the aged.

The potential of the nutrition program to become the leader is evident. Its political powerbase at all levels of government and in the community has made its short-term growth and impact on savings, socialization, morale, and life satisfaction among the aged possible and in part assures the program's long-term viability. The program's viability could be secured by demonstrating its effectiveness in the physical health and nutritional areas. This remains a major consideration as the Nutrition Program for Older Americans enters its sixth year and a challenge for the future.

Notes

1. Segal, J.: "Food for the Hungry: The Reluctant Society," Baltimore: Johns Hopkins Press, 1970; and Mayer, J., ed.: *U.S. Nutrition Policies of the Seventies*, San Francisco: W.H. Freeman & Co., 1973.

2. "Toward a National Policy on Aging," Proceedings of the 1971 White House Conference on Aging, vol. 2, 1971.

3. *White House Conference on Food, Nutrition, and Health*, Government Printing Office, 1969.

4. Watkin, D.M.: "A Year of Developments in Nutrition and Aging," *Med. Clin. North Am.* 54:1589-97, 1970.

5. U.S. Senate Committee on Labor and Public Welfare: "Research in Aging and Nutrition Programs for the Elderly," 92d Congress, 1st sess., June 1971.

6. "National Policy on Aging."

7. Bechill, W.D.: "The Program Highlights of the Research and Development of Nutrition Programs Funded under Title IV of the Older Americans Act of 1965," University of Maryland School of Social Work and Community Planning, 1971; and PL 92258, 92d Congress, S 1163, Mar. 22, 1972.

8. Bechill: "Nutrition Programs."

9. Watkin, D.M.: "The NPOA: A Successful Application of Current Knowledge in Nutrition and Gerontology," *World Rev. Nutr. Diet.* 26:26-40, 1977.

10. PL 92258, 92d Congress.

11. Ibid.

12. Watkin: "The NPOA."

13. Ibid.

14. Ibid.

15. Lakoff, S.A.: "The Future of Social Intervention," in *Handbook of Aging and the Social Sciences*, chapter 25, eds. R.H. Binstock and E. Shanas, New York: Van Nostrand Reinhold Co., 1976.

16. U.S. Senate Select Committee on Nutrition and Human Needs: "Nutrition and the Elderly," June 19, 1974.

17. Harper, J.M., and Jansen, G.R.: "Nutrient Standard Menus," *Food Technol.* 27:48-52, 1973; Jansen, G.R., and Harper, J.M.: "Nutritional Aspects of Nutrient Standard Menus," *Food Technol.* 28:62-67, 1974; and Frey, A.L., et al.: "Comparison of Type A and Nutrient Standard Menus for School Lunch. I: Development of the Nutrient Standard Method (NSM)," *J.A.D.A.* 66:242-48, 1975.

18. General Accounting Office: "Actions Needed to Improve the Nutrition Program for the Elderly," HRD-78-58, Feb. 23, 1978.

19. Ibid.

20. Ibid.

21. Ibid.

22. Watkin, "The NPOA."

23. GAO: "Nutrition Program for Elderly."

24. Ibid.

25. Howard, L.: "The National Title VII Evaluation Study," paper presented at the Annual American Dietetic Association Meetings, October 1977.

26. GAO: "Nutrition Program for Elderly."

27. Branch, L.G.: "Understanding the Health and Social Service Needs of People over Age 65," Center for Survey Research, a Facility of the University of Massachusetts and the Joint Center for Urban Studies of MIT and Harvard University, 1977.

28. PL 92258, 92d Congress.

29. Hosowkawa, M.C., et al.: "Central Missouri Nutrition Assessment Project," 1975; idem: "Nutrition Project Assessment," Central Missouri AAA, 1976; and Postma, J.S.: "The Characteristics and Needs of the Eugene-Springfield Elderly Nutrition Congregate Meals Program Participants and Their Perceptions of the Program's Effects and Operation," doctoral dissertation, University of Oregon, 1974.

30. Ibid.

31. Kohrs, M.B.: "Influence of the Congregate Meal Program in Central Missouri on Dietary Practices and Nutritional Status of Participants," Jefferson City, Mo.: Lincoln University, Department of Agriculture and Natural Resources, Human Resources, Human Nutrition Research Program, August 1976a; Kohrs, M.B., et al.: "Contribution of the Nutrition Program for Older Americans to Nutritional Status," paper delivered at American Gerontological Society Meetings, New York City, 1976b; and Kohrs, M.B.: "Nutrition Data from an

'Aging Program': Implications for Planning," paper presented at the Society for Nutrition Education Annual Meeting, Kansas City, Mo. 1976c.

32. Kohrs: "Congregate Meal Program"; Kohrs et al.: "Nutrition Program"; and Kohrs: "Nutrition Data."

33. GAO: "Nutrition Program for Elderly."

34. Ibid.

35. Branch: "Health and Social Service Needs"; Katz, S., et. al.: "Progress in the Development of the Index of ADL," *The Gerontologist* 10:20-30, 1970; and Branch, L.G., and Fowler, F.J.: "The Health Care Needs of the Elderly and Chronically Disabled in Massachusetts," Survey Research Program, a Joint Facility of the University of Massachusetts/Boston and the Joint Center for Urban Studies of MIT and Harvard, March, 1975.

36. Branch: "Health Care Needs."

37. Branch: "Health and Social Service Needs."

38. GAO: "Nutrition Program for Elderly."

39. Lakoff: "Future of Social Intervention."

40. GAO: "Nutrition Program for the Elderly."

41. Linder, F.E.: "The Health of the American People," *Sci. Am.*, vol. 214, June 1966.

42. Fowler, F.J., and McCalla, M.E.: "Need and Utilization of Services among the Aged in Greater Boston," AoA, 1969.

43. Ibid.

44. Kohrs: "Congregate Meal Program"; Kohrs et al.: "Nutrition Program"; Kohrs: "Nutrition Data"; Katz et al.: "Index of ADL"; and Branch: "Health Care Needs."

45. National Academy of Sciences, Food and Nutrition Board: *Recommended Dietary Allowances*, 8th ed., Washington, D.C.: 1974.

46. Haffron, D., et al.: "Title VII Nutrition Program: Profiles of Non-participants, Participants, and Dropouts in a Midwestern Community," paper presented at the American Gerontological Society Annual Convention, October 1976.

47. Watkin, personal communication, 1978.

48. GAO: "Nutrition Program for Elderly."

49. Ibid.

50. Watkin, D.M.: "Aging, Nutrition and the Continuum of Health Care," *Ann. N.Y. Acad. Sci.*, 300: 290-297, 1977.

51. U.S. Senate Select Committee on Aging: "Developments in Aging," Apr. 7, 1977.

52. Watkin: personal communication, 1978.

53. Haffron: "Title VII Program."

54. GAO: "Nutrition Program for Elderly."

Appendix
Federal Definitions of Title
VII Supportive Services

Definitions of Title VII Supportive Services

*Federal Regulation Definition of Information and
Referral Services*

Information sources or services which provide a location where state, area, or other public or private agencies or organizations: (1) *maintain current information systems* with respect to the opportunities available to older persons, and *develop current lists of older persons in need of services and opportunities*; and (2) *employ a specially trained staff*, including bilingual individuals as appropriate, *to inform older persons of the opportunities and services which are available*, and *assist them* to take advantage of such opportunities and services.

Referral services which assist individuals to identify the type of assistance needed, place individuals in contact with appropriate services and follow up to determine whether services were received and met the need identified, and which provide for the *maintenance of proper records* for use in identifying services offered and gaps in existing service systems (903.2(g)2).

Federal Regulation Definition of Outreach

A. Outreach service means an activity designed to seek out and identify, on an ongoing basis, the maximum number of the hard-to-reach, isolated, and withdrawn target group eligible individuals throughout the project area in greatest need of nutrition and supporting social services, and to provide the opportunity for them to participate in the project.

B. Such services must provide for: (1) the designation of a *project staff person to be responsible* for the conduct of this activity from each congregate meal site; (2) adequate numbers of *outreach workers* knowledgeable in dealing with and identifying needs of older persons, (3) the use of a variety of methods that will assure a *systematic coverage of the project area* and contact with the *maximum possible number of older persons*; and (4) arranging for *referral* and *follow-up of* individuals found to be in need of services (Part C 23.2(b)1).

Federal Regulation Definition of Objectives Related to
Counseling Services for the Elderly

Counseling services which provide direct guidance and assistance in the utilization of needed health and social services, and help in coping with personal
problems which threaten personal health and social functioning (503.2(g)6).

Federal Regulation Definition of Objectives Related to
Recreation Services

Recreational services which foster the health and social well-being of individuals
through social interaction and the satisfying use of time.

Federal Regulation Definition of Transportation

Transportation services designed to transport older persons to and from community facilities and resources for the purpose of applying for and receiving services, reducing isolation, or otherwise promoting independent living, but not
including a direct subsidy for an overall transit system or a general reduced fare
program for a public or private transit system. Such transportation services shall
be, insofar as possible, part of an area transportation plan (903.2(g)4).

Federal Regulation Definition of Escort Services

Escort services which assist individuals who, for a variety of factors, are unable
to use conventional means of transportation to reach needed services, or require
such assistance for reasons of personal security or protection.

Federal Regulation Definition of Nutrition Education Services

A. Nutrition education means a formal program of *regularly scheduled meetings*
to make available facts about the kinds and amounts of foods that are required
to meet one's daily nutritional needs. It shall be an accompanying feature of the
meal program, with close coordination between the two components to improve
the nutritional intake of older persons through *better eating habits by making*
them aware of the relative nutritional value of different food groups.
B. *Such activity must provide for: (1)* visual information to be available on a
continuing basis; and (2) regularly scheduled meetings conducted in an appropriate manner to meet the needs of the participants (Part C 23.2(b)7).

Federal Regulation Definition of Shopping Assistance

A. Shopping assistance means making help available to project participants in getting to and from food markets and in the selection of proper food items so as to improve their nutrition intake.

B. Such activity must provide for: (1) the service to be regularly available; (2) the service to be available at a time convenient to older persons; and (3) the opportunity to shop at a food market of the individual's choice (Part C 23(b)8).

Additional Definitions

Home Care Corporations (HCC) are community-based nonprofit agencies that are involved primarily in the implementation of the homemaker service program that is funded under Title III of the Older Americans Act. They have boards of directors made up of elders and professionals from the community who advise on policy. The HCC is however responsible to and dependent upon the State Office on Aging for its funding. In addition to the management of the homemaker service program which included assessment of needs for homemaker services and monitoring of ongoing service provision, additional HCC activities may include chore service programs, medical transportation, and outreach.

Homemakers are individuals who are specially trained and certified to provide the following activities to elderly clients: light housekeeping, shopping, cooking, and laundry assistance. Homemaker services are reimbursed through Title XX (Social Security Act).

Home Health Aides are trained and certified individuals who in addition to light housekeeping provide personal care activities under the supervision of a registered nurse. These activities involve handling the client such as bathing, assistance with walking, etc. Client assessments for home health aide services are made by the Visiting Nurse Association. Reimbursement for home health aide services is provided by Medicare and Medicaid.

Index

About the Author

Barbara Millen Posner is an assistant professor of nutrition at Sargent College of Allied Health Professions, Boston University and Boston University School of Medicine. She completed her doctoral studies in nutrition at the Harvard School of Public Health. Dr. Posner has been a consultant in nutrition policy and program planning as well as clinical nutrition to the Administration on Aging, the National Academy of Sciences, the World Bank, the Massachusetts Department of Elder Affairs and Public Health, the Massachusetts Office of Deaf Seniors, and Grocery Manufacturers of America. She has also worked as a clinical and research nutritionist at Harvard University, the Massachusetts General Hospital, and the Newton-Wellesley Hospital.